BIKING *in Vikingland*

Minnesota & Western Wisconsin Trails

Where to Go · What to Expect · How to Get There

By Marlys & Phil Mickelson

10669504

Second Printing
All rights reserved.
Adventure Publications, Inc.
PO Box 269
Cambridge, Minnesota 55008

Copyright 1999
ISBN 1-885061-20-X
Front cover photo: Bill Marchel

Printed in Canada

Dedication:

This book is dedicated to a diverse group of energetic individuals whose mutual interest in physical activity, ecology, conservation and the great outdoors evolved into an ever-widening circle of friends who call themselves the Weakenders. (TM)

Acknowledgements:

Our sincere appreciation for the cooperation and assistance given by the Departments of Transportation and Natural Resources and the Office of Tourism of the State of Minnesota. Also the Division of Tourism and the Department of Natural Resources Bureau of Parks and Recreation of the State of Wisconsin.

We also acknowledge the cooperation and information provided by the many state, city and county parks and/or engineering departments whose assistance was invaluable in assembling many of the trail descriptions contained in this book.

In Celebration of Cycling

To wheel quietly up and down hill and across the valley, miles away from so-called civilization, and yet knowing that with a good bicycle miles mean but little; to wheel along drinking in the perfumes of the morning with the song of the birds, and at even, thankful for the matchless glow in the west and the music of cow-bells; to wheel silently at sunset into some peaceful village where your guidebook bids you expect a welcome — all this is worth celebrating.

Philip C. Hubert, Jr.
Scribners Magazine, 1895

Introduction:

Whether you are now a bicyclist, or about to become one, this book is for you. If you value friendships, good exercise, the outdoors or just economic transportation, you will find this guide a reliable reference to enhance your enjoyment.

Minnesota is the leader in the development of paved bicycle trails with over 600 miles now available to you. Wisconsin is not far behind.

The Minnesota and Wisconsin DNRs and Bureaus of Parks & Recreation have worked with interested communities and groups to convert railroad right-of-ways to bike trails, offering great biking that offers a quiet biking experience through scenic areas on level to minor grade rail beds.

Whatever your age or biking skill, whether you want to bike a short distance or several hours, this book is your guide to leisurely biking on safe trails, away from motorized traffic.

The trail maps, trail length and access information in this book tell you where to go, what to expect and how to get there.

Contents

General Information 10
Northwest Minnesota 13
Alexandria City Trails 14
Central Lakes Rail-Trail 16
Heartland State Rail-Trail 20
Itasca State Park 24
Mi-Gi-Zi Trail-Chippewa National Forest 26
Moorhead/Fargo City Trails 28
Northeast Minnesota 31
Duluth City Trails 32
Jay Cooke State Park 34
Laveau Memorial Bike Trail 36
Mesabi Trail, Itasca Bicycle Trail, Taconite Trail 42
Willard Munger-Carlton to Duluth Segment 46
Central Minnesota 49
Brainerd City Trails 50
Lake Wobegon Rail-Trail 52
Paul Bunyan State Rail-Trail 56
Soo Line Rail-Trail 60
St. Croix State Park 62
Sunrise Prairie Trail-Hardwood Creek Rail-Trail 64
Willard Munger-Hinckley Fire Trail Segment 70
Southwest Minnesota 73
Glacial Lakes State Rail-Trail 74
Lake Shetek State Park 76
Luce Line State Rail-Trail 78
Mankato City Trails 82
Marshall City Trails 84
Red Jacket Rail-Trail 86
Sakatah Singing Hills State Rail-Trail 88
Sakatah State Park 92
Sibley State Park 94
Southeast Minnesota 97
Cannon Valley Rail-Trail 98
Douglas State Rail-Trail 102
Faribault City Trails 104
Harmony-Preston Valley State Rail-Trail 113
Owatonna City Trails 106
Rochester City Trails 108
Root River State Rail-Trail 112
Winona City Trails 116
Metro Minnesota 119
Minneapolis & St. Paul Metro Bike Trails 120
Afton State Park 124
Baker Park Reserve 126
Bassets Creek 128
Battle Creek Regional 134
Big River Trail 135
Bunker Hills Regional 136

Burlington Northern Regional 138
Carver Park Reserve 140
Cedar Lake Trail 129
Cleary Lake Regional Park 141
Clifton E. French Park Reserve 142
Como Park 143
Coon Rapids Dam Regional Park 144
Crosby Farm/Hidden Falls Regional Park 145
Elm Creek Park Reserve 146
Fish Lake Park Reserve 147
Fort Snelling State Park 148
Gateway Segment-Willard Munger State Trail 150
Hastings City Trails 154
Hyland Lake Park Reserve 155
Kenilworth 138
Lake Phalen Regional Park 156
Lake Rebecca Park Reserve 157
Lebanon Hills Regional 158
Long Lake Regional Park-New Brighton 159
Lower Afton Road 160
McKnight Road 162
Midtown Greenway 131
Minneapolis Grand Rounds 164
Minnesota Valley State Park 170
Mississippi Regional Trail Corridor 172
North Hennepin Trail Corridor 176
Phalen Creek Regional 178
Rice Creek West Regional 179
Southwest Region LRT, North Corridor 180
Southwest Region LRT, South Corridor 181
St. Paul Grand Rounds 184
Summit Avenue Trail 188
William O'Brien State Park 190
Western Wisconsin 193
Wisconsin Information 194
400 State Trail 196
Chippewa River State Park Trail 200
Elroy-Sparta State Park Trail 204
Gandy Dancer 208
Governor Dodge State Park 219
Great River State Park Trail 212
LaCrosse River State Park Trail 216
Military Ridge State Park Trail 218
Omaha Trail 222
Red Cedar State Park Trail 201
Sugar River State Park Trail 224
Future Trails 228
Bike Safety & Equipment 230
Additional Information 234

Minnesota Trails

1. Afton State Park, p. 124
2. Alexandria (City), p. 14
3. Baker Park Reserve, p. 126
4. Bassets Creek, p. 128
5. Battle Creek Reg'l, p. 134
6. Big River, p. 135
7. Brainerd (City), p. 50
8. Bunker Hill Reg'l, p. 136
9. Burlington Northern Reg'l, p. 138
10. Cannon Valley, p. 98
11. Carver Park Reserve, p. 140
12. Cedar Lake Park, p. 129
13. Central Lakes, p. 16
14. Cleary Lake Reg'l Park, p. 141
15. Clifton E. French Reg'l Park, p. 142
16. Como Park, p. 143
17. Coon Rapids Dam Reg'l Park, p. 144
18. Crosby Farm/ Hidden Falls Reg'l Park, p. 145
19. Douglas State, p. 102
20. Duluth (City), p. 32
21. Elm Creek Park Reserve, p. 146
22. Faribault (City), p. 104
23. Fish Lake Reg'l Park, p. 147
24. Fort Snelling State Park, p. 148
25. Gateway, p. 150
26. Glacial Lakes State, p. 74
27. Hardwood Creek, p. 65
28. Harmony-Preston Valley, p. 113
29. Hastings (City), p. 154
30. Heartland State, p. 20
31. Hyland Lake Park Reserve, p. 155
32. Itasca State Park, p. 24
33. Jay Cooke State Park, p. 34
34. Kenilworth, p. 138
35. Lake Phalen Reg'l Park, p. 156
36. Lake Rebecca Park Reserve, p. 157
37. Lake Shetek State Park, p. 76
38. Lake Wobegon State, p. 52
39. Laveau Memorial Bike, p. 36
40. Lebanon Hills Reg'l Park, p. 158
41. Long Lake Reg'l Park, p. 159
42. Lower Afton Road, p. 160
43. Luce Line State, p. 78
44. Mankato (City), p. 82
45. Marshall (City), p. 84
46. McKnight Road, p. 162
47. Midtown Greenway, p. 131
48. Mi-ge-zi Trail- Chippewa Nat'l Forest, p. 26
49. Minneapolis Grand Rounds, p. 164
50. Minnesota Valley State Park, p. 170
51. Mississippi Reg'l Corridor, p. 172
52. Moorhead/Fargo (City), p. 28
53. North Hennepin Corridor, p. 176
54. Owatonna (City), p. 106
55. Paul Bunyan State, p. 56
56. Phalen Creek Reg'l, p. 178
57. Red Jacket, p. 86
58. Rice Creek West Reg'l, p. 179
59. Rochester (City), p. 108
60. Root River, p. 112
61. Sakatah Singing Hills State, p. 88
62. Sakatah State Park, p. 92
63. Sibley State Park, p. 94
64. Soo Line, p. 60
65. S.W. Reg'l LRT-No. Corridor, p. 180
66. S.W. Reg'l LRT-So. Corridor, p. 181
67. St. Croix State Park, p. 62
68. St. Paul Grand Rounds, p. 184
69. Summit Avenue, p. 188
70. Sunrise Prairie, p. 64
71. Taconite, Itasca Mesabi, p. 42
72. W. Munger-Carlton, p. 46
73. W. Munger-Hinckley Fire, p. 70
74. Wm. O'Brien State Park, p. 190
75. Winona (City), p. 116

Western Wisconsin Trails

W1. 400 State, p. 196
W2. Chippewa River State Park, p. 200
W3. Elroy Sparta State Park, p. 204
W4. Gandy Dancer, p. 208
W5. Governor Dodge State Park, p. 219
W6. Great River State Park, p. 212
W7. LaCrosse River State Park, p. 216
W8. Military Ridge State Park, p. 218
W9. Omaha, p. 222
W10. Red Cedar State Park Park, p. 201
W11. Sugar River State Park, p. 224

The map below shows the location of the Minnesota and Wisconsin trails described within this book. See the following pages to view each quadrant of the state in more detail.

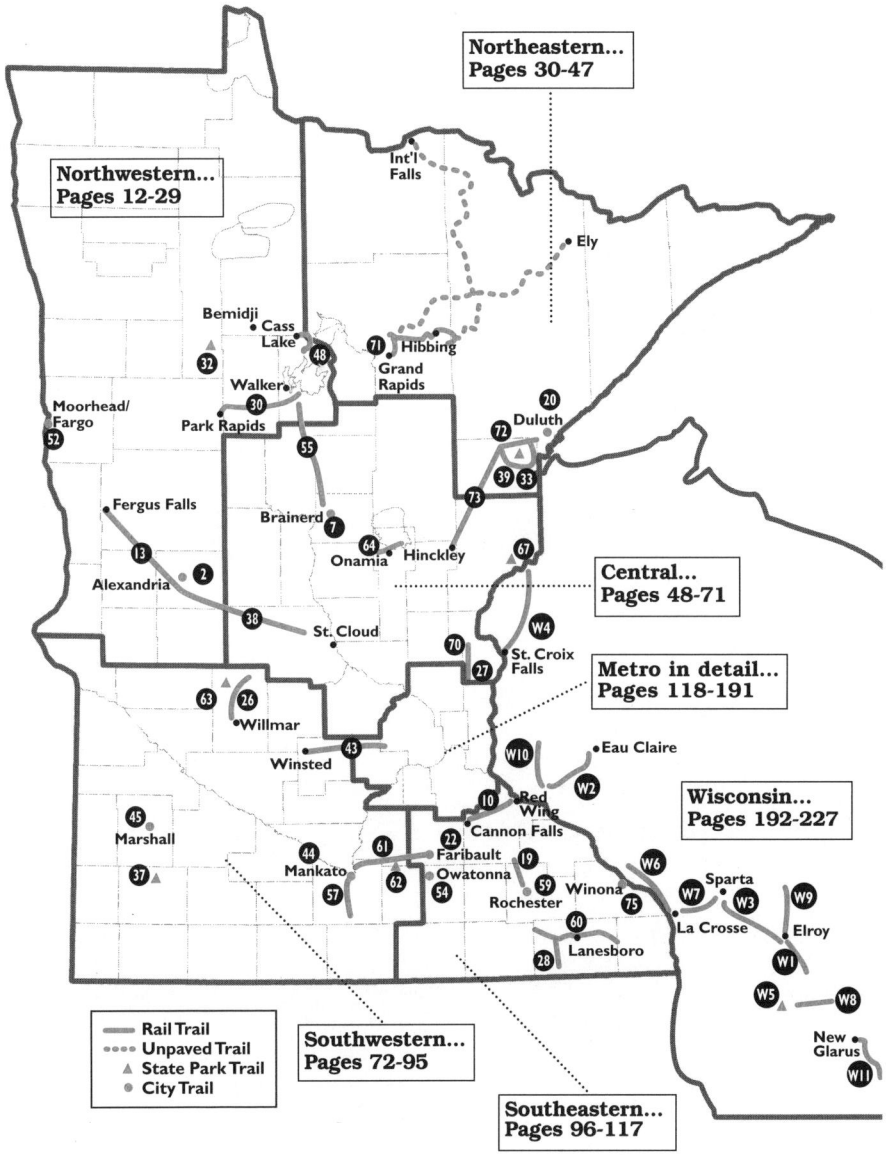

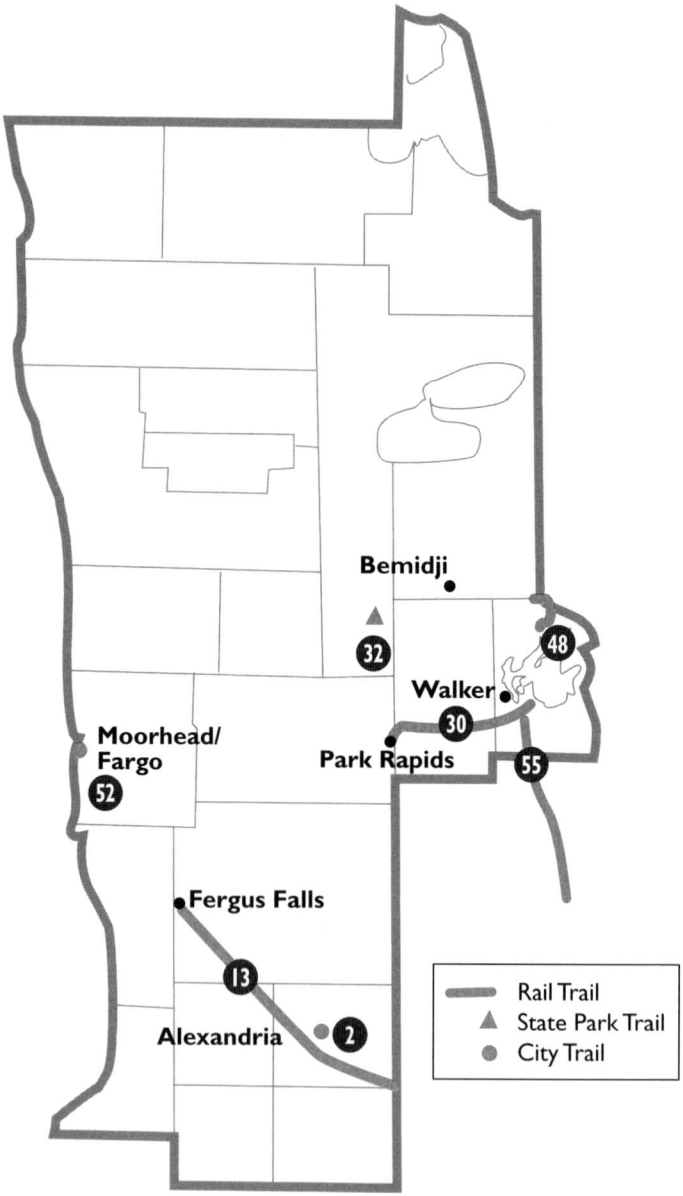
Bemidji
32
48
Walker
30
Moorhead/
Fargo
52
Park Rapids
55
Fergus Falls
13
Alexandria
2
Rail Trail
State Park Trail
City Trail

Northwest Minnesota

Trail

2. Alexandria City Trail . . . . . .page 14
13. Central Lakes Rail-Trail . . . . . .page 16
30. Heartland State Rail-Trail . . . . . .page 20
32. Itasca State Park Trail . . . . . .page 24
48. Mi-Ge-Zi State Rail-Trail-Chippewa Nat'l Forest . . .page 26
52. Moorhead/Fargo City Trails . . . . . .page 28
55. Paul Bunyan State Rail-Trail (see Central section) . . . page 56

*** Numbers refer to large map on page 11 and opposite page**

ALEXANDRIA (CITY)

WHERE: City of Alexandria
LENGTH: Several miles
SURFACE: Crushed rock through Polk County
TRAIL USE:

Alexandria has several miles of well marked roadside trails, specifically along county roads 22, 23 and 82. The city is also spanned east to west by the Central Lakes Rail-Trail (page 16) which will eventually run from Lake Wobegon Trail (page 52) in Sauk Centre all the way to Fergus Falls. Presently, the Central Lakes Trail is suitable for only snowmobiles or mountain bikes, but paving is planned.

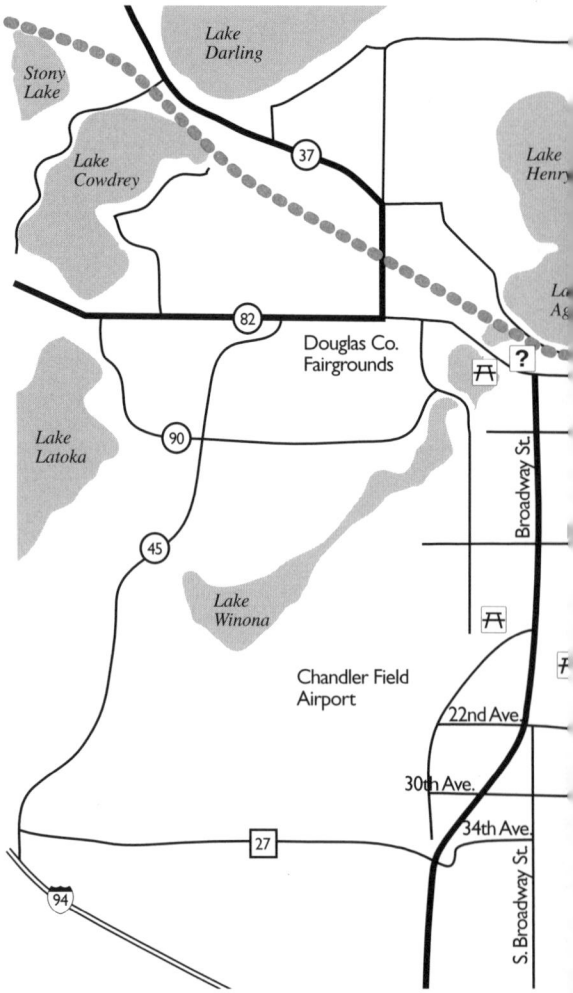

FOR MORE INFORMATION:

Alexandria Lakes Area Chamber of Commerce
206 Broadway
Alexandra, MN 56308
1-800-235-9441
E-Mail: alexrecr@rea-alp.com

Alexandria Lakes Community Recreation
P.O. Box 801
Alexandria, MN 56308
320-762-2868

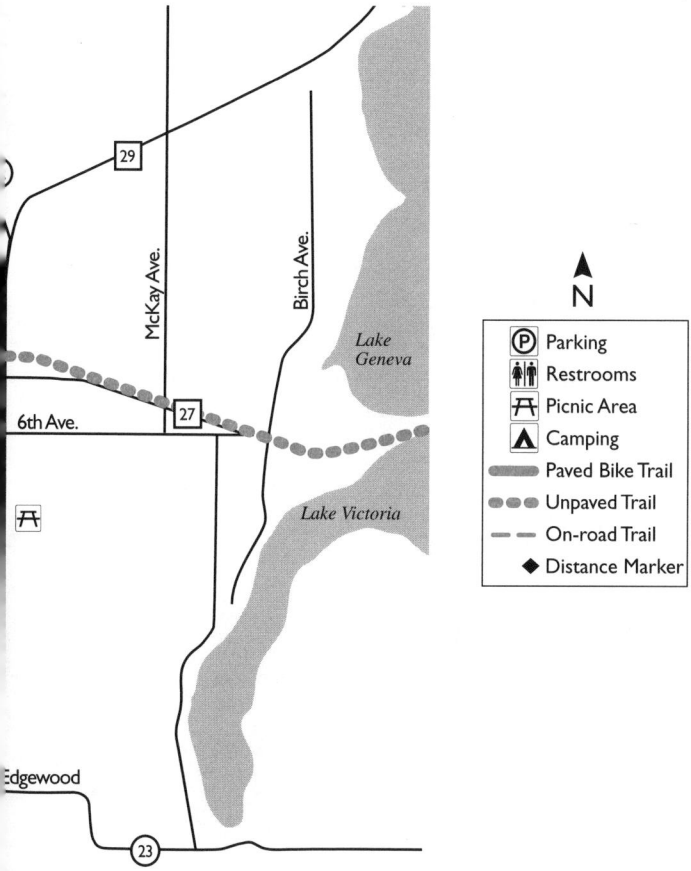

CENTRAL LAKES

WHERE: Osakis to Fergus Falls
LENGTH: 69 miles (when completed)
SURFACE: Crushed rock
TRAIL USE: 

Trailhead East: Osakis at intersection of Hwy 27 and rail corridor adjacent to the Osakis Chamber of Commerce where there is parking.

Mid Access: Small towns along the route accessible from I-94 include Nelson, Garfield, Brandon, Evansville, Ashby and Dalton. The trail will traverse the entire city of Alexandria, east to west.

Trailhead West: Fergus Falls going north on I-94 exit 61 which is County Road 82. Proceed north to DeLagoon Park where there are facilities, parking and overnight camping

Mn DOT currently owns this right-of-way. The counties of Douglas, Grant and Otter Tail will construct and administer their sections just as is being done by Stearns County for the Lake Wobegon Trail to which this will eventually connect.

The surface is presently gravel suitable only for mountain bikes. Paving and parking, etc. will follow if projected maintenance costs do not prohibit it because of the reinstatement of studded snowmobiles.

This will rank very high on the list of most scenic rail-trails when completed. The rail bed winds its way along or near many lakes, streams and wooded areas.

FOR MORE INFORMATION:

Central Lakes Trail Office
320-763-6001

Osakis Chamber of Commerce
P.O. Box 327
Osakis, MN 56360
320-859-3777

Fergus Falls Area Chamber of Commerce
202 S. Court St.
Fergus Falls, MN 56537
218-736-6951

Alexandria Lakes Area Chamber of Commerce
206 Broadway
Alexandria, MN 56308
800-235-9441

Hand and arm signal methods

Left turn: left hand and arm extended horizontally

Right turn: hand and arm extended upward or extend right hand and arm horizontally to right side of bicycle

Stop or decrease speed: left hand and arm extended downward

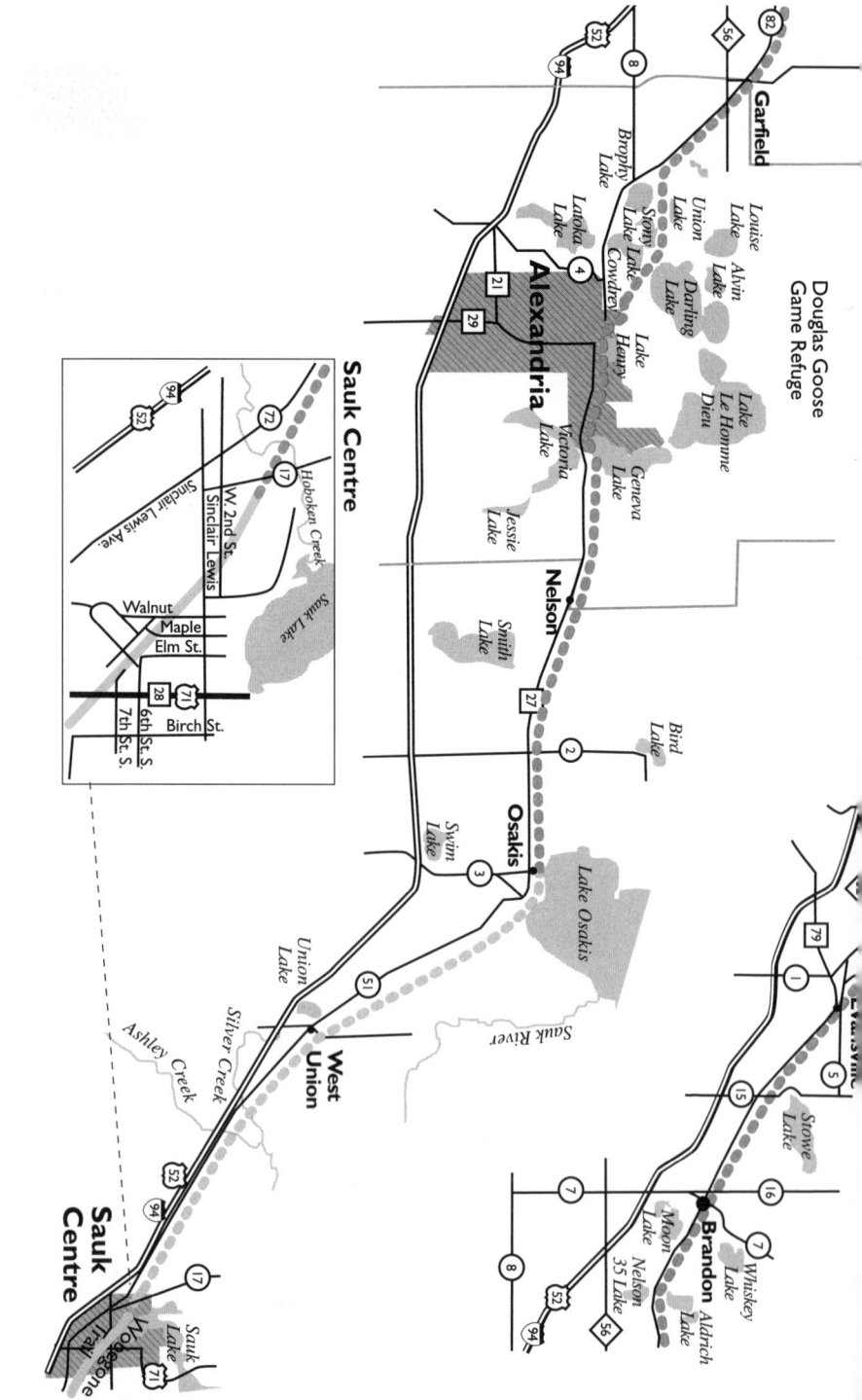
Douglas Goose Game Refuge
Garfield
Louise Lake
Alvin Lake
Union Lake
Darling Lake
Stony Lake
Lake Le Homme Dieu
Brophy Lake
Lake Henry
Cowdrey
Latoka Lake
Alexandria
Victoria Lake
Geneva Lake
Jessie Lake
Nelson
Smith Lake
Bird Lake
Osakis
Swim Lake
Lake Osakis
Sauk River
Union Lake
West Union
Silver Creek
Ashley Creek
Sauk Centre
Sauk Lake
Wolgosone Trail
Stowe Lake
Brandon
Whiskey Lake
Aldrich Lake
Moon Lake
Nelson 35 Lake
Sauk Centre
Hoboken Creek
Sauk Lake
W. 2nd St.
Sinclair Lewis
Sinclair Lewis Ave.
Walnut
Maple
Elm St.
Birch St.
6th St. S.
7th St. S.

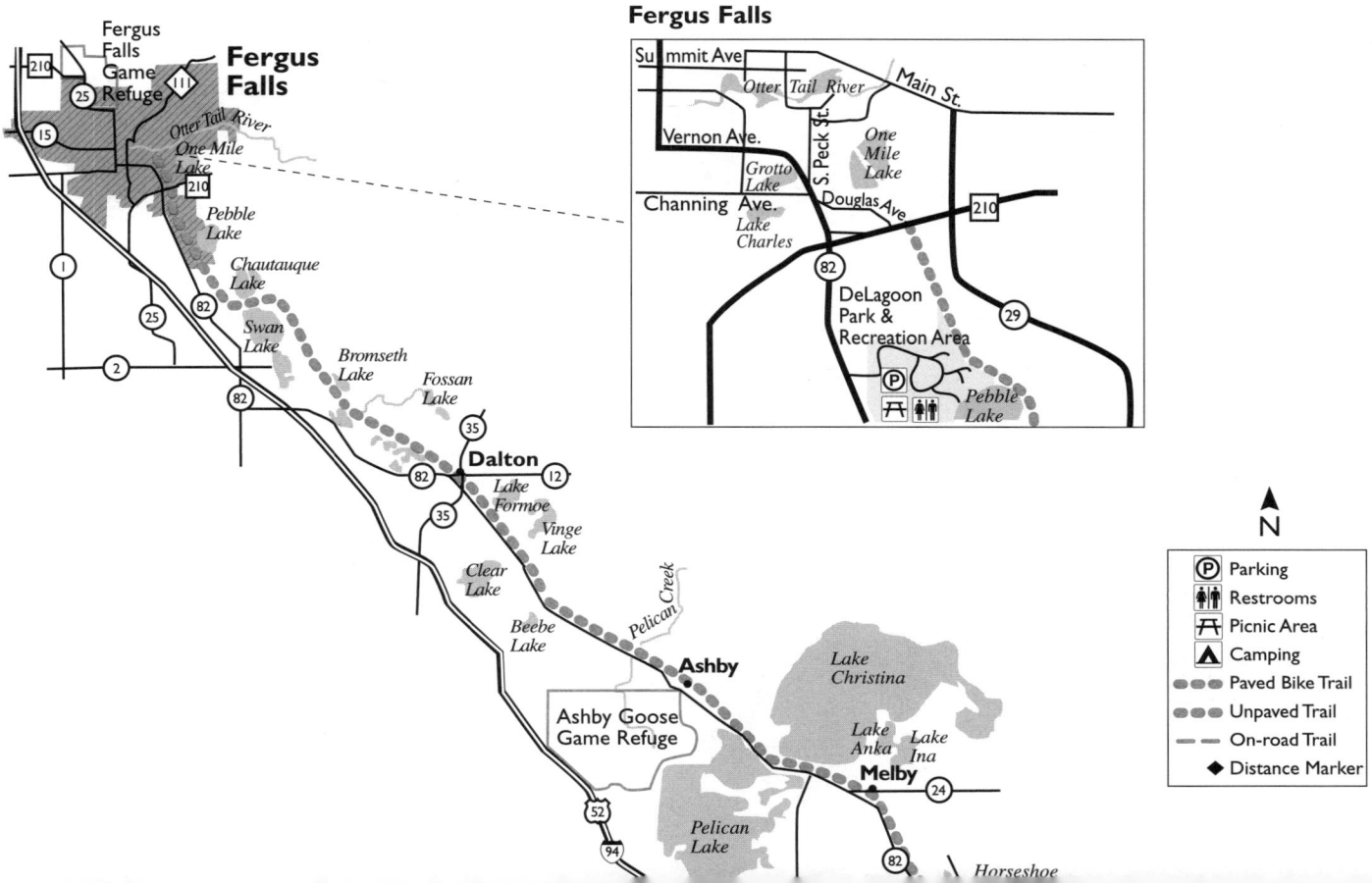
Fergus Falls
Fergus Falls Game Refuge
Fergus Falls
Otter Tail River
One Mile Lake
Pebble Lake
Chautauque Lake
Swan Lake
Bromseth Lake
Fossan Lake
Dalton
Lake Formoe
Vinge Lake
Clear Lake
Beebe Lake
Pelican Creek
Ashby
Ashby Goose Game Refuge
Lake Christina
Lake Anka
Lake Ina
Melby
Pelican Lake
Horseshoe
Summit Ave.
Otter Tail River
Main St.
Vernon Ave.
S. Peck St.
One Mile Lake
Grotto Lake
Channing Ave.
Douglas Ave.
Lake Charles
DeLagoon Park & Recreation Area
Pebble Lake
N
Parking
Restrooms
Picnic Area
Camping
Paved Bike Trail
Unpaved Trail
On-road Trail
Distance Marker

HEARTLAND

WHERE: Park Rapids to Walker
LENGTH: 28 miles
SURFACE: Blacktop
TRAIL USE:

Trailhead West: The trail begins at Heartland Park in Park Rapids. Going east on Highway 34 through Park Rapids, you turn north on Central Avenue. There is a sign on Central Avenue indicating the Heartland Trail. You turn left (west) on North Street which leads right into the park. There is a large paved parking lot here, with excellent facilities. Overnight parking is permitted.

Mid Access: Dorset, Nevis and Akeley, just off Highway 34.

Trailhead East: In Walker, where Highway 371 intersects with County Road 12. The access is one-half mile west on County Road 12. The parking lot, with restrooms, is set back from the street.

If you enjoy the north woods, glacial lakes and flowing streams, you will like the Heartland Trail. The Trailhead West is located just 21 miles from one of the major attractions in northern Minnesota, Itasca State Park and the origin of the mighty Mississippi River.

Originally paved in 1975, this was the first blacktopped trail in Minnesota, perhaps in the country. The Heartland is a popular trail for snowmobilers in winter. The surfaced bike portions are part of many miles of trail for winter recreation which are not suitable for biking unless your are a real mountain bike enthusiast. These trails do, however, offer an opportunity to get off your bicycle and take a quiet walk in the woods.

The 28 miles of paved bike trail is an easy half-day ride through the Chippewa State Forest and also lends itself to a two-way, one day ride. Our group prefers to ride to Walker one day and back to Park Rapids the next. This is partly because of the driving distance from home, but also because of the interesting towns, scenery and the area in general. For overnight trips, reservations are highly recommended if you want a motel room during the tourist season.

If you plan to ride two days, we recommend starting at Heartland Park in Park Rapids where you may leave your car overnight. Heading east out of Park Rapids you will soon find yourself in deep woods with only an occasional farm field or residence in sight. About 10½ miles brings you into Nevis where you can have lunch.

Another 5½ miles puts you in Akeley, where you will want to ride one block off the trail and have your picture taken while sitting on the hand of a huge Paul Bunyan statue at the municipal park on Main Street. On the north side of the trail at Akeley, there is a picnic shelter, tables and restrooms. A well with hand pump will give you good water.

From Akeley to Walker is probably the most scenic section. You leave the proximity of Highway 34 (and an occasional residence) and ride by numerous lakes. The east end of the trail ends rather abruptly and it is necessary to ride the last one-quarter mile into Walker on city streets.

In Walker, we found excellent accommodations at reasonable rates and a family restaurant just a short distance from the marina on beautiful Leech Lake.

The entire trail from Park Rapids to Walker was resurfaced in 1997. Future plans include extending the trail from Walker to Cass Lake. The Paul Bunyan Trail, which now runs from Brainerd to Hackensack, will eventually intersect with the Heartland on its way to Bemidji.

Itasca State Park is just 21 miles north of Park Rapids. There are 17 miles of bike paths in the park (see page 24). Closer to Walker, the scenic and unfortunately named Leech Lake is located in Minnesota's beautiful Chippewa National Forest.

FOR MORE INFORMATION:

Trail Office
P.O. Box 112
Nevis, MN 56467
218-652-4054

Leech Lake Area Chamber of Commerce
P.O. Box 1089
Walker, MN 56484
218-547-1313
800-833-1118

Park Rapids Chamber of Commerce
Highway 71 South
P.O. Box 249
Park Rapids, MN 56470
800-247-0054

Bemidji Area Trails & Waterways
6603 Birchmont Beach Rd. N.
Bemidji, MN 56601
218-755-2265

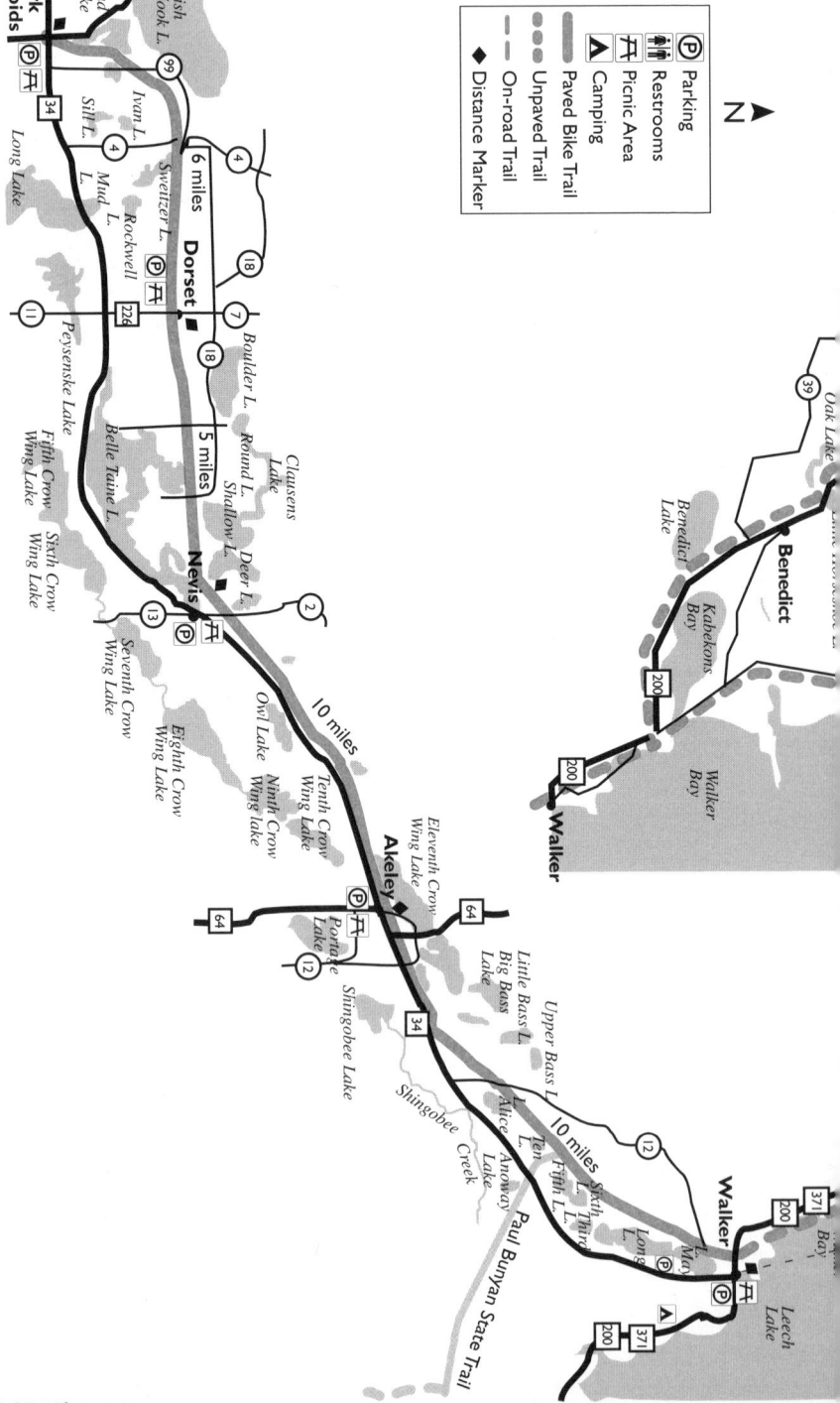

Administered by Minnesota Department of Natural Resources

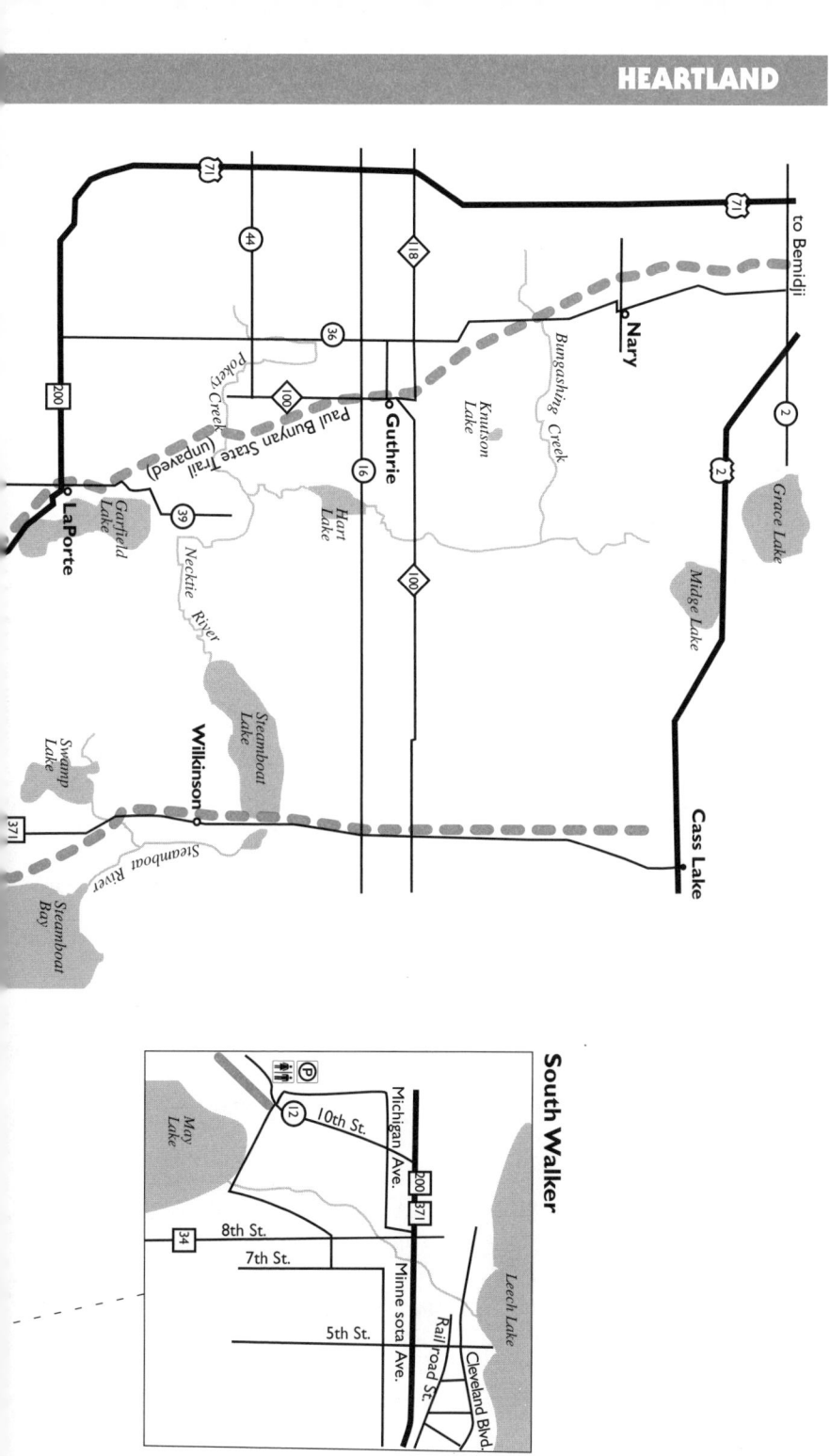
to Bemidji
71
2
Grace Lake
Midge Lake
Cass Lake
Nary
Bungashing Creek
Knutson Lake
118
36
Guthrie
16
100
Hart Lake
Paul Bunyan State Trail (unpaved)
Poker Creek
44
71
200
39
Garfield Lake
LaPorte
Necktie River
Steamboat Lake
Wilkinson
Swamp Lake
371
Steamboat River
Steamboat Bay
South Walker
Leech Lake
Cleveland Blvd.
Railroad St.
Minnesota Ave.
Michigan Ave.
200
371
10th St.
12
May Lake
8th St.
34
7th St.
5th St.

ITASCA STATE PARK

WHERE: 21 miles north of Park Rapids on Highway 71
LENGTH: 17 miles, 6.5 miles off-road
SURFACE: Paved
TRAIL USE:

Here is a chance to combine a really scenic bike ride with a visit to one of the more famous state parks in the nation. Not only is the scenery impressive, but the park offers a wide variety of other attractions. In 1991 this park celebrated its 100th birthday.

The off-road path is only 6.5 miles, with an additional 10.5 miles designated on low traffic roads. This permits a complete circle ride around Lake Itasca. Bike rentals are available in the park. The Trailhead South starts at the information center on the east entrance road, and the Trailhead North starts in the parking lot for the interpretive center at the headwaters of the Mississippi River near the north entrance road.

The location lends itself well to a companion trip with the Heartland Trail (see page 20). Biking enthusiasts may want to consider staying in Park Rapids or riding to Park Rapids. It is only 20 miles via U.S. Highway 71 from the south edge of the park. The highway has paved shoulders specifically marked for biking or hiking and it would be an interesting ride.

The virgin pines, lakes and other attractions of the park make this trail a real gem for outdoor enthusiasts and nature lovers. Be sure of your reservations, including campgrounds, during the summer season.

FOR MORE INFORMATION:

Itasca State Park
HCO 5, Box 4
Lake Itasca, MN 56460
218-266-3654

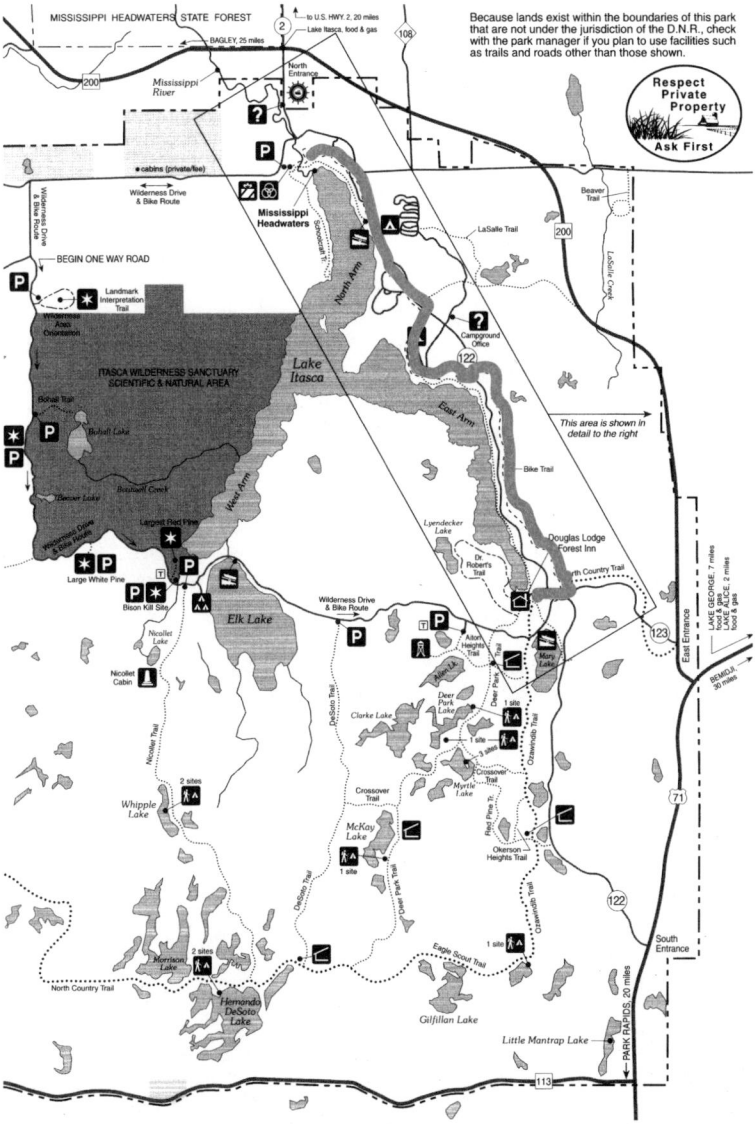
MISSISSIPPI HEADWATERS STATE FOREST
to U.S. HWY. 2, 20 miles
Lake Itasca, food & gas
BAGLEY, 25 miles
Because lands exist within the boundaries of this park that are not under the jurisdiction of the D.N.R., check with the park manager if you plan to use facilities such as trails and roads other than those shown.
Respect Private Property
Ask First
Mississippi River
North Entrance
cabins (private/fee)
Wilderness Drive & Bike Route
Mississippi Headwaters
Spurrier Tr.
North Arm
LaSalle Trail
Beaver Trail
LaSalle Creek
BEGIN ONE WAY ROAD
Landmark Interpretation Trail
Area Orientation
Campground Office
ITASCA WILDERNESS SANCTUARY SCIENTIFIC & NATURAL AREA
Lake Itasca
East Arm
This area is shown in detail to the right
Bohall Trail
Bohall Lake
Bohall Creek
Beaver Lake
West Arm
Bike Trail
Largest Red Pine
Lyendecker Lake
Douglas Lodge Forest Inn
Dr. Robert's Trail
North Country Trail
Large White Pine
Bison Kill Site
Elk Lake
Wilderness Drive & Bike Route
Nicollet Lake
Nicollet Cabin
Nicollet Trail
Adam Heights Trail
Mary Lake
East Entrance
LAKE GEORGE, 7 miles
BEMIDJI, 30 miles
LAKE JULIE, 2 miles
food & gas
DeSoto Trail
Clarke Lake
Deer Park Lake
Deer Park Trail
Olaverson Trail
Crossover Trail
Myrtle Lake
Whipple Lake
Crossover Trail
McKay Lake
Red Pine Tr.
Olaverson Heights Trail
Deer Park Trail
Eagle Scout Trail
South Entrance
Morrison Lake
North Country Trail
Hernando DeSoto Lake
Gilfillan Lake
Little Mantrap Lake
PARK RAPIDS, 20 miles
LEGEND
SUMMER TRAILS
Hiking
Biking/Hiking
Interpretive
North Country National Scenic Trail
GREAT RIVER ROAD
National Route
FACILITIES
Information/Office
Point of Interest
Picnic Area
Interpretive Area
Boat Ramp
Historic Site
Shelter
Observation Tower
Lodge
Campground
Group Camp
Backpack Camping
Parking
Gift Shop
Toilet
Private Property
Public Use Prohibited

MI-GE-ZI TRAIL CHIPPEWA NATIONAL FOREST

WHERE: Chippewa National Forest–Cass Lake
LENGTH: Approximately 3 miles (18 miles when complete)
SURFACE: Asphalt 8' wide, 10' wide through the campground
TRAIL USE: 

Trailhead North: From the North, the Wanaki Campground and Knutsen Dam at north end of the Norway Beach recreation area on Cass Lake (open seasonally).

Trailhead South: The trail presently dead ends just over one-half mile south of Highway 2 on east side of Pike Bay. No parking at this point.

This is a new trail built and administered by the U.S. Forest Service. Although presently short, we include it here because of its future potential and its eventual connection with the city of Cass Lake and the Heartland Trail into Walker. Mi-ge-zi is Anishinabe for "Bald Eagle."

Although not constructed on a rail bed, this trail is flat and scenic, overlooking and/or adjacent to the shore of Cass Lake at frequent intervals. The trail passes through dense woods and large pines. This is especially true around the east side, and will also hold true of the south shore of Pike Bay when that section is completed.

The Chippewa National Forest also has many miles of paved road shoulders marked as bike routes, if you wish to extend your ride.

FOR MORE INFORMATION:

Chippewa National Forest
Ranger Work Station
Route 3, Box 219
Cass Lake, MN 56633
218-335-8618

Chippewa National Forest
Ranger Station
HCR 73, Box 15
Walker, MN 56484
218-547-1044

Cass Lake Area Civic and
Commerce Association
PO Box 548
Cass Lake, MN 56633
218-335-6723 (season only)

Bemidji Area Chamber of Commerce
300 Bemidji Ave.
Bemidji, MN 56619
218-751-3541
800-458-2223

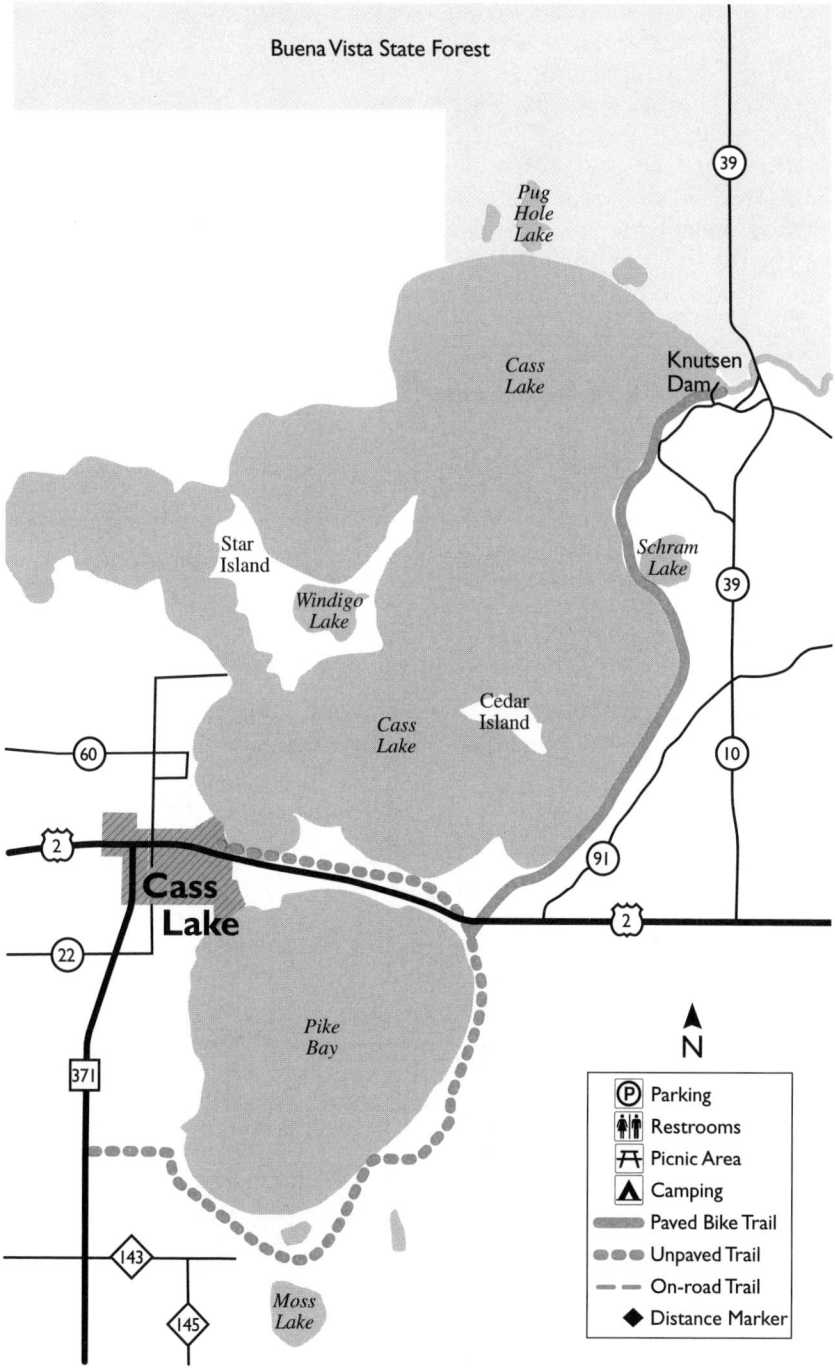

Administered by Minnesota Department of Natural Resources

MOORHEAD/FARGO (CITY)

WHERE: Cities of Moorhead and Fargo
LENGTH: Moorhead-12.5 miles, Fargo-25 miles
SURFACE: Paved
TRAIL USE:

Both Moorhead and Fargo have quite extensive dedicated bicycle and recreational trails along with on-street trails. Both cities take advantage of the scenery and green space provided by the Red River of the North which divides the two cities. Dedicated trails also continue east from Moorhead into Dilworth along Highway 10.

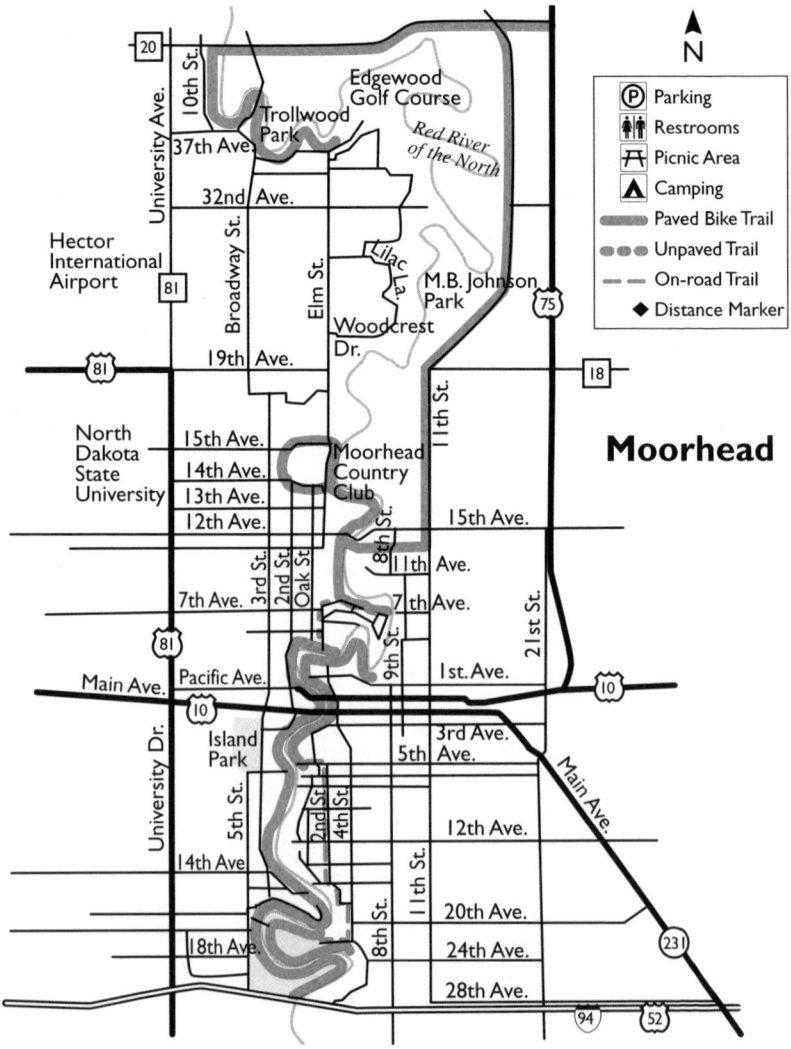

Fargo

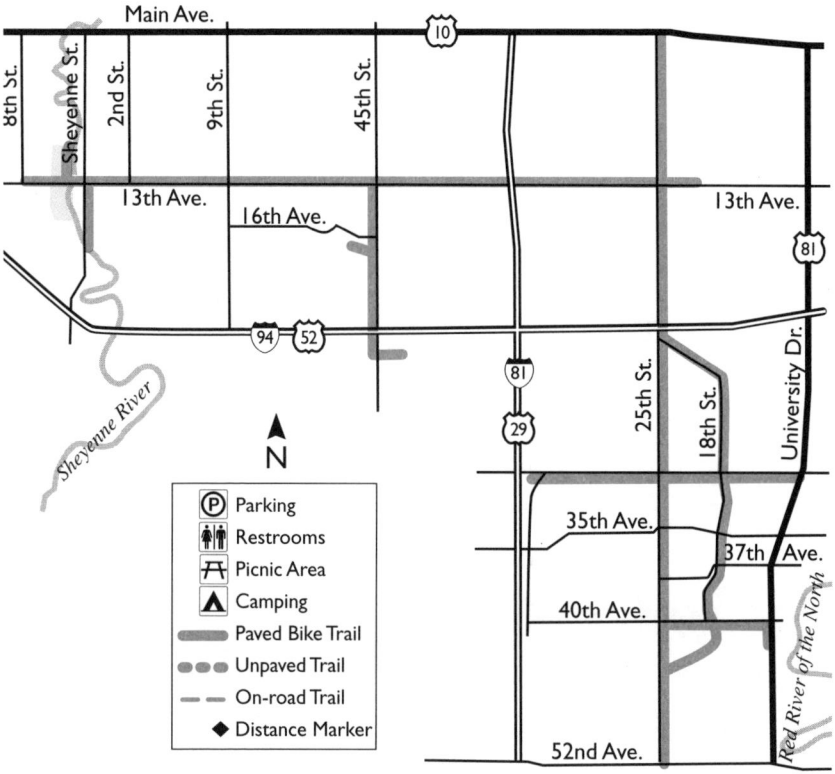

FOR MORE INFORMATION:

Fargo/Moorhead
Chamber of Commerce
P.O. Box 2443
Fargo, ND 58108
701-237-5678

Moorhead Parks Department
324-24th St. S.
Moorhead, MN 56560
218-299-5340

Fargo Parks Department
P.O. Box 1796
Fargo, ND 58107
701-241-1350

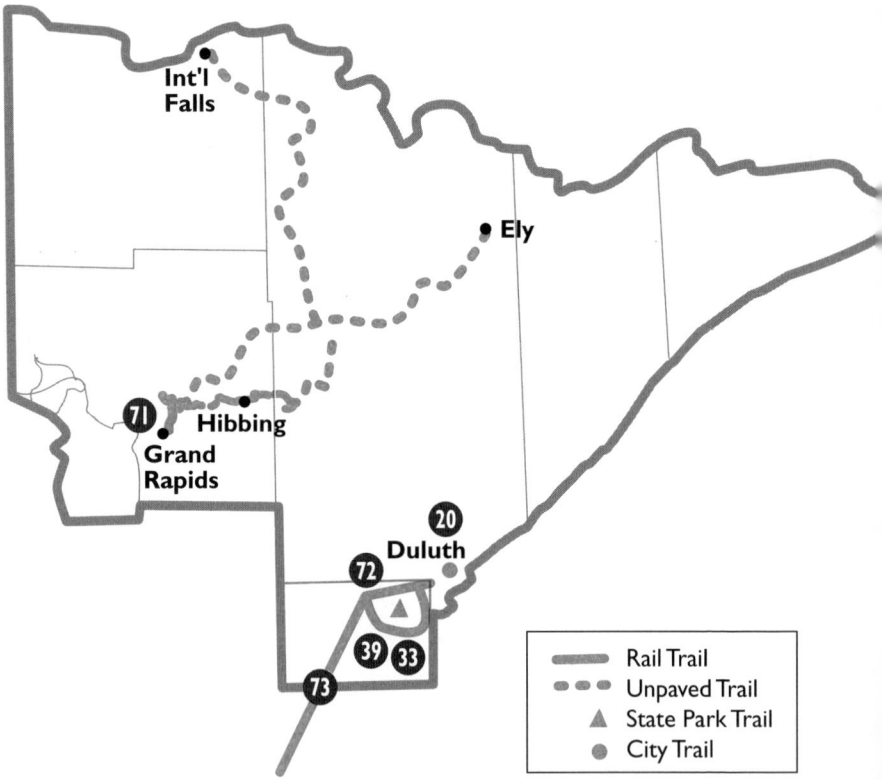
Int'l Falls
Ely
71
Hibbing
Grand Rapids
20
Duluth
72
39
33
73
Rail Trail
Unpaved Trail
State Park Trail
City Trail

Northeast Minnesota

Trail

20. Duluth City Trails . . . . . .page 32
33. Jay Cooke State Park Trail . . . . . .page 34
39. Laveau Memorial Rail-Trail . . . . . .page 36
71. Mesabi, Itasca, Arrowhead, Taconite Bike Trails . . .page 42
72. Willard Munger-Carlton to Duluth Segment . . . . . .page 46
73. Willard Munger-Hinckley Fire Trail Segment
(see Central section) . . . . . .page 70

*** Numbers refer to large map on page 11 and opposite page**

DULUTH (CITY)

WHERE: City of Duluth
LENGTH: Trails range from 1.5 miles-23 miles
SURFACE: Varies between trails
TRAIL USE: 

Access: Canal Park and off several city streets (see maps).

There are several bike routes in the Duluth-Superior area in addition to the Willard Munger Trail which you can follow some 65 miles to Hinckley (see page 46) and the Alex Laveau Memorial Trail (see page 36) which travels to Wrenshall. Lakewalk (see below) is a very popular path located next to Lake Superior and the busy Canal Park area. A section of this 3-mile trail has a boardwalk for pedestrians and an asphalt trail for bikers and skaters. Western Waterfront Trail (next page) is unpaved and about 5 miles long with the portion designated for bicycling shown on the map. Trails and paths you may want to consider that we haven't mapped include Central Entrance Bicycle Path (near Central High School, about 1.5 miles long), Bong Bridge Path (about 2.5 miles long, crossing the St. Louis Bay next to the Bridge's eastbound lane), and the Osaugie Trail (multi-purpose trail next to State Highway 53 in Superior). You can also bike along some 21 miles of the North Shore Drive by following the designated bike route signs. In addition, numerous scenic parks in town have hiking and cross-country ski trails, and nearby Jay Cooke State Park (see page 34) also has beautiful trails.

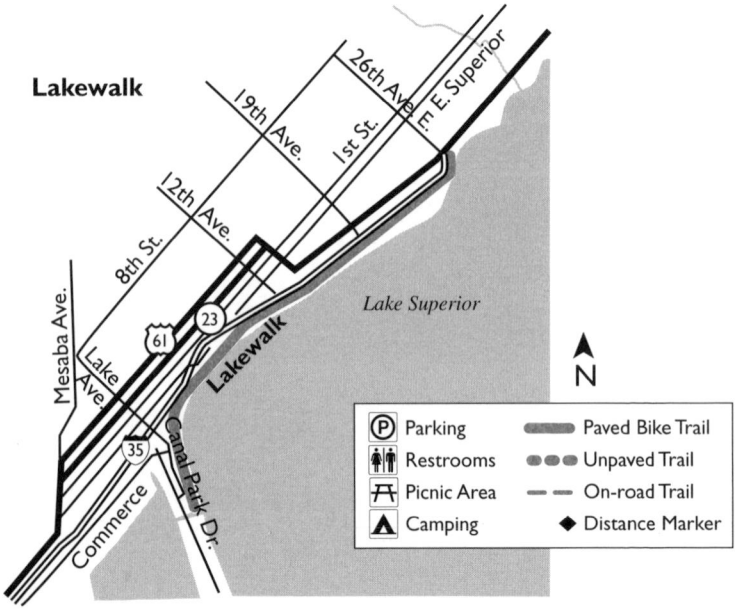

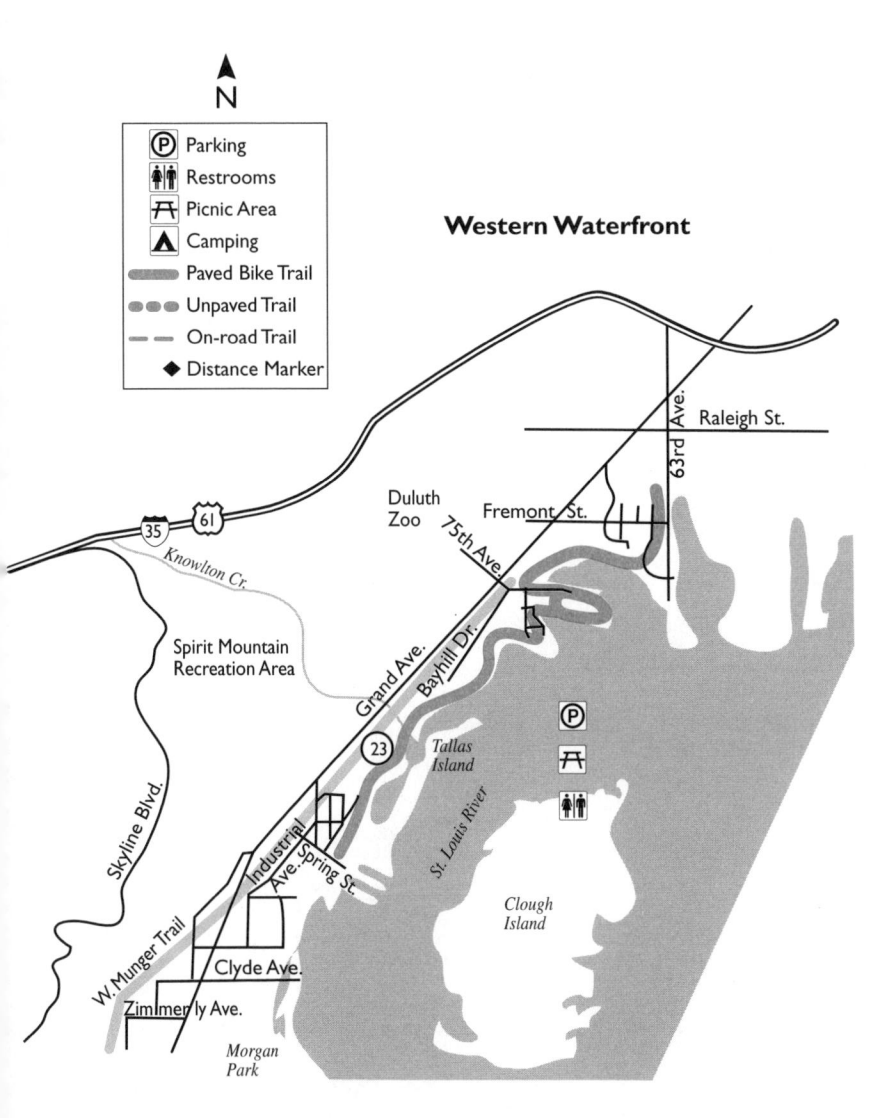

FOR MORE INFORMATION:

Duluth CVB
Endion Station
100 Lake Place Drive
Duluth, MN 55802
218-722-4011
1-800-438-5884
www.visitduluth.com

Parks and Recreation
330 City Hall
Duluth, MN 55802
218-723-3612

JAY COOKE STATE PARK

WHERE: Carlton
LENGTH: 3 miles
SURFACE: Paved roadside only within park
TRAIL USE:

Access: Park entrance is off Hiway 210, 3 miles east of Carlton.

Although there are very few separate bicycle trails within the park, it is an excellent base for a bicycle outing. It is surrounded on all four sides by state rail-trails and/or improved roadside lanes. The Munger from Carlton to Duluth traverses the north side, and the Alex Laveau skirts the west, south and east sides.

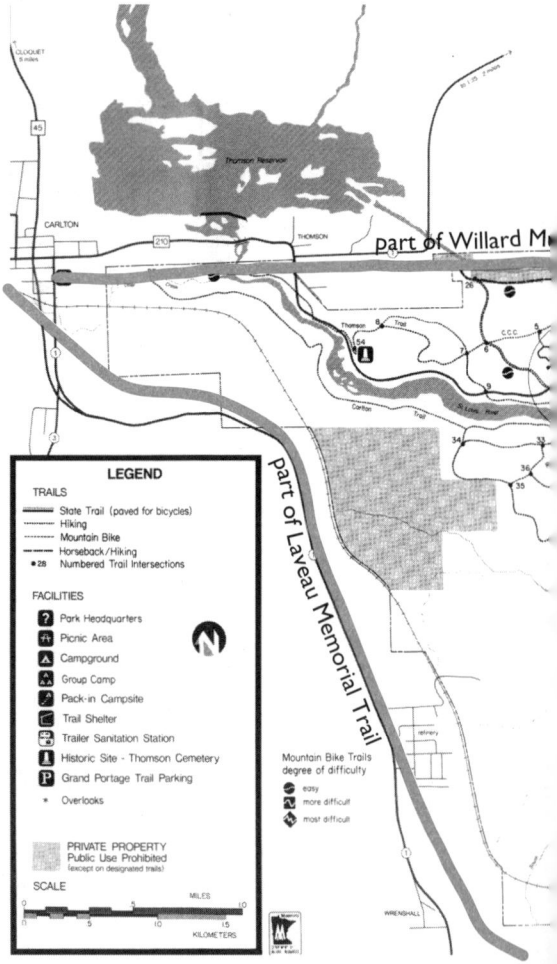

FOR MORE INFORMATION:

Jay Cooke State Park
500 E. Highway 210
Carlton, MN 55718
218-384-4610

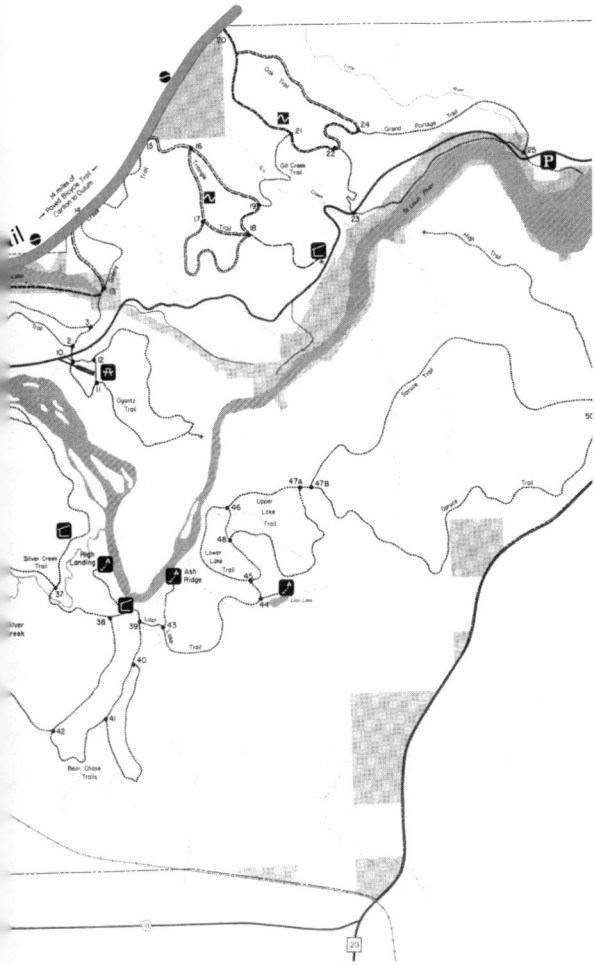

LAVEAU MEMORIAL

WHERE: Carlton to Duluth
LENGTH: 6 miles to Highway 23, 12 miles from Highway 23 into S. Duluth
SURFACE: Paved 10' wide on rail bed to Highway 23, paved road shoulder from Highway 23 into Duluth.
TRAIL USE:

Trailhead West: Carlton, 1 block south of Carlton Depot and the Munger Trail.

Mid Access: Wrenshall, off County Road 1.

Trailhead North: South Duluth. Via paved street shoulders, the Laveau presently joins the Munger at the bridge over Commonwealth Avenue (also Highway 23), but they will eventually intersect at Beaudry Street.

Utilizing the Munger State Trail, this new addition provides an excellent circle route for a total ride of just over 35 miles. This trail will give you a different view of Jay Cooke State Park and the St. Louis River Estuary in South Duluth.

This trail is somewhat unique in that the Carlton to Highway 23 segment is owned by the DNR, and the construction from the Highway 23 trail into Duluth is the combined effort of the MN DOT, Carlton, St. Louis counties and the City of Duluth.

The DNR portion follows an old rail bed from Carlton through Wrenshall and on to Highway 23. From that point, the DOT portion is a wide paved shoulder following Highway 23 into South Duluth.

The trail name honors the memory of a former County Commissioner and dairy farmer who was a strong advocate of the idea of reusing abandoned railways as public trails.

FOR MORE INFORMATION:

DNR Trail Office
Route 2, 701 S. Kenwood
Moose Lake, MM
218-485-5410

Duluth Area Visitors Bureau
800-4-DULUTH

Duluth Area Chamber of Commerce
118 E. Superior St.
Duluth, MN 55802
218-722-5501

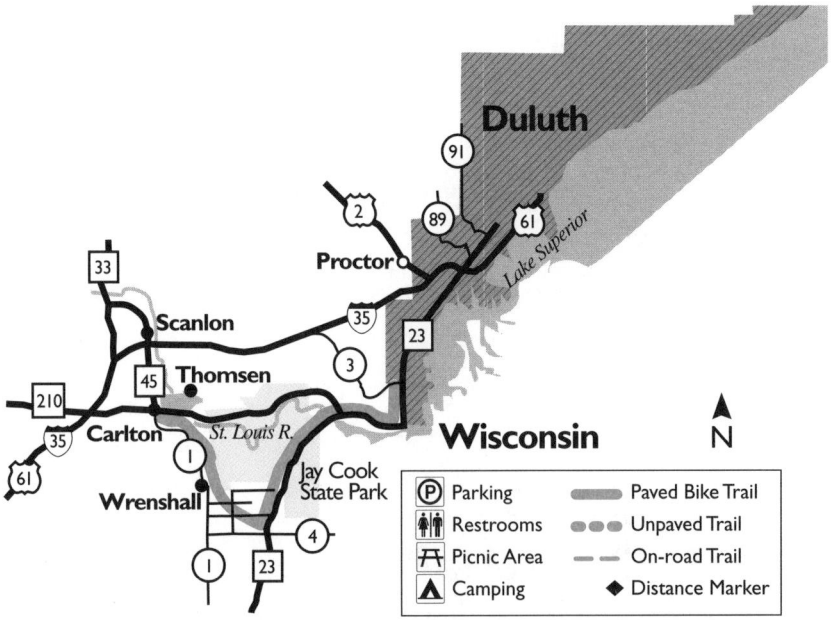

Administered by Minnesota Department of Natural Resources

Bike Shorts

If you are not fully familiar with the area or trail you plan to ride, a good map or bicycle guide book can be very important. Not all trails and routes are well marked.

Mesabi Trail (see map page 44)

WHERE: Grand Rapids to Ely
LENGTH: 132 miles when completed
SURFACE: bituminous, 10-14 feet wide
TRAIL USE:

Itasca Bicycle Trail (see map page 40)

WHERE: Grand Rapids to Gunn Park
LENGTH: 6 miles
SURFACE: Paved
TRAIL USE:

Arrowhead Trail (no detailed map included)

WHERE: Tower to International Falls
LENGTH: 128 miles
SURFACE: unimproved
TRAIL USE:

Taconite Trail (see map page 40)

WHERE: Grand Rapids to Ely
LENGTH: 165 miles
SURFACE: 5 miles paved
TRAIL USE:

While the Taconite and Itasca Trails are coordinated and administered by the DNR, the Mesabi Trails is coordinated and administered by the St. Louis and Lake Counties Regional Railroad Authority, implementing plans some of which go as far back as the 1970s. They have undertaken an ambitious project to connect the population centers of this sparsely settled region and the combined efforts of city, county, state and private industry is gradually getting it done. Approximately 40% will be on rail bed.

Three of the trails (Mesabi, Itasca and Taconite) begin as one trail at the fairgrounds in Grand Rapids and continue for 3½ miles north to the Prairie River Dam. At that point, the Itasca Trail goes another 2 miles west to Gunn Park (open seasonally). The Taconite and Mesabi trails take two different routes to the east to Tower, where the Arrowhead goes north to International Falls. The Mesabi and Taconite proceed to Ely.

The Taconite and Arrowhead Trails are winter snowmobile trails with many parts unusable in summer. The Itasca Trail is paved for all of its 6 miles and the Mesabi Trail to date has paved and completed segments totaling approximately 55 miles.

MESABI, ITASCA, ARROWHEAD AND TACONITE TRAILS

FOR MORE INFORMATION:

DNR
1201 East Highway 2
Grand Rapids, MN 55744
218-327-4408

Mesabi
St. Louis and Lake Counties Regional
Railroad Authority
US Bank Place Suite 6B
230 First Street South
Virginia, MN 55792
218-749-0697

DNR
Box 388
406 Main St.
Tower, MN 55790
218-753-6257

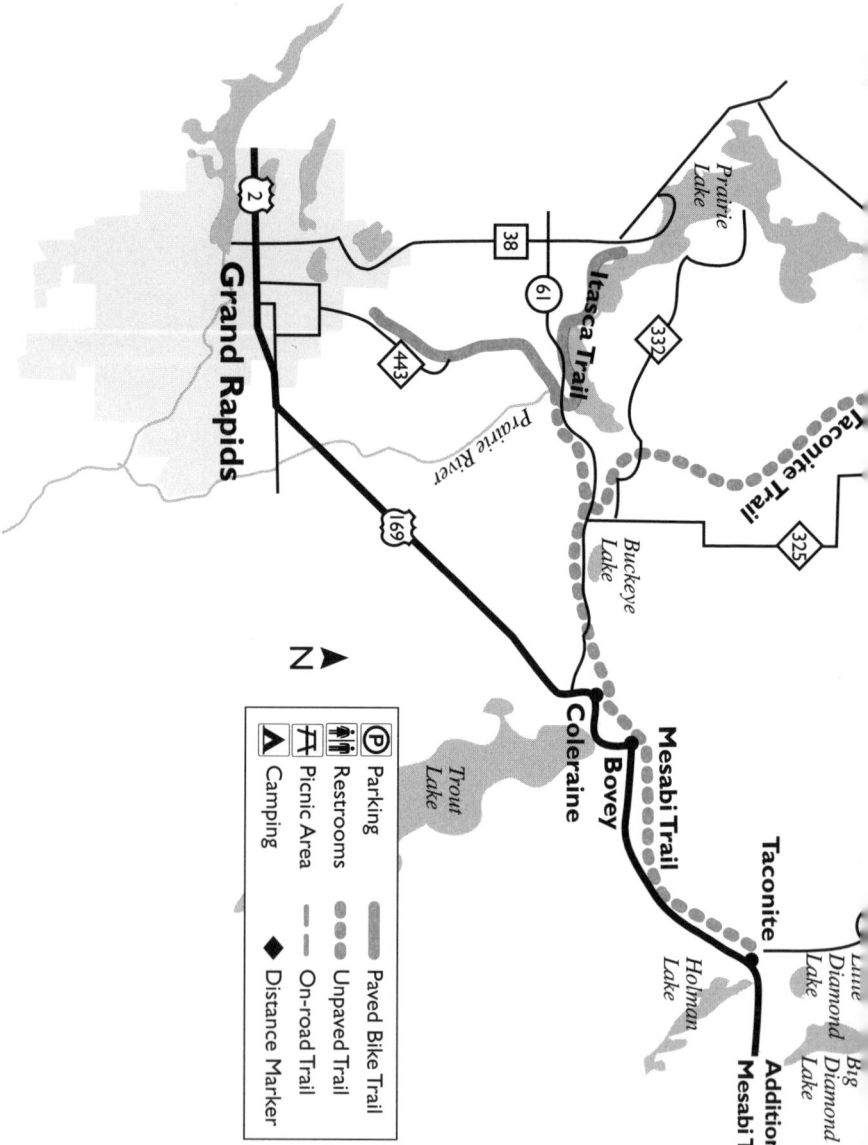
Big Diamond Lake
Little Diamond Lake
Holman Lake
Additional portions of Mesabi Trail on next page
Taconite
Mesabi Trail
Bovey
Coleraine
Trout Lake
Taconite Trail
325
Buckeye Lake
Prairie River
169
Itasca Trail
61
38
443
332
Prairie Lake
2
Grand Rapids
N
Parking
Restrooms
Picnic Area
Camping
Paved Bike Trail
Unpaved Trail
On-road Trail
Distance Marker

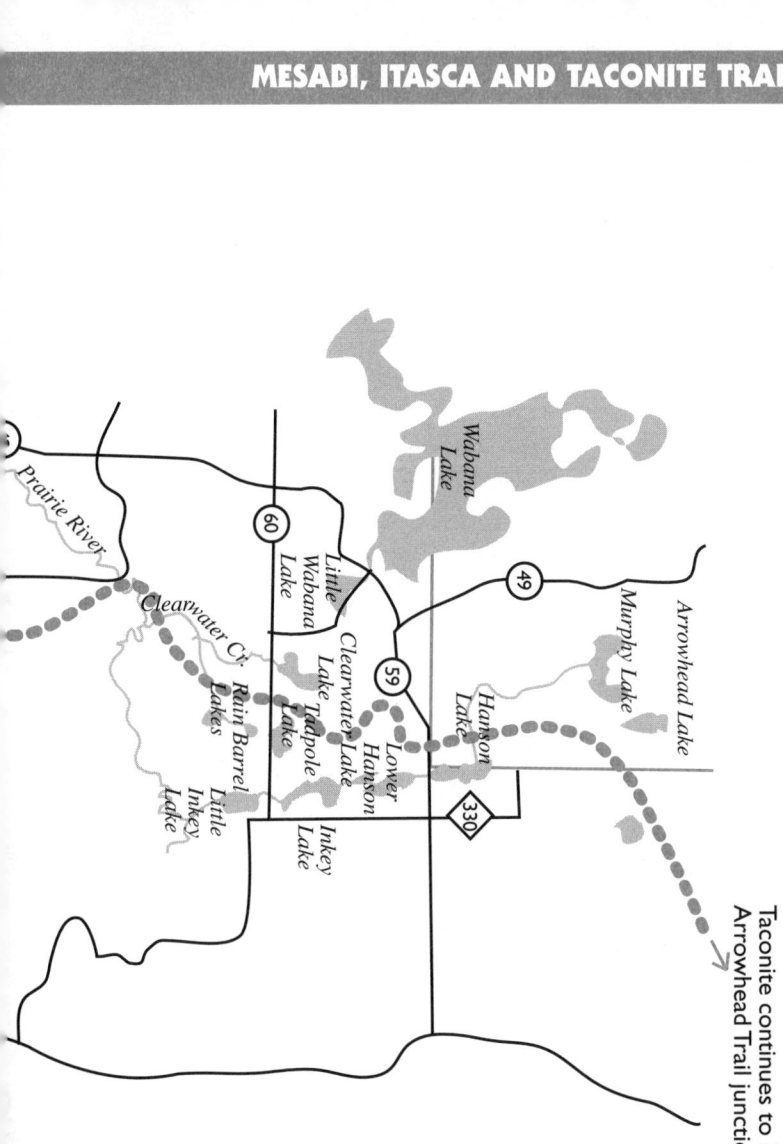
Taconite continues to Ely
Arrowhead Trail junction near Tower
Arrowhead Lake
Murphy Lake
49
Hanson Lake
330
Wabana Lake
59
Lower Hanson Lake
Clearwater Lake
Little Wabana Lake
Tadpole Lake
Inkey Lake
60
Rain Barrel Lakes
Little Inkey Lake
Clearwater Cr.
Prairie River

The Mesabi Trail

This will be a 132-mile, multi-use recreational trail linking over 22 communities across the Iron Range area. Utilizing abandoned railways, logging and mine haul roads and existing bike trails, the trail will provide safe and healthy recreational opportunities.

The trail alignment will emphasize the historic, scenic, environmental and educational aspects of the region while providing alternate transportation possibilities for local communities. Along the trail will be learning centers where users can stop to learn about the forest, area geology and the region's fascinating history. The trail will be routed past established tourist attractions, where feasible.

The Mesabi Trail is destined to become a star quality attraction to the tourism industry and give an economic boost to the entire region. The estimated cost to complete this entire system is $10 million. Completion of the 132-mile length will be determined by funding availability.

The Mesabi Trail is a brand new trail and therefore the access points and descriptions that follow are tentative, pending further trail development. By the time of this printing, the following sections of the Mesabi will be paved and will allow biking and hiking. Please consult the Regional Railroad Authority at the address/phone number below for current trail status.

Grand Rapids to Taconite Segment

WHERE: Grand Rapids to Taconite
LENGTH: 13 miles

Trailhead West: Grand Rapids Fairgrounds. From combined Hwys. 169 and 2, turn north onto 3rd Ave. NE to Itasca County Fairgrounds. Trail access at north side of fairgrounds.

Mid Access: Coleraine. From Hwy. 169, exit onto Curley Ave., trail access at intersection with Curley Ave. and Cole St. Bovey. From Hwy. 169 exit onto 2nd St (west) go one block to 1st. Ave., trail on left.

Trailhead East: Taconite. From Hwy. 169, exit onto Cty. 15 into town. Turn left on Haines Ave. to Community Center. Trail access at the Community Center.

Nashwauk to Kinney Segment

WHERE: Nashwauk to Kinney
LENGTH: 28 miles

Trailhead West: Nashwauk. From Hwy.169 exit on Cty. 65. Continue north 7 blocks to the city park where you will find the trail access.

Mid Access: Keewatin. From Hwy. 169 exit Cty. 82 (7th St.). Continue north about .3 of a mile. Trail access at corner of 3rd Ave. and 7th St. Hibbing. From Hwy. 169 take Howard St. exit, and follow to 3rd Ave. E (Greyhound Blvd.). Turn right and continue 1 mile, trail on right. Chisholm. Exit Hwy. 169 onto 4th Ave. SE (downtown exit). Trail access on right about 150 feet from Highway.

Trailhead East: Kinney. From Hwy. 169 exit onto Hwy. 25 North. Continue .75 mile, with the trail access on left.

Mt. Iron to Gilbert

WHERE: Mt. Iron to Gilbert
LENGTH: 11 miles

Trailhead West: Mt. Iron. From Hwy. 169 exit at Cty. 102 toward downtown. Trail access about .1 of a mile on right.

Mid Access: Virginia. From Hwy. 53 exit onto 9th St. North, travel 1.5 miles to 3rd St., and turn left. Trail access one block on left.

Trailhead East: Gilbert. From Hwy. 53, exit onto Hwy. 135 to Gilbert. Continue 3 miles to intersection of Hwy. 37 (Broadway), turn left. Trail access on right.

Gilbert to Ely

Small sections are completed but most of this segment is still under construction.

FOR MORE INFORMATION:

Mesabi
St. Louis and Lake Counties Regional Railroad Authority
US Bank Place Suite 6B
230 First Street South
Virginia, MN 55792
218-749-0697

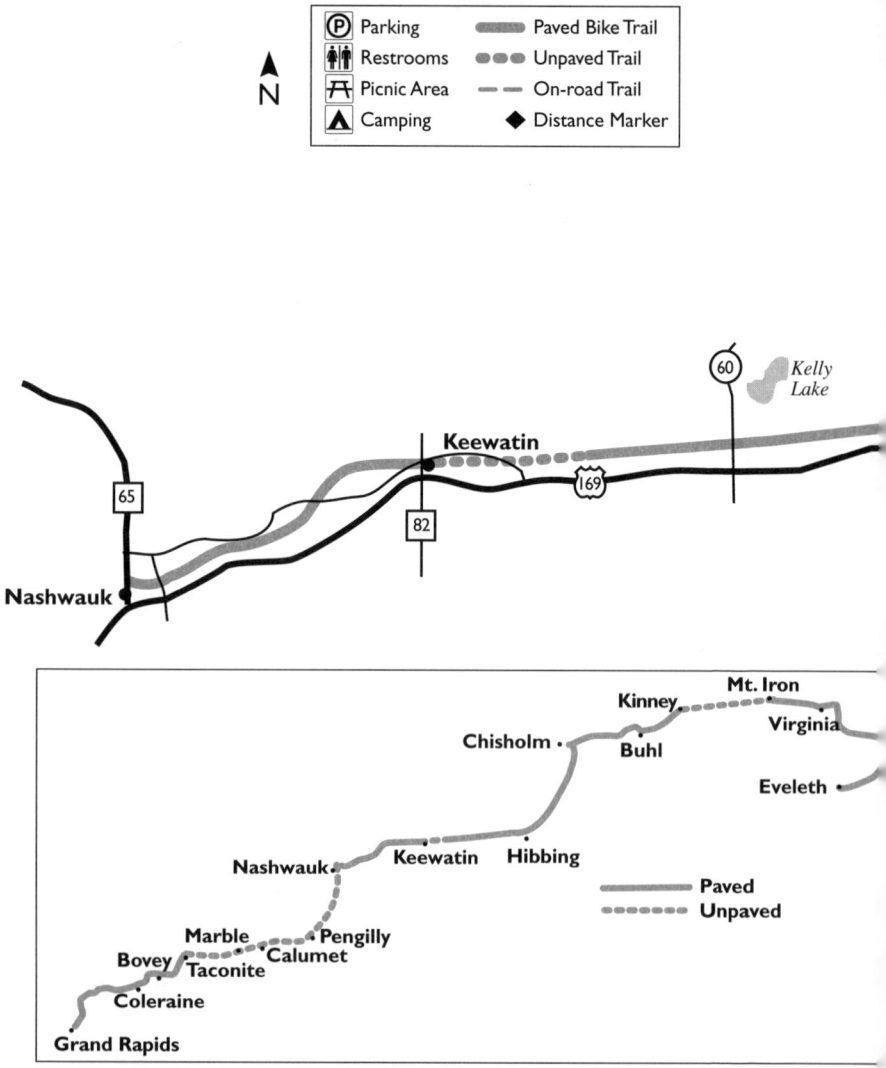
Parking
Restrooms
Picnic Area
Camping
Paved Bike Trail
Unpaved Trail
On-road Trail
Distance Marker
N
60
Kelly Lake
Keewatin
169
65
82
Nashwauk
Mt. Iron
Kinney
Virginia
Chisholm
Buhl
Eveleth
Nashwauk
Keewatin
Hibbing
Paved
Unpaved
Marble
Pengilly
Bovey
Calumet
Taconite
Coleraine
Grand Rapids

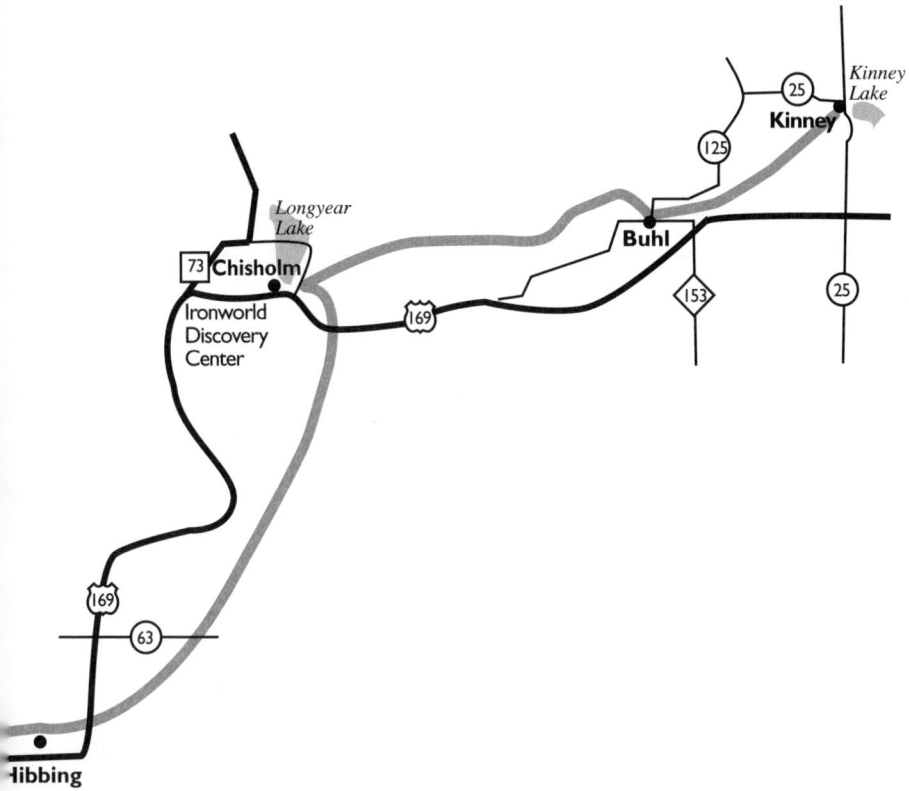
Kinney Lake
25
Kinney
125
Longyear Lake
Buhl
73
Chisholm
153
25
Ironworld Discovery Center
169
169
63
Hibbing

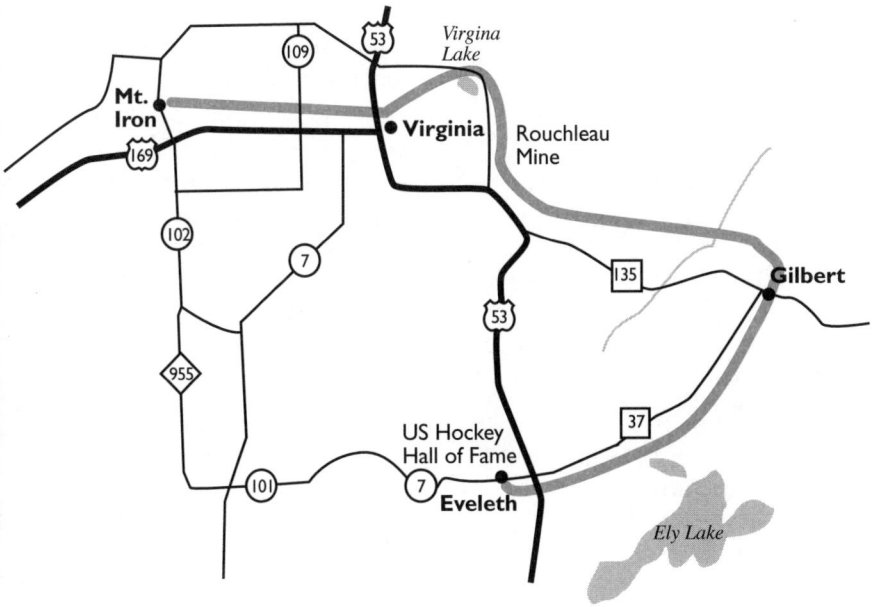
53
Virgina Lake
109
Mt. Iron
Virginia
Rouchleau Mine
169
102
7
135
Gilbert
53
955
37
US Hockey Hall of Fame
101
7
Eveleth
Ely Lake

WILLARD MUNGER-CARLTON TO DULUTH SEGMENT

WHERE: Carlton to West Duluth
LENGTH: 14.5 miles
SURFACE: Paved
TRAIL USE:

Trailhead North: Driving north on I-35, take Cody Street exit (251-A). Turn right on 63rd (south), you will intersect with Grand Avenue. The trail access is directly behind the Willard Motel at 75th Avenue and Grand Avenue. Also, at this location, you will see the Lake Superior Zoological Garden on the west side of Grand. Parking is available at the trail access. If driving south on I-35, take the Grand Avenue exit (S-23).

Trailhead West: Exit from I-35, on Highway 210, and drive east to Carlton. At the four-way stop, turn onto County Road 1, and proceed about one block south to the trail access depot and parking lot.

The Carlton to West Duluth segment is the very northern 14½ miles of what is eventually planned to be a single trail from St. Paul to Duluth (and perhaps beyond). Now completed and paved from Duluth to Hinckley, we have a super 68 mile distance ride.

The first time we selected this trail, we started at Duluth. While 14½ miles makes an easy two-way ride, the first 9 miles seem more of an uphill grade than the 3% slope. We recommend starting in Duluth so you can do that section while you are still fresh and because it permits you to start and end your ride in Duluth. While the ride up is a bit strenuous, the long coast back down makes up for it.

Along the way, there are some interesting cuts through solid rock, a great view of Lake Superior and Wisconsin, and other scenic vistas. The trail takes you through woods, alongside Jay Cooke State Park and over a high bridge overlooking a spectacular gorge where you may see park visitors swimming and fishing. We did not join them, but not much further west, we did cool off by wading into a cool, clear stream paralleling our path. One pleasant surprise en route was a mobile refreshment stand run by an enterprising individual complete with ice cream, pop, candy, food and picnic tables.

If you choose a one-way ride, there is ample parking one block from downtown Carlton. Because of the long down grade, you will find the Carlton to Duluth ride will take quite a bit less time so you may want to include a side trip into Jay Cooke State Park or ride the Laveau Memorial Bike Trail.

Also of interest along the way are the National Kayak School in Thomson, Whitewater rafting opportunities near Cloquet, and the Black Bear Casino, in Carlton. Finally, The Alex Laveau Memorial Bike trail access is just one block south of the Willard Munger depot trail access in Carlton. (See page 70).

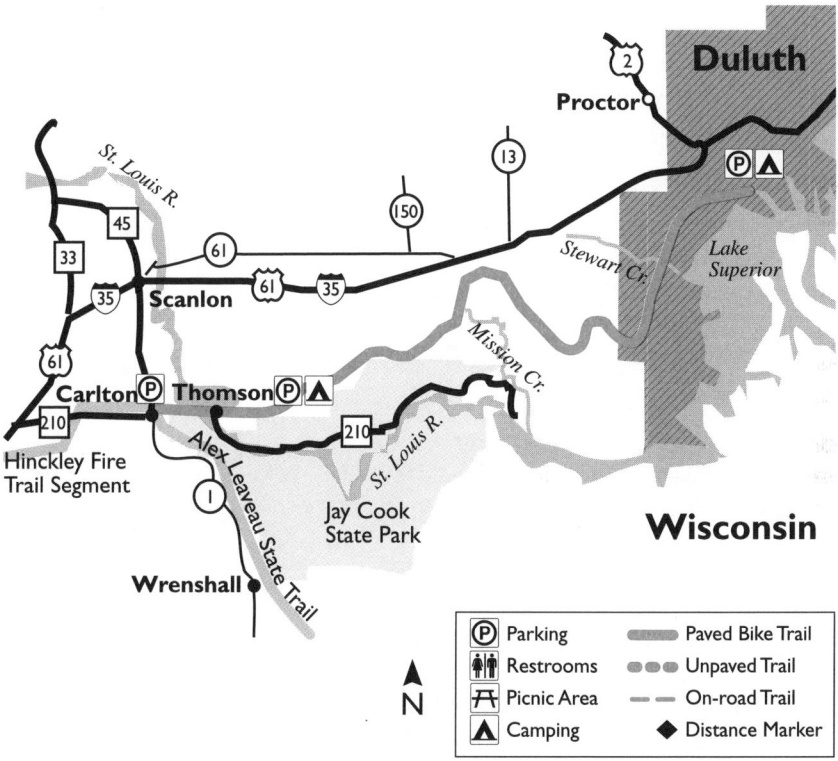

Administered by Minnesota Department of Natural Resources

FOR MORE INFORMATION:

DNR Trail Office
Route 2, 701 S. Kenwood
Moose Lake, MN 55767
218-485-5410

Duluth Visitors Bureau
1-800-4-DULUTH

Duluth Area Chamber of Commerce
118 E. Superior St.
Duluth, MN 55802
218-722-5501

Western Waterfront Trail
Duluth Park and Recreation
218-723-3337

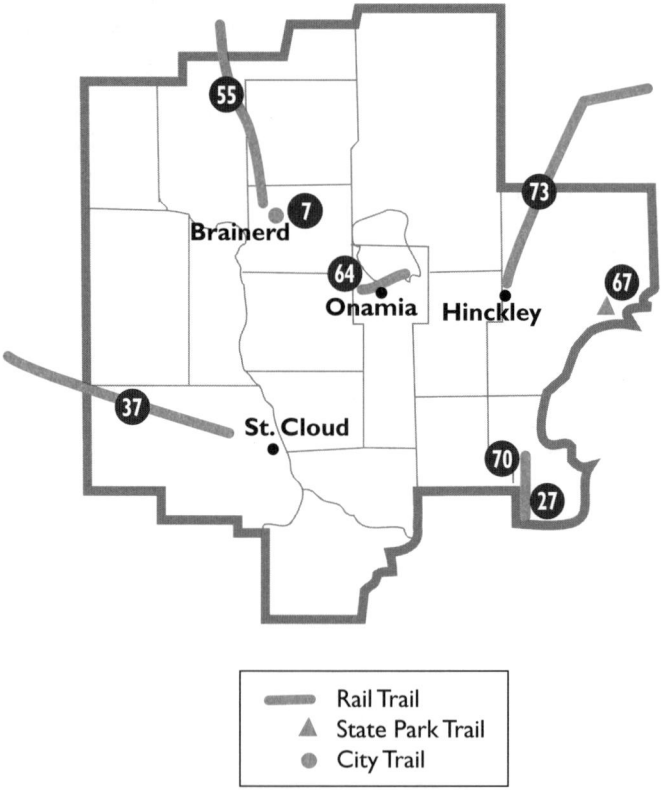
55
7
Brainerd
73
64
Onamia
Hinckley
67
37
St. Cloud
70
27
Rail Trail
State Park Trail
City Trail

Central Minnesota

Trail

7. Brainerd City Trails . . . . . .page 50
27. Hardwood Creek Trail . . . . . .page 65
37. Lake Wobegon State Rail-Trail . . . . . .page 52
55. Paul Bunyan State Rail-Trail . . . . . .page 56
64. Soo Line Rail-Trail . . . . . .page 60
67. St. Croix State Park Trail . . . . . .page 62
70. Sunrise Prairie Trail . . . . . .page 64
73. Willard Munger-Hinckley Fire Trail Segment . . . . . .page 70

*** Numbers refer to large map on page 11 and opposite page**

BRAINERD (CITY)

WHERE: City of Brainerd
LENGTH: Several miles
SURFACE: Paved
TRAIL USE: 

The City of Brainerd has some excellent off-road and roadside trails. Its proximity to the south trailhead of the northbound Paul Bunyan DNR trail (see page 56) make this an excellent location for a bicycle outing.

There are many attractions and historic sites in the Brainerd Lakes Area including the Brainerd International Raceway, the Paul Bunyan Amusement Center, miniature golf courses or some 450 holes of golf, including several championship courses.

Over 465 sand bottom lakes within a 30-mile radius of Brainerd are very popular for boating, canoeing and fishing in the summer, cross-country skiing, snowmobiling and ice fishing in the winter.

FOR MORE INFORMATION:

Brainerd Lakes Area C/CVB
124 North 6th Street
Brainerd, MN 56401
218-829-2838 ext. 483
www.brainerd.com

Parks and Recreation
1619 N.E. Washington
Brainerd, MN 56401
218-828-2320

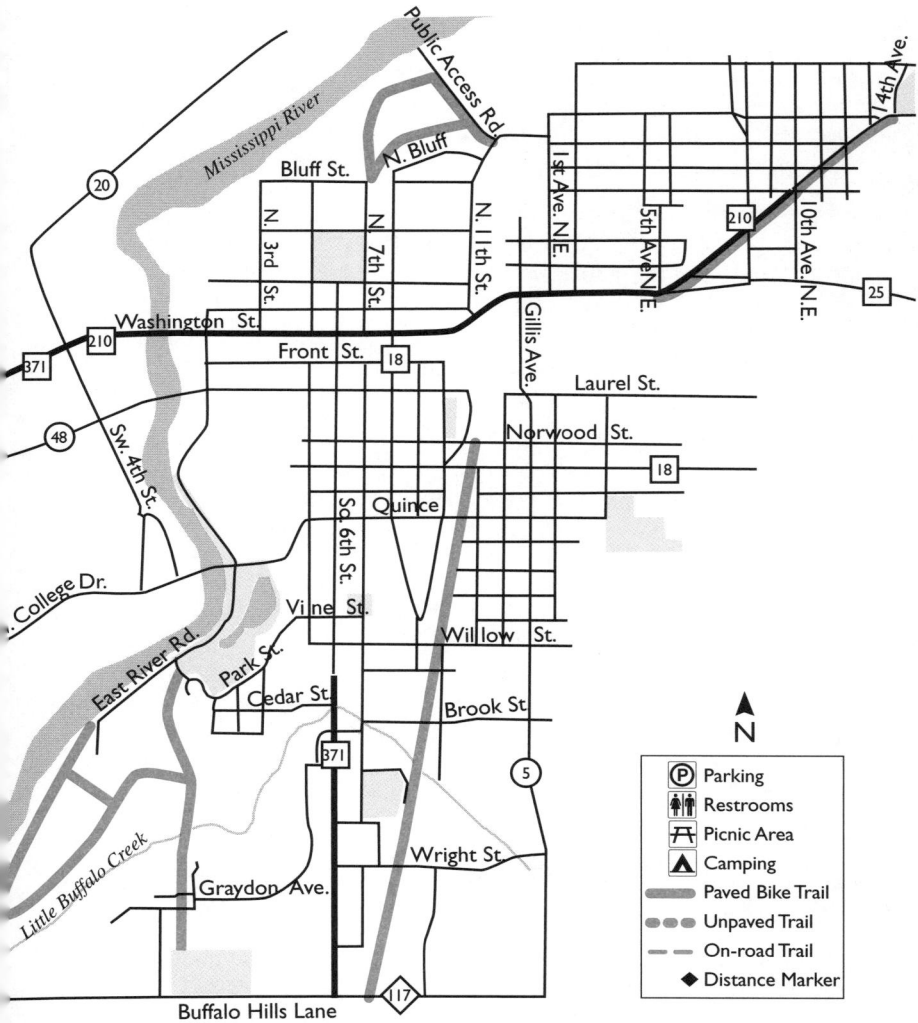
Public Access Rd.
Mississippi River
N. Bluff
Bluff St.
N. 3rd St.
N. 7th St.
N. 11th St.
1st Ave. N.E.
5th Ave. N.E.
10th Ave. N.E.
14th Ave.
Washington St.
Front St.
Gillis Ave.
Laurel St.
Norwood St.
Sw. 4th St.
So. 6th St.
Quince
College Dr.
Vine St.
Willow St.
East River Rd.
Park St.
Cedar St.
Brook St.
Wright St.
Graydon Ave.
Little Buffalo Creek
Buffalo Hills Lane
20
371
210
18
48
5
117
25
N
Parking
Restrooms
Picnic Area
Camping
Paved Bike Trail
Unpaved Trail
On-road Trail
Distance Marker

LAKE WOBEGON

WHERE: Sauk Centre to Avon
LENGTH: 28 miles
SURFACE: Asphalt, 10' wide
TRAIL USE:

Trailhead East: Avon, with a soon to be paved parking lot just across County Road 9 in downtown Avon. Facilities also planned. Exit I-94 at Highway 157 or 9.

Mid Access: Albany, with parking on Second Street. Melrose and Freeport exits from I-94.

Trailhead West: Sauk Centre. There is parking and access on city streets, but presently there is none at the actual pavement end on Highway 17 in west Sauk Centre. Funds have been secured for a connecting off-road spur from Highway 17 on the west to the city park at the south end of Sauk Lake. This will be the actual trailhead and provide parking, facilities and camping when completed.

The Lake Wobegon Trail was dedicated in September 1998. It was built and is managed by Stearns County Parks Department. It received its name by special permission from Garrison Keillor who located his fictional lake in this area. Financed with an ISTEA Grant, local donations and some DNR funds, this is an excellent addition to Minnesota's trail system.

It is by far the best marked trail we have ridden, with mile markers every one-half mile and warning signs in advance of every stop sign. It is also unique to us to find smooth asphalt paved bridges. Much of the local fund-raising as well as the impetus to build the trail was provided by the Albany Jaycees and each community enthusiastically supports it. This includes a neat rest stop with special tables beside the trail in Melrose provided by a local businessman.

FOR MORE INFORMATION:

Lake Wobegon Regional Trail
Trail Office
Stearns County Parks
455-28th Ave. S.
Waite Park, MN 56387
320-255-6172

Sauk Centre Chamber of Commerce
1220 S. Main St.
P.O. Box 222
Sauk Centre, MN 56378
320-352-5201

Melrose Chamber of Commerce
407 E. Main
Melrose, MN 56352
320-245-7174

Albany Chamber of Commerce
P.O. Box 634
Albany, MN 56307
320-845-7777

A municipal building is under construction in Albany which will provide parking and facilities. The right-of-way has been secured for an eventual continuation all the way to Fergus Falls on the west with a rail bed connection into St. Cloud on the east also a possibility.

This is mostly an open rail-trail with very few country roads crossing it. However, the close proximity of I-94 along most of the route does little to promote serenity and this is mostly an open rail-trail. Consider wind direction when you plan your ride. We found the first 6 miles out of Avon to be the most sheltered and scenic, but don't miss the Sinclair Lewis Interpretive Center in Sauk Centre near the I-94 exit to Highway 71 and 28.

New Trail headquarters and City Hall at Albany

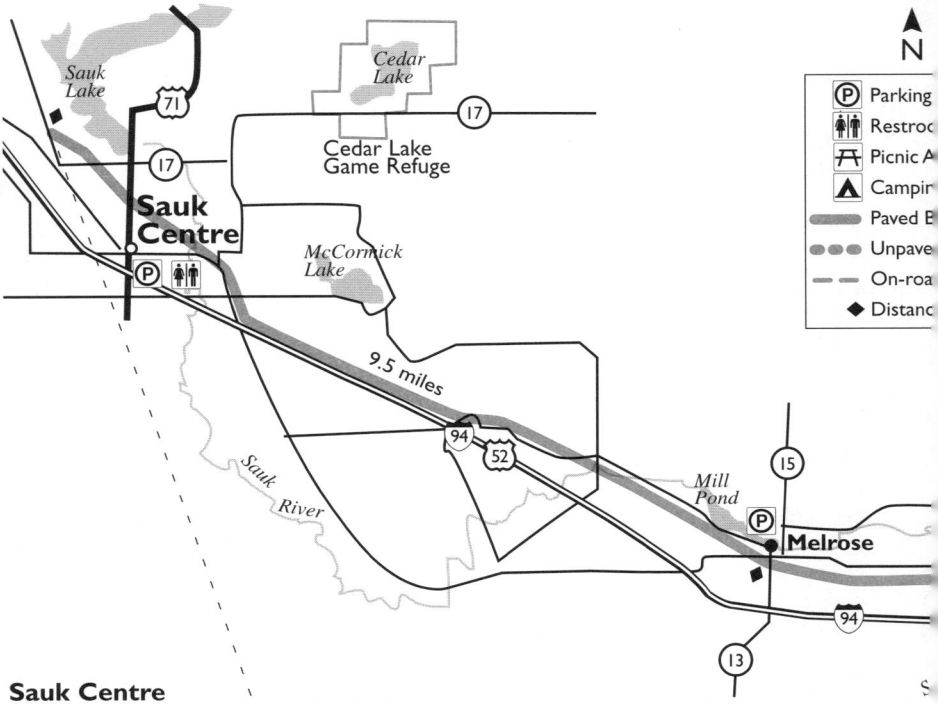
N
Parking
Restroo
Picnic A
Campir
Paved B
Unpave
On-roa
Distanc
Sauk Lake
71
17
Cedar Lake
17
Cedar Lake Game Refuge
Sauk Centre
McCormick Lake
9.5 miles
94
52
Sauk River
Mill Pond
15
Melrose
94
13

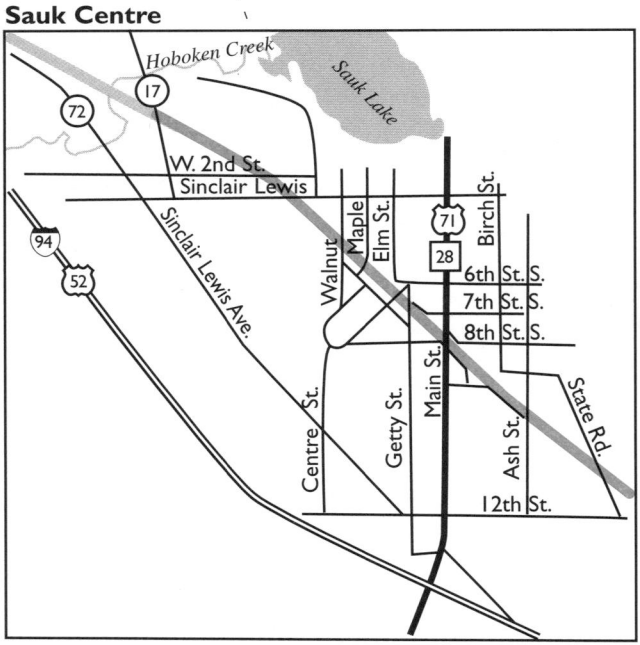
Sauk Centre
Hoboken Creek
Sauk Lake
17
72
W. 2nd St.
Sinclair Lewis
Sinclair Lewis Ave.
94
52
Walnut
Maple
Elm St.
71
28
Birch St.
6th St. S.
7th St. S.
8th St. S.
Main St.
State Rd.
Centre St.
Getty St.
Ash St.
12th St.

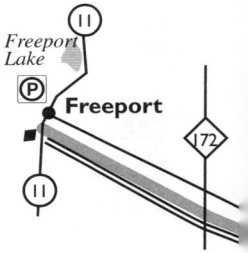
11
Freeport Lake
Freeport
172
11

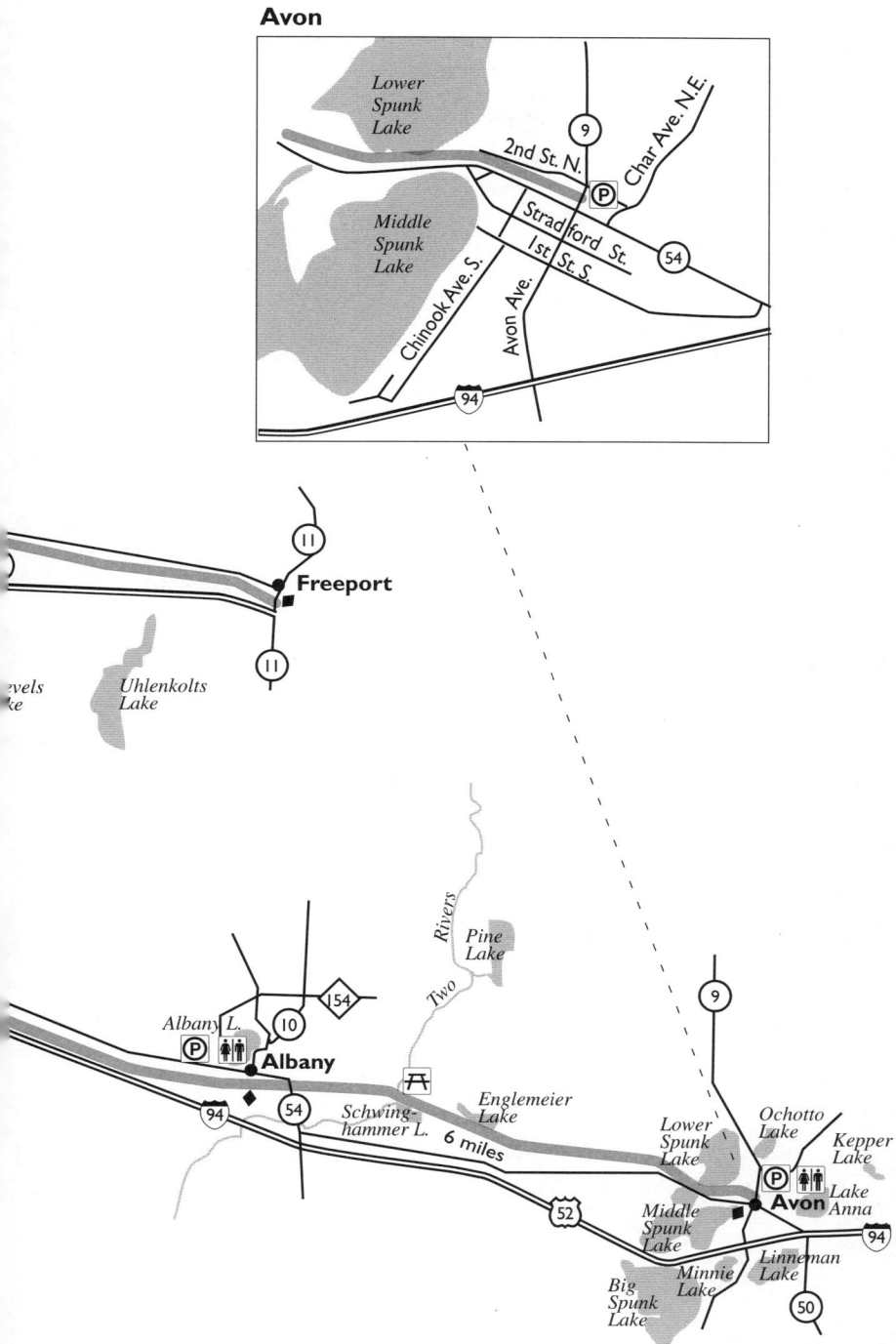
Avon
Lower Spunk Lake
Middle Spunk Lake
2nd St. N.
Char Ave. N.E.
Stradford St.
1st St. S.
Chinook Ave. S.
Avon Ave.
9
54
94
Freeport
11
Uhlenkolts Lake
Rivers
Two
Pine Lake
Albany L.
Albany
154
10
Schwing-hammer L.
Englemeier Lake
6 miles
Lower Spunk Lake
Ochotto Lake
Kepper Lake
Lake Anna
Avon
Middle Spunk Lake
Linneman Lake
Minnie Lake
Big Spunk Lake
52
50

PAUL BUNYAN

WHERE: Baxter to Hackensack
LENGTH: 46.4 miles
SURFACE: Blacktop 10' wide
TRAIL USE:

Trailhead North: Currently the paved trail terminates at Hackensack. The DNR has yet to complete the connection between Hackensack and the Heartland State Trail just southwest of Walker where the two trails will meet.

Trailhead South: Baxter. From Brainerd, go west on State Highway 210 about three-quarter miles. Turn north (right) on State Highway 371 to the first stoplight (Excelsior Rd). Turn east (right) and continue to the parking lot adjacent to the Paul Bunyan Arboretum.

Mid Access: At Merrifield, which is 9 miles north of Baxter. There is parking at the public access for North Long Lake, where you will find various resorts and businesses. Nisswa, Pequot Lakes, Jenkins, Pine River and Backus all offer parking, resorts, businesses and city parks. Presently, the trail terminates at Hackensack, paralleling Highway 371. Be sure to watch for signs. Parking and city facilities are available here.

Completed from Baxter/Brainerd to Hackensack in 1995, this DNR trail lies along an historic rail bed from the lumbering heydays of northern Minnesota. The trail generally parallels Highway 371 (particularly through the towns) but provides frequent views and accesses to lakes and wetlands for which Minnesota is famous.

The emphasis of this trail is on the pine forests, lakes and wetlands of North Central Minnesota, along with its wildlife, fishing and other recreational opportunities. It is a great addition to the upper Midwest rail-trail system.

In addition to numerous lakes and wetlands, the area traveled has tourist attractions such as well-known resorts (i.e. Grand View Lodge), Nisswa, the Hay Lake Mound District (a Native American burial ground near Jenkins), and the Paul Bunyan Arboretum, which is very near the trail's beginning in Baxter. There is a photo opportunity of Paul Bunyan's girlfriend at Hackensack and of course, Paul Bunyan and Babe, his Blue Ox, in Baxter.There are many fishing and swimming opportunities on this trail. Accommodations of all kinds abound in the resort area, with large and small resort communities located at reasonable intervals throughout.

Although there will be some interruptions, the rail bed from Hackensack to Bemidji is already secured assuring an eventual 100 mile trail which will showcase northern Minnesota attractions. Plans include connecting to the Heartland State Trail west of Walker (see page 20) as well as other points north from Walker and Bemidji. Someday Walker may be a central point for some very extensive bicycle trail riding.

Bike Shorts

Yield the right-of-way to vehicles or pedestrians. Be prepared to do so even if you have the right-of-way. A bicycle is hardly the vehicle for practicing that a good offense is the best defense.

FOR MORE INFORMATION:

DNR Trail Office
1601 Minnesota Drive
Brainerd, MN 56401
218-828-2693

Brainerd Chamber of Commerce
P.O. Box 356
Brainerd, MN 56401
218-829-2838
800-450-2838

Nisswa Chamber of Commerce
549 Main St.
P.O. Box 185
Nisswa, MN 56468
218-963-2620
800-950-9610

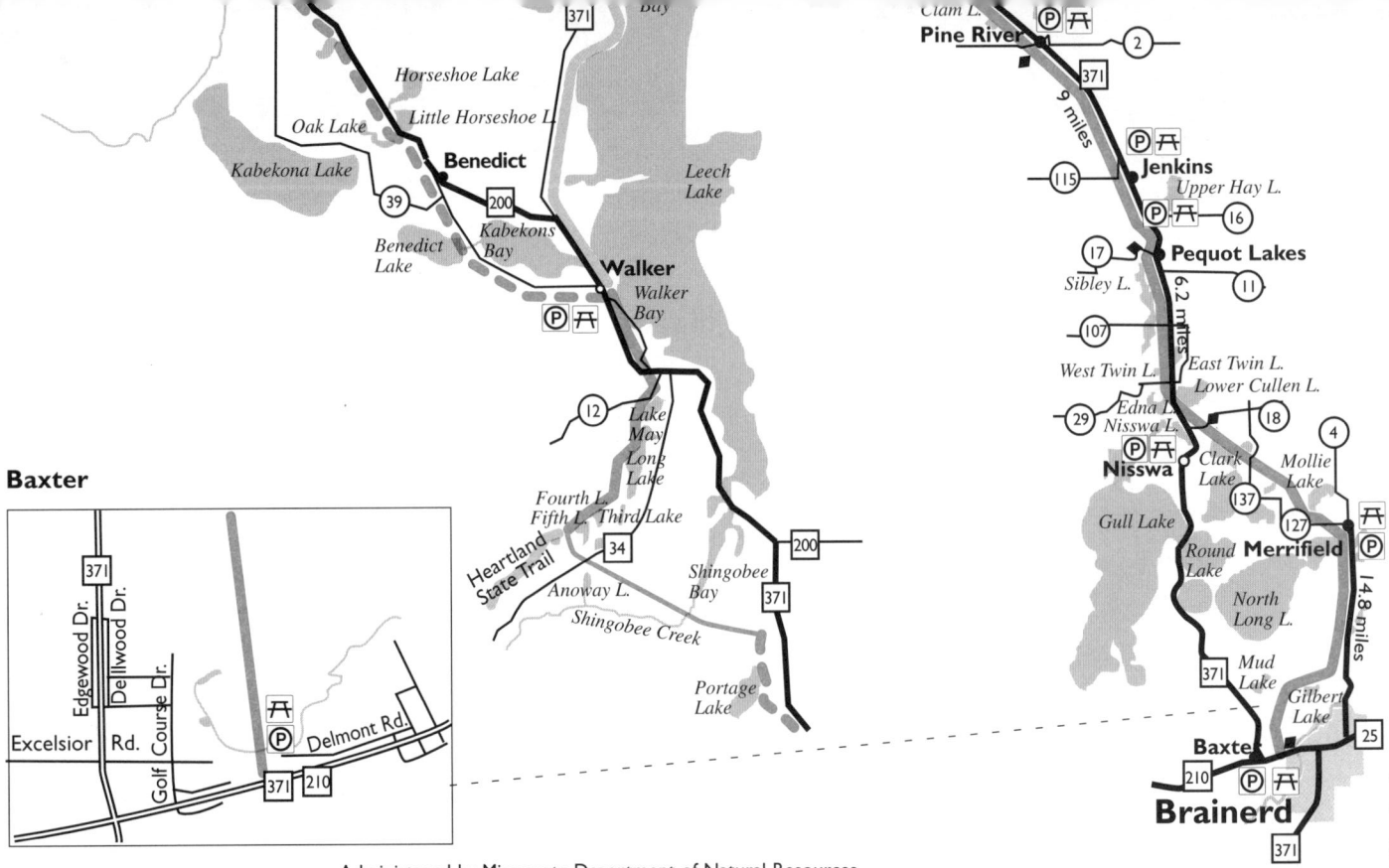

Administered by Minnesota Department of Natural Resources

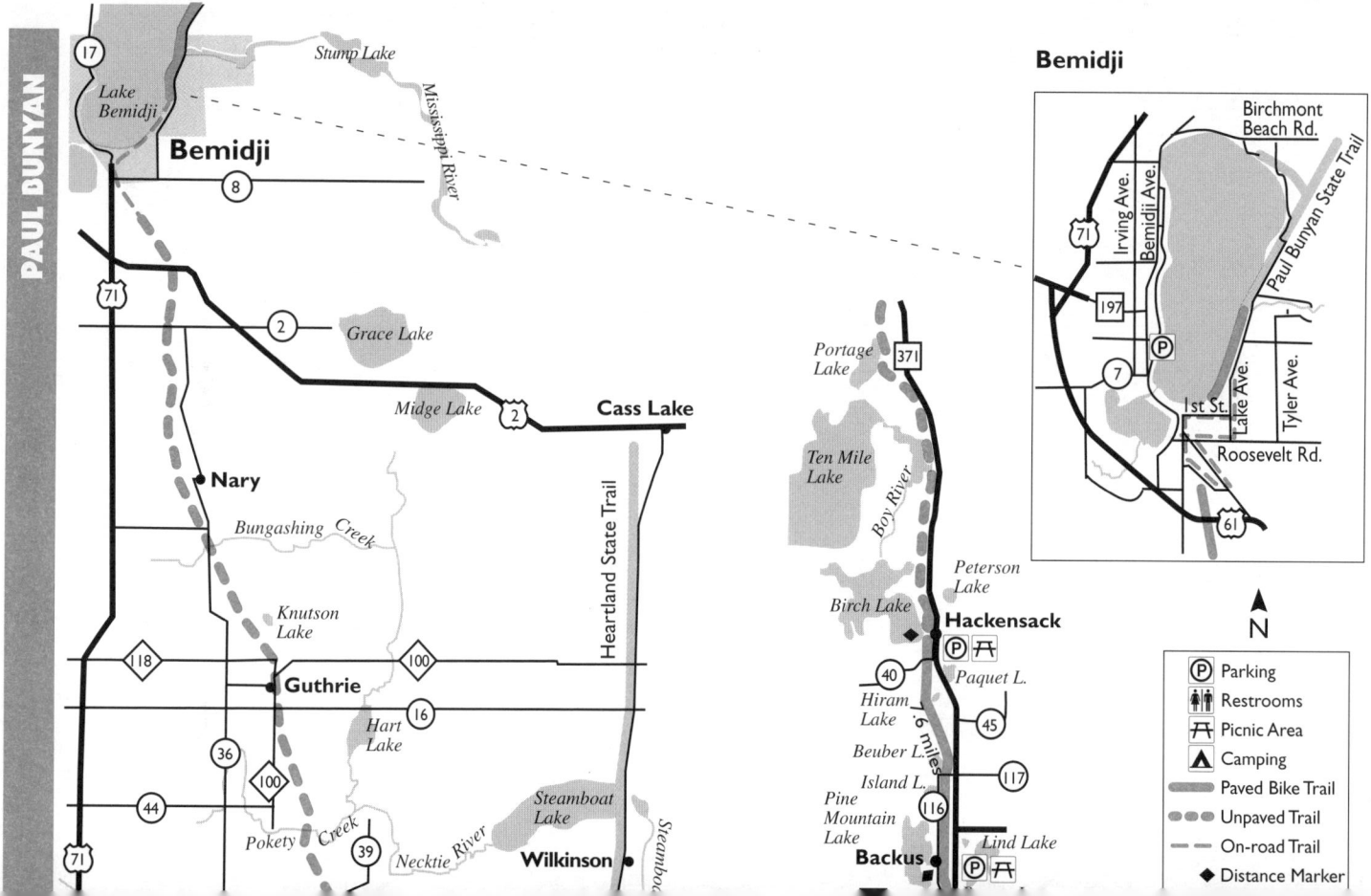
Bemidji
Lake Bemidji
Stump Lake
Mississippi River
Grace Lake
Midge Lake
Cass Lake
Nary
Bungashing Creek
Knutson Lake
Guthrie
Hart Lake
Pokety Creek
Necktie River
Steamboat Lake
Wilkinson
Heartland State Trail
Steamboat
Portage Lake
Ten Mile Lake
Boy River
Peterson Lake
Birch Lake
Hackensack
Paquet L.
Hiram Lake
6 miles
Beuber L.
Island L.
Pine Mountain Lake
Backus
Lind Lake
Birchmont Beach Rd.
Irving Ave.
Bemidji Ave.
Paul Bunyan State Trail
1st St.
Lake Ave.
Tyler Ave.
Roosevelt Rd.
N
Parking
Restrooms
Picnic Area
Camping
Paved Bike Trail
Unpaved Trail
On-road Trail
Distance Marker

SOO LINE

WHERE: Onamia to Isle
LENGTH: 11 miles
SURFACE: Paved, 8' wide
TRAIL USE:

Trailhead West: At Onamia, at the depot on Pike St. where there is parking available. The trail actually extends one-quarter mile west to 125th Avenue.

Mid Access: At Wahkon, County Road 17, south end of Main Street.

Trailhead East: At Isle, follow 17 one block south of business district to the ball park, where parking is available. You may choose to follow green bike route signs west of the ball park to Father Hennepin State Park.

Opened in the spring of 1995, this new trail is located just 90 miles north of the Twin Cities. It was developed by Mille Lacs County on the old Soo Line rail bed and is the first phase of a project that will eventually link Kathio State Park northwest of Onamia with Father Hennepin State Park east of Lake Mille Lacs. The goal is to provide a continuous bike, snowmobile and ATV path from one State Park to the other. Presently, one can connect to Kathio State Park from Onamia via County roads and to Father Hennepin State Park via 4 blocks of Isle city streets.

The trail follows a straight line between Onamia and Isle, and is very flat. Much of it is through open farmland so wind might be a factor. A note of caution: this trail is also open to ATV travel so watch for motorized traffic.

The Soo Line Trail is an 11-mile segment, part of the 100-mile Genola-Superior snowmobile trail. The beginning of the trail at Genola is located on Highway 25 by the lumber yard. It is narrow, single file and the surface suitable for mountain bikes. Genola is approximately 20 miles west of Onamia via the trail.

For more recreational activities, you might consider the two local state parks, Father Hennepin and Kathio, in addition to Lake Mille Lacs, with its many resorts.

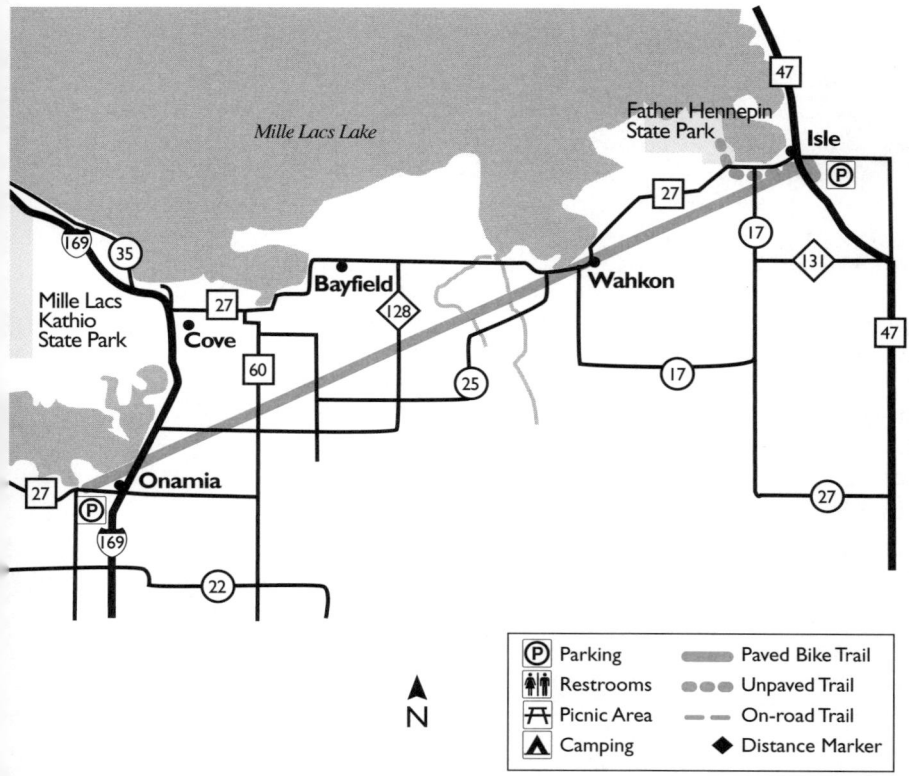

FOR MORE INFORMATION:

Mille Lacs Bureau of Tourism
565 Eighth St. N.E.
Milaca, MN 56353
320-983-8201
800-350-2692

ST. CROIX STATE PARK

WHERE: Hinckley
LENGTH: 5.5 miles
SURFACE: Paved
TRAIL USE:

Access: 16 miles east of Hinckley on State Highway 48.

The largest state park in Minnesota also contains one of the longer paved trails. During the ride, you will see lots of woods and several streams. The park offers the most complete facilities of any Minnesota State Park. Also included within the park is a canoe rental concession which is extremely popular as is a river boat tour operation nearby. Fishing, swimming and camping all take advantage of the scenic St. Croix River.

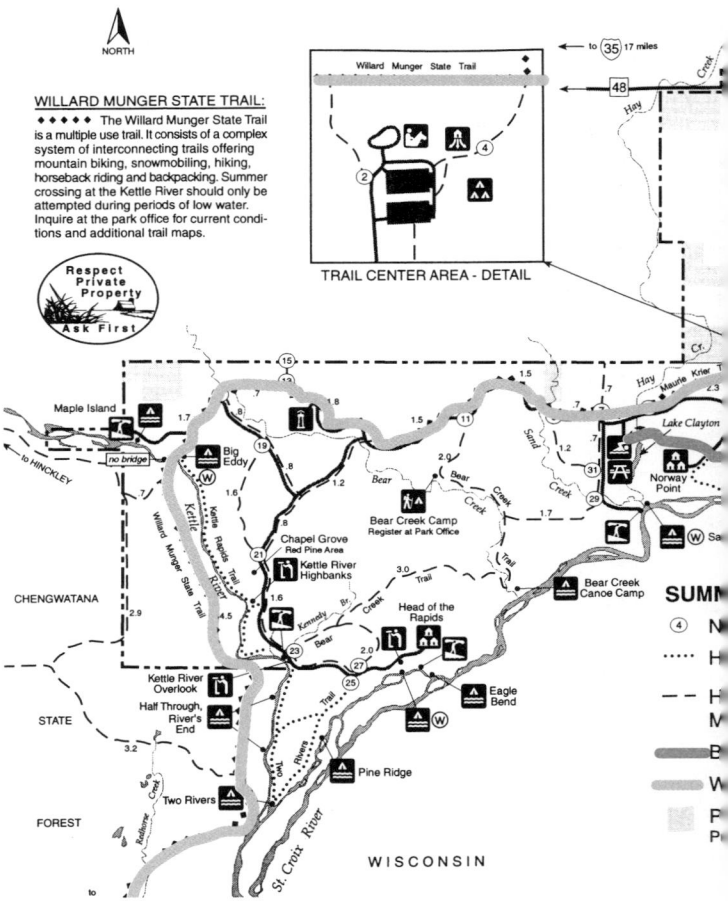

FOR MORE INFORMATION:

St. Croix State Park
Route 3, Box 450
Hinckley, MN 55037
320-384-6591

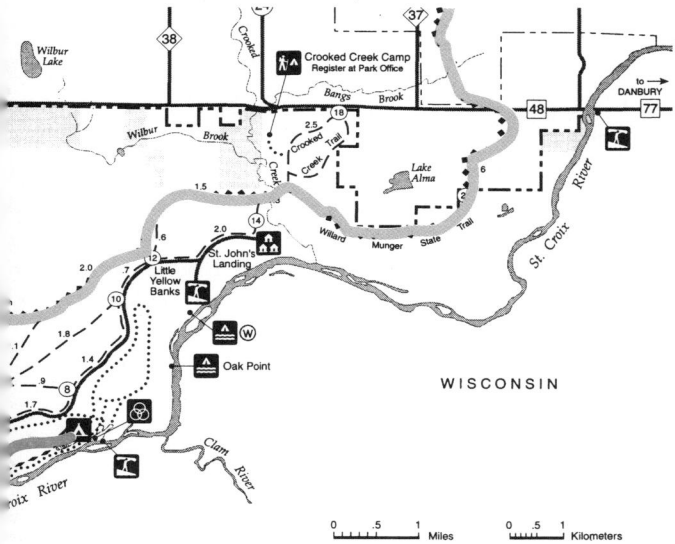

FACILITIES

- Park HQ / Ranger Station
- Picnic Area
- Overlook
- Observation Tower
- Trail Center
- Swimming
- Canoe Access
- Campground
- Group Center
- Primitive Group Camp
- Backpack Camping
- Equestrian Area
- Watercraft Camping
- Interpretive Center
- Drinking Water

SUNRISE PRAIRIE

WHERE: North Branch to Forest Lake
LENGTH: 15.5 miles
SURFACE: Paved, 10' wide
TRAIL USE:

Trailhead North: At North Branch. The trail terminates at the junction of Highway 95 and 61 with parking just south of Highway 95.

Mid Access: At Wyoming, where you will find parking and restrooms. Also at Stacy, adjacent to Lion Park, there is parking and restrooms available.

Trailhead South: At the Washington County line where it connects to the Washington County trail system (see page 65). The best place to start or finish your ride would be on Broadway in the city of Forest Lake, which is actually on the Hardwood Trail.

On this trail, you will ride through a variety of natural areas including native prairie remnants, woodlands and marsh areas. Bridges cross both a west and south branch of the Sunrise River and there are frequent opportunities for spotting wildlife and birds.

Sunrise Trail is administered by Chisago County, another example of counties developing multi-use trails on their own initiative. At the south county line it connects to the Washington County Hardwood Creek Trail. Both trails are on the same rail bed so your transition from one to the other will not be noticeable except for signage. The total of 25 miles for both trails make a nice ride.

See map page 66.

FOR MORE INFORMATION:

Trail Office
Chisago County Park and Recreation
1356 Main St.
North Branch, MN 55056
651-674-2345

Forest Lake Chamber of Commerce
92 S. Lake St.
P.O. Box 474
Forest Lake, MN 55025
651-464-3200

WHERE: Forest Lake to Hugo
LENGTH: 9.5 miles
SURFACE: Paved, 10' wide
TRAIL USE:

Trailhead North: Forest Lake. Although the Hardwood Trail actually starts at the county line 1½ miles north of Forest Lake, the best place to start or end your trip is in the city where parking is available. The paved trail is one block west of Highway 61 on Broadway.

Mid Access: 170th Street (County Road 4)

Trailhead South: Hugo at County Road 8. Parking is available on city streets. There are rest rooms here, as well.

The Hardwood Creek Trail is a sister trail to the Sunrise Trail and connects directly to it on the same rail bed. Washington County has allocated funds to complete paving from Forest Lake into Hugo. Until this trail is finished call 651-430-4325 for trail status. After completion call trail office at 651-430-8368.

The Hardwood Trail was developed by Washington County with the assistance of the DNR and is administered by the county parks department. The trail goes through generally open countryside, crossing three bridges en route.

Parking and facilities will be added as funds permit and extensions to connect with the Ramsey County and St. Paul trails will come eventually.

See map page 66.

FOR MORE INFORMATION:

Trail Office
Washington County Parks
1515 Keats Avenue North
Lake Elmo, MN 55042
651-430-8368

Forest Lake Chamber of Commerce
92 South Lake Street
P.O. Box 474
Forest Lake, MN 55025
651-464-3200

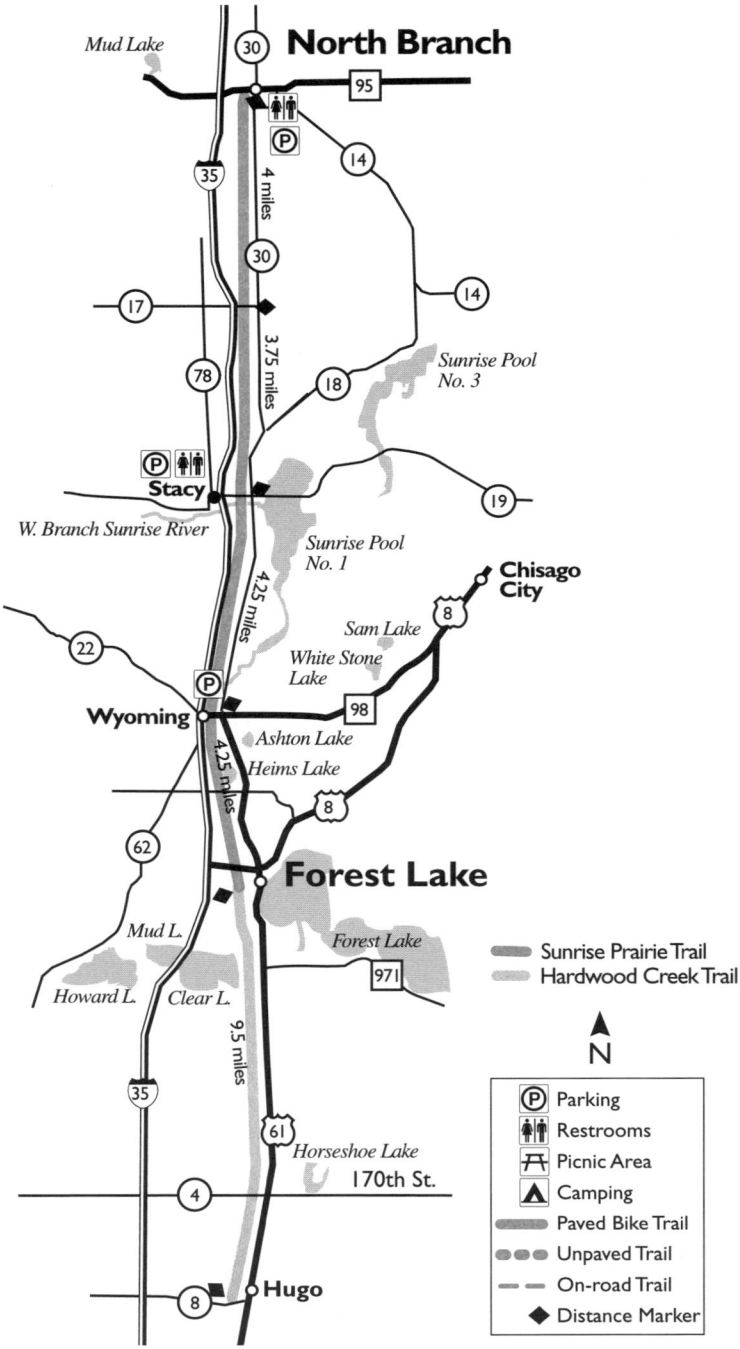
North Branch
Mud Lake
30
95
14
35
4 miles
30
14
17
3.75 miles
78
18
Sunrise Pool No. 3
Stacy
19
W. Branch Sunrise River
Sunrise Pool No. 1
Chisago City
8
4.25 miles
Sam Lake
22
White Stone Lake
98
Wyoming
Ashton Lake
Heims Lake
4.25 miles
8
62
Forest Lake
Mud L.
Forest Lake
971
Howard L.
Clear L.
9.5 miles
35
61
Horseshoe Lake
170th St.
4
Hugo
8
Sunrise Prairie Trail
Hardwood Creek Trail
N
Parking
Restrooms
Picnic Area
Camping
Paved Bike Trail
Unpaved Trail
On-road Trail
Distance Marker

Trail Use Tips

Respect the rights of other trail users. Always yield to hikers, horses and other animals.

Pass with care to avoid startling other users.

Stay on trails to preserve fragile ecosystems.

Control your speed, especially on hills and around curves.

Don't litter, put in proper place.

Plan ahead for your own safety.

Drug or alcohol use is prohibited.

Camping and fires are not allowed.

Be careful of poisonous plants.

Don't feed the wild animals.

Leave wild flowers alone. Do not pick!

Never eat wild berries.

Respect privately owned land adjacent to trail.

WILLARD MUNGER-HINCKLEY FIRE

WHERE: Hinckley to Carlton
LENGTH: 55 miles
SURFACE: Paved, except for 3 miles (signed) on the road shoulder south from Carlton
TRAIL USE: 

Trailhead South: Exit I-35 at Hinckley and go west to old Highway 61. Turn north and continue to County Road 18, then turn west across the tracks to a parking lot with restrooms on the Grindstone River.

Mid Access: Since this segment closely parallels I-35, accesses at a number of towns and freeway exits are available. South to north they include Finlayson, Willow River, Sturgeon Lake, Moose Lake, Barnum and County Road 4 (Exit 227). There is a 2.2 mile paved bikeway connecting the trail to Sandstone and Banning State Park.

Trailhead North: At Carlton with parking and new facilities one block south of County Road 1 near downtown. It took considerable time and expense to span this former short trail interruption near this city.

We list this as a separate segment of the present 70-mile Willard Munger Trail since it is both the longest part and quite different from the Carlton-Duluth Segment. You will find a very flat rail bed with scattered forest, open farmlands, while the Carlton-Duluth portion has a steady incline and is more wooded and winding. With all segments combined, the Munger Trail is currently the longest paved trail in the world.

As you ride north of Hinckley, you are riding on the same rail bed which played a very important role during the Hinckley Forest Fire of 1894. Do plan to spend some extra time and tour the Hinckley Fire Museum near downtown. Also, within a short ride from Hinckley is the Mission Creek 1894 Theme Park and Tobies restaurant and complex on the east side of I-35.

FOR MORE INFORMATION:

DNR Trail Office
Route 2, 701 S. Kenwood
Moose Lake, MN 55767
218-485-5410

Munger Trail Towns Association
205 Elm Avenue
P.O. Box 110
Moose Lake, MN 55767
888-263-0586

North from Barnum the trail is more sheltered and scenic including a tunnel under Highway 61. This is the most recently completed portion of this trail. Local landowner and community opposition prevented acquisition of the rail bed for quite some time after first proposed in the early 80s. Subsequent observation of the success and economic impact of the completed portions of the trail convinced all involved that bicyclists support local economies.

This is a long trail, but there are many opportunities to tour shorter portions. There are good motels in Moose Lake, Hinckley, Barnum and Carlton. An overnight will permit you to include the 14½ mile Carlton-Duluth segment and/or the Alex Laveau Trail, both of which go in and near the Jay Cooke State Park east of Carlton.

Bike Shorts

A word about dogs, many of whom seem to take particular objection to bicycles. If you encounter one, the first requirement is not to panic. If the dog is only testing, and not actually attacking, a shout or order may keep it at bay. If it is very aggressive, the best defense is to dismount, keeping the bike between you and the dog. Grab any thing available to throw or pretend to throw. Most of all, keep moving as a dog is only going to defend what it perceives to be the limits of its territory.

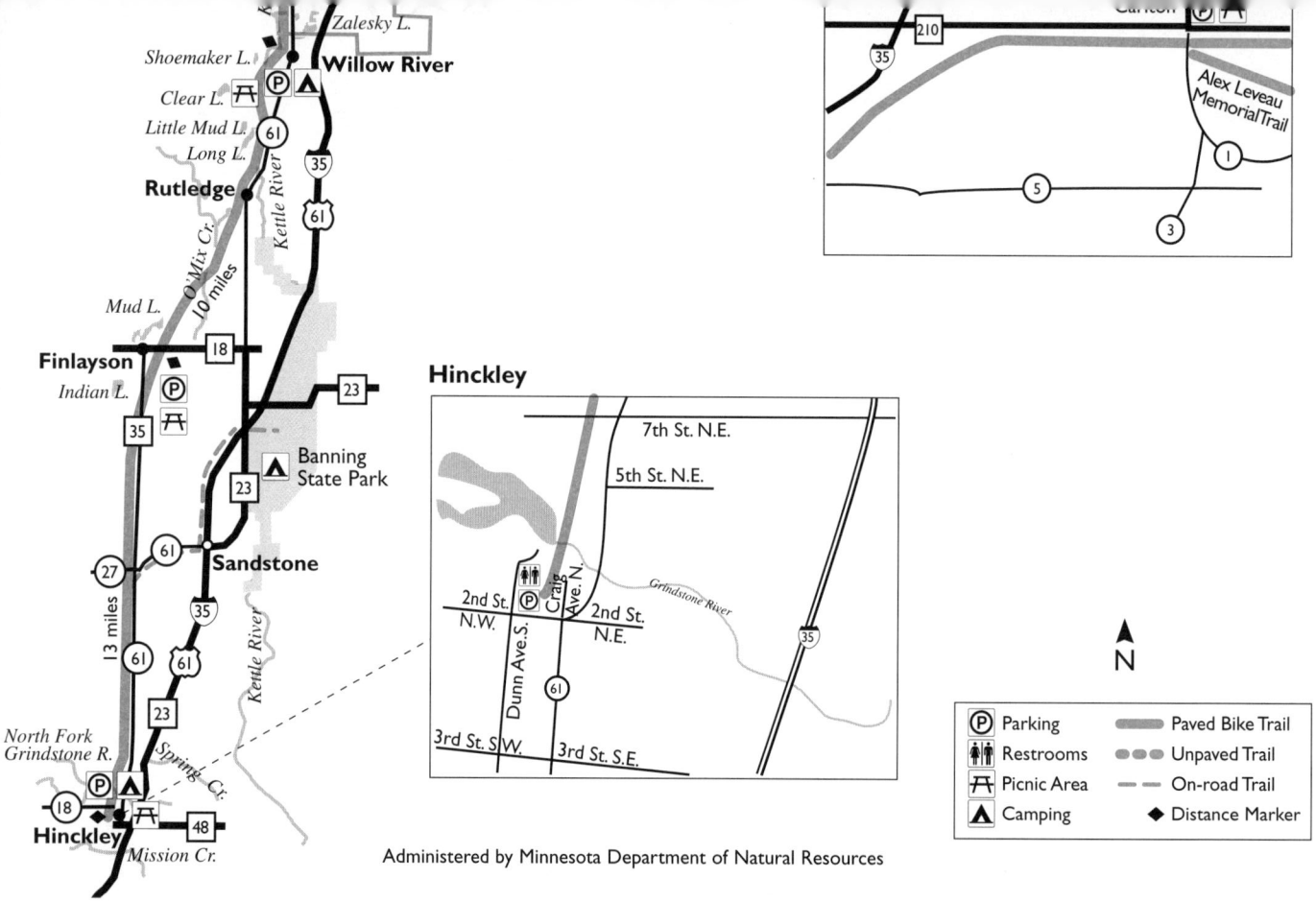

Administered by Minnesota Department of Natural Resources

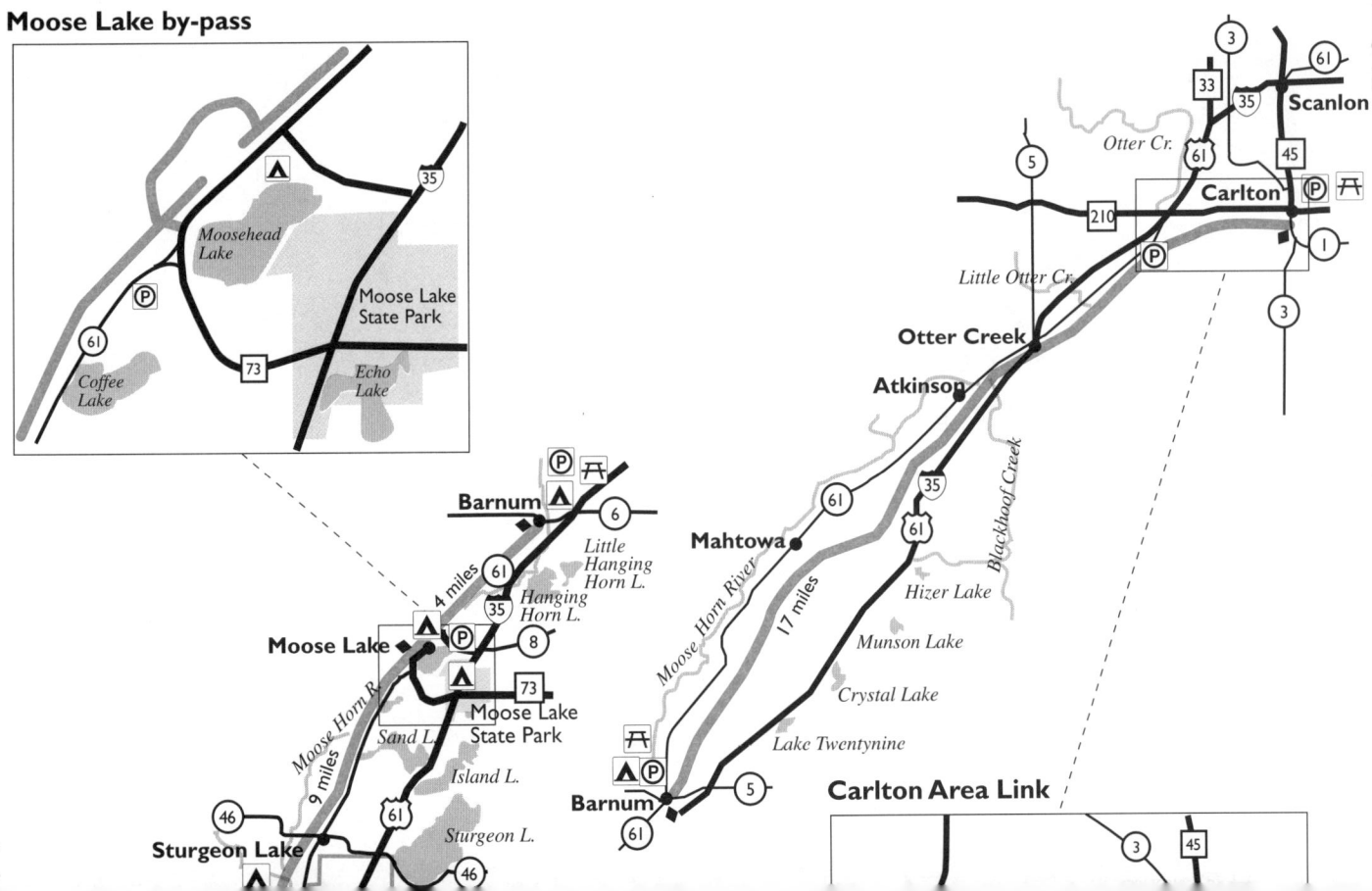
Moose Lake by-pass
Moosehead Lake
Moose Lake State Park
Coffee Lake
Echo Lake
35
61
73
Barnum
6
Little Hanging Horn L.
Hanging Horn L.
4 miles
Moose Lake
8
Moose Lake State Park
Moose Horn R.
9 miles
Sand L.
Island L.
Sturgeon L.
Sturgeon Lake
46
Mahtowa
Moose Horn River
17 miles
Blackhoof Creek
Hizer Lake
Munson Lake
Crystal Lake
Lake Twentynine
5
Carlton Area Link
Otter Cr.
Little Otter Cr.
Otter Creek
Atkinson
Carlton
Scanlon
33
45
210
1
3

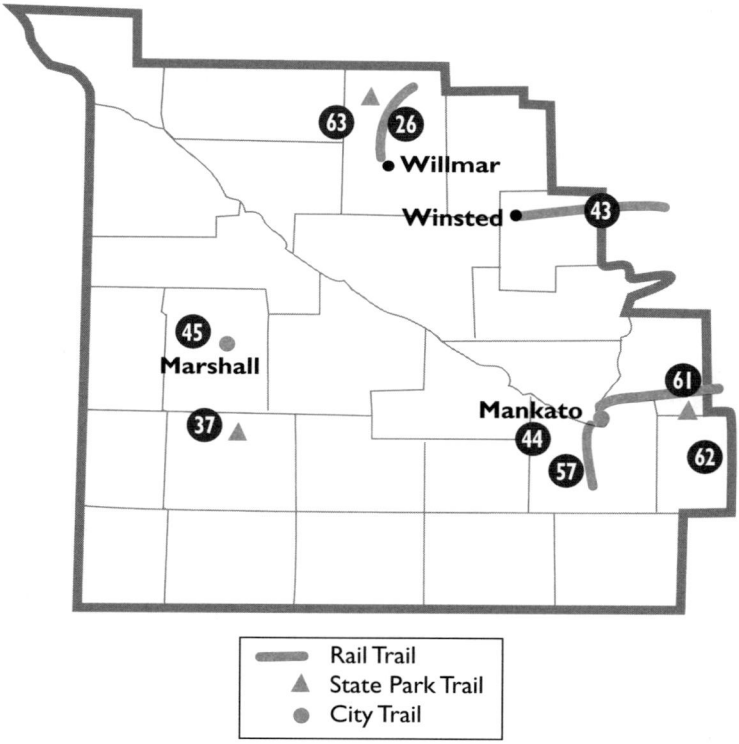
63
26
Willmar
Winsted
43
45
Marshall
61
Mankato
37
44
57
62
Rail Trail
State Park Trail
City Trail

Southwest Minnesota

Trail

26. Glacial Lakes State Rail-Trail . . . . . .page 74
37. Lake Shetek State Park . . . . . .page 76
43. Luce Line State Rail-Trail . . . . . .page 78
44. Mankato City Trails . . . . . .page 82
45. Marshall City Trails . . . . . .page 84
57. Red Jacket Rail-Trail . . . . . .page 86
61. Sakatah Singing Hills State Rail-Trail . . . . . .page 88
62. Sakatah State Park . . . . . .page 92
63. Sibley State Park . . . . . .page 94

*** Numbers refer to large map on page 11 and opposite page**

GLACIAL LAKES

WHERE: Willmar to Hawick
LENGTH: 18 miles, 12 paved
SURFACE: Blacktop, 10' wide
TRAIL USE: 

Trailhead South: The Willmar Civic Center 3 miles NE of downtown. Take Highway 71 and 23 north from downtown Willmar and turn east on Civic Center Road or take the bypass 71 and 23 from east Willmar to Civic Center Road. You will find ample parking and restrooms here.

Mid Access: At Spicer, the trail parallels Highway 23 on the west side all the way through town. You will find ample parking and restrooms here. Be careful, though, since there are a few street crossings. Future plans include moving the "Whistle Stop" depot, presently three miles out, to the intersection of the trail and County Road 10.

At New London, the trail skirts the SE edge of this charming town, with access on County Road 9 and at County Road 40 (just off 4th avenue SE).

Trailhead North: Across Highway 23 from Hawick is the present terminus and the northern end of the DNR improvements to date. There is parking south of Highway 23 in Hawick.

Completed in 1995, this relatively short rail-trail traverses the heart of the lake and resort area of Kandiyohi County. North of New London you will ride open vistas, but it is generally scenic with opportunities for refreshments and rest stops. You will find this trail a great initial step toward establishing some off-road and/or rail-trails in western Minnesota. Adjacent to the trail the DNR has included a separate horse riding trail between Willmar and New London which will be groomed for snowmobiling. You may occasionally encounter horseback riders.

Green Lake is truly one of the great swimming and boating lakes in Minnesota, with an excellent public swimming beach including facilities in Spicer. A stop for a swim is highly recommended — weather permitting. Consider packing fishing gear also, since there is excellent fishing at several locations along the trail.

Plan to include a street side trip through New London. Its wooded hills and several glacial ponds make a charming community. Sinclair Lewis described New London as "sitting among its ponds like a Cape Cod village." Take Main Street (Highway 9) to downtown and Birch Street back to the trail.

The DNR has acquired the abandoned trail bed as far as Richmond, and plans to extend the trail corridor all the way to St. Cloud providing some 50 miles overall. The New London to Hawick segment is crushed granite.

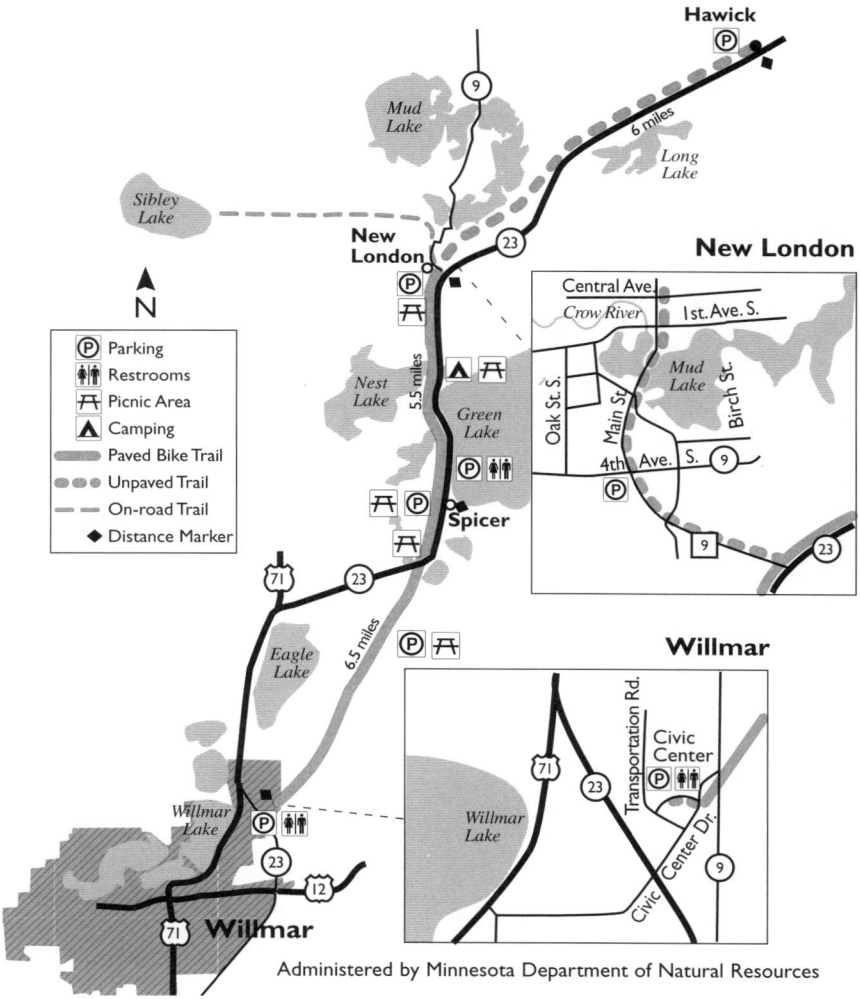

Administered by Minnesota Department of Natural Resources

FOR MORE INFORMATION:

Trail Office
P.O. Box 508
New London, MN 56273
320-354-4940

Willmar Chamber of Commerce
2104 East Highway 12
Willmar, MN 56201
320-235-0300

LAKE SHETEK STATE PARK

WHERE: Currie
LENGTH: 6 miles
SURFACE: Paved
TRAIL USE:

Access: County Road 17 at Currie

The paved trail system includes 3 miles from Currie north to the park and 3 miles within the park.

This park takes you back through time. A granite monument marks the burial site of victims of the Dakota uprising of 1862. View the relocated "Koch" cabin, home of the Koch family during the Dakota Uprising. There are also four pioneer cabin sites along the interpretive trail. After a picnic overlooking Lake Shetek, hike the trail heading north to the boat ramp. From there, a self-guided interpretive trail heads out and circles Loon Island. There is another trail from the boat landing back to the picnic area and the swimming beach, which has a changing house for those wishing to cool off.

FOR MORE INFORMATION:

Lake Shetek State Park
R.R.1, Box 164
Currie, MN 56123
507-763-3256

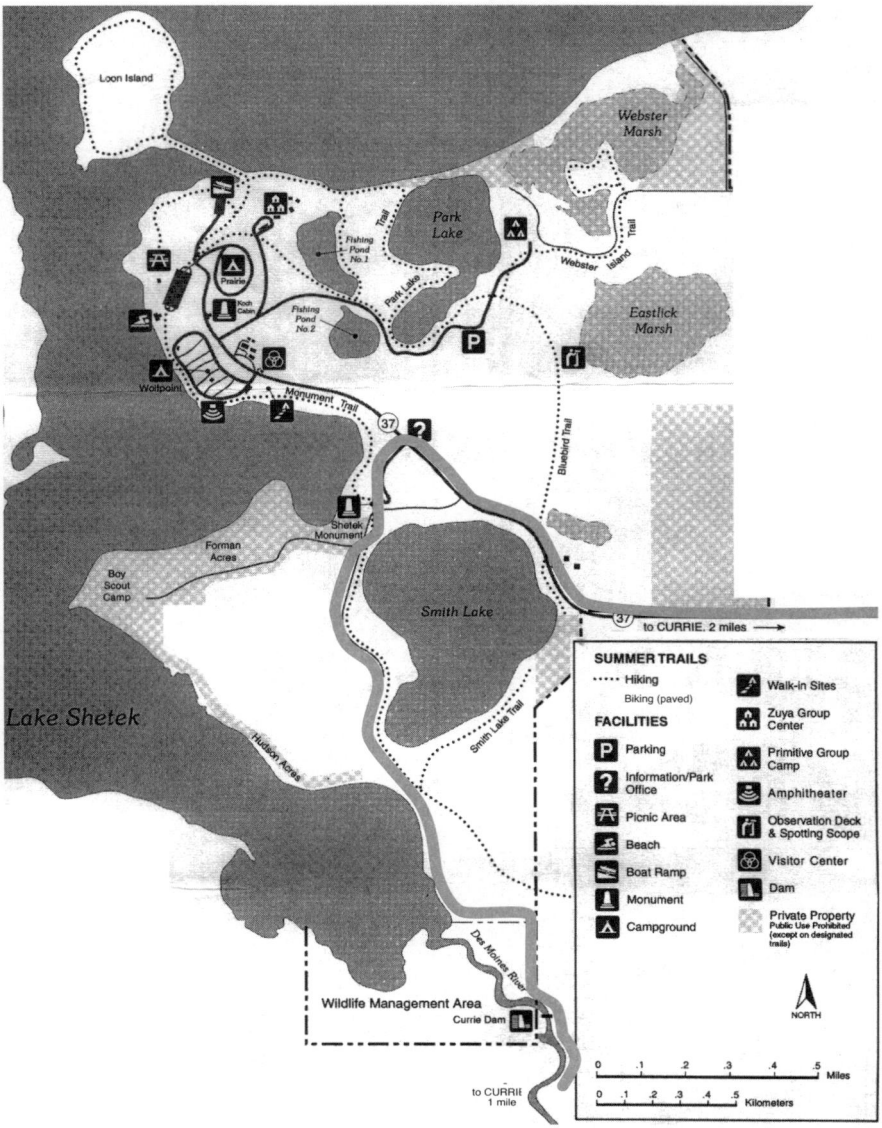
Loon Island
Webster Marsh
Park Lake
Fishing Pond No. 1
Trail
Park Lake
Webster Island Trail
Prairie
Roth Cabin
Fishing Pond No. 2
Eastlick Marsh
Wolfpoint
Monument Trail
37
Bluebird Trail
Shetek Monument
Forman Acres
Boy Scout Camp
Smith Lake
37
to CURRIE, 2 miles
Lake Shetek
Hudson Acres
Smith Lake Trail
Des Moines River
Wildlife Management Area
Currie Dam
to CURRIE 1 mile
SUMMER TRAILS
Hiking
Biking (paved)
FACILITIES
Parking
Information/Park Office
Picnic Area
Beach
Boat Ramp
Monument
Campground
Walk-in Sites
Zuya Group Center
Primitive Group Camp
Amphitheater
Observation Deck & Spotting Scope
Visitor Center
Dam
Private Property
Public Use Prohibited (except on designated trails)
NORTH
0 .1 .2 .3 .4 .5 Miles
0 .1 .2 .3 .4 .5 Kilometers

LUCE LINE

WHERE: Plymouth to Winsted
LENGTH: 30 miles
SURFACE: Crushed Limestone
TRAIL USE: 

Trailhead East: From I-494, exit west on Highway 12 (Wayzata Boulevard) to County Road 15 (Gleason Lake Road). Exit and turn north on Vicksburg Lane. Continue north to 10th Avenue North (there is a sign), and turn west one-half block to the parking lot with restrooms. The City of Plymouth has paved a spur east to I-494 as part of their development of Parkers Lake. If you are traveling west on Highway 55, west of I-494, turn south at Vicksburg Lane.

Mid Access: Several county roads cross this trail, but the best parking is at Winsted, Silver Lake, Hutchinson and Stubbs Bay Road in Watertown.

Trailhead West: The limestone surface actually ends at County Road 9 in Winsted but the parking lot is a short distance east on Lake Winsted. There is a county park with facilities at the southern tip of Lake Winsted. Best parking is at the boat ramp parking lot. Parking and facilities are planned for Cedar Mills.

The Luce Line State Trail actually begins at the parking lot on 10th Avenue North just off Vicksburg Lane, but the City of Plymouth paved a short section east to I-494.

Through the foresight of the Luce Line Trail Association and subsequently the State Legislature, the right of way continues west from Plymouth for 51 miles. There has been considerable recent activity by the DNR to improve and expand this trail. Many bridges have been replaced including one to be built over the new bypass road around Hutchinson. Improvements to the trail from Winsted west to Cedar Mills will be continuing so you may want to postpone biking west of Winsted until completed. Call 320-234-7616 for current information west of Winsted. The trail is crushed rock from Wayzata west with 3 miles paved through Hutchinson and current plans include paving 14 miles from Silver Lake through Hutchinson to Cedar Mills. The balance of the trail will probably remain crushed rock for some time.

Fifty-one miles may necessitate a two vehicle outing unless you want to make it a long trip or take only a portion of the trail. Throughout most of the Plymouth to Winsted route, the rail bed is lined with trees on both sides and sometimes with cuts through thick woods. This provides a generally sheltered and cool ride. En route, you will ride through the Wayzata Country Club and past lakes and marshes. The further west you go, the more open it becomes.

Current DNR plans are to extend this trail to its full 63 miles when funds are available. Paving is probably a few years away, but bridge work and grade improvements are being done.

We prefer to start at the east end but wind direction may be a consideration. Although there are few towns, Lyndale is an interesting stop for refreshments. Be sure to bring your water bottle and have snacks in your pack for this trail.

See map page 80.

Bike Shorts

Give an audible sound (we recommend a bike bell) before passing pedestrians or other cyclists.

FOR MORE INFORMATION:

DNR Trail West
20596 Highway 7
Hutchinson, MN 55350
320-234-7616

Luce Line Trail Office
3980 Watertown Road
Maple Plain, MN 55359
612-475-0371

Twin West Chamber of Commerce
10550 Wayzata Blvd.
Minnetonka, MN 55343
612-540-0234

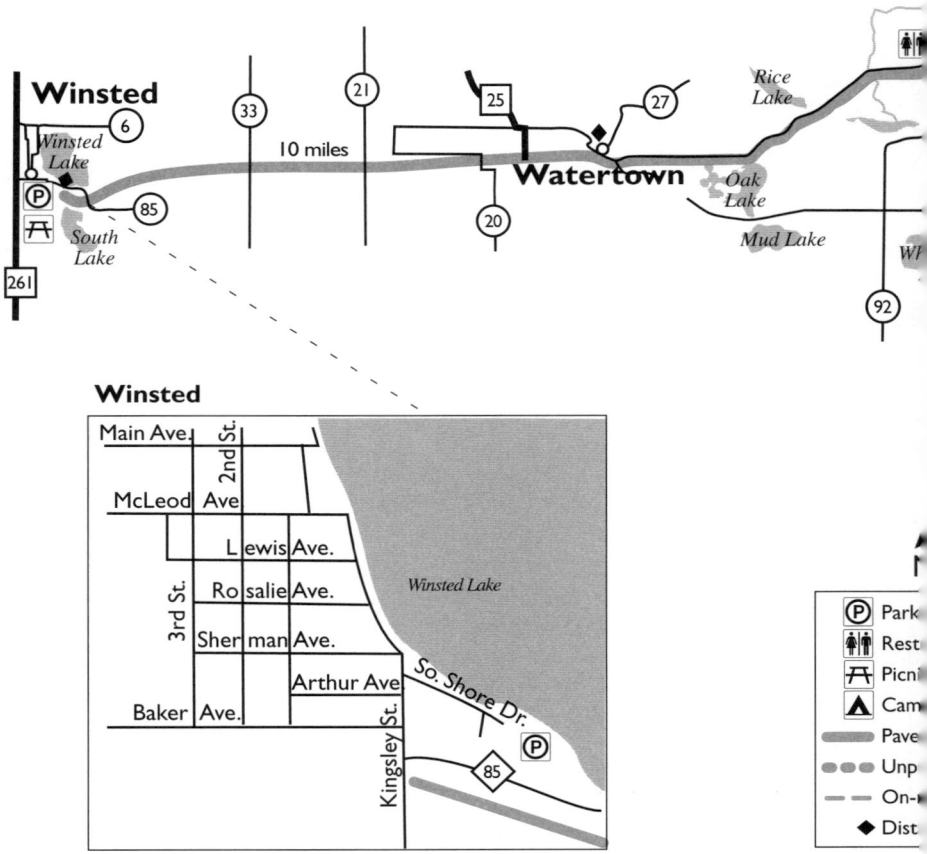

Administered by Minnesota Department of Natural Resources

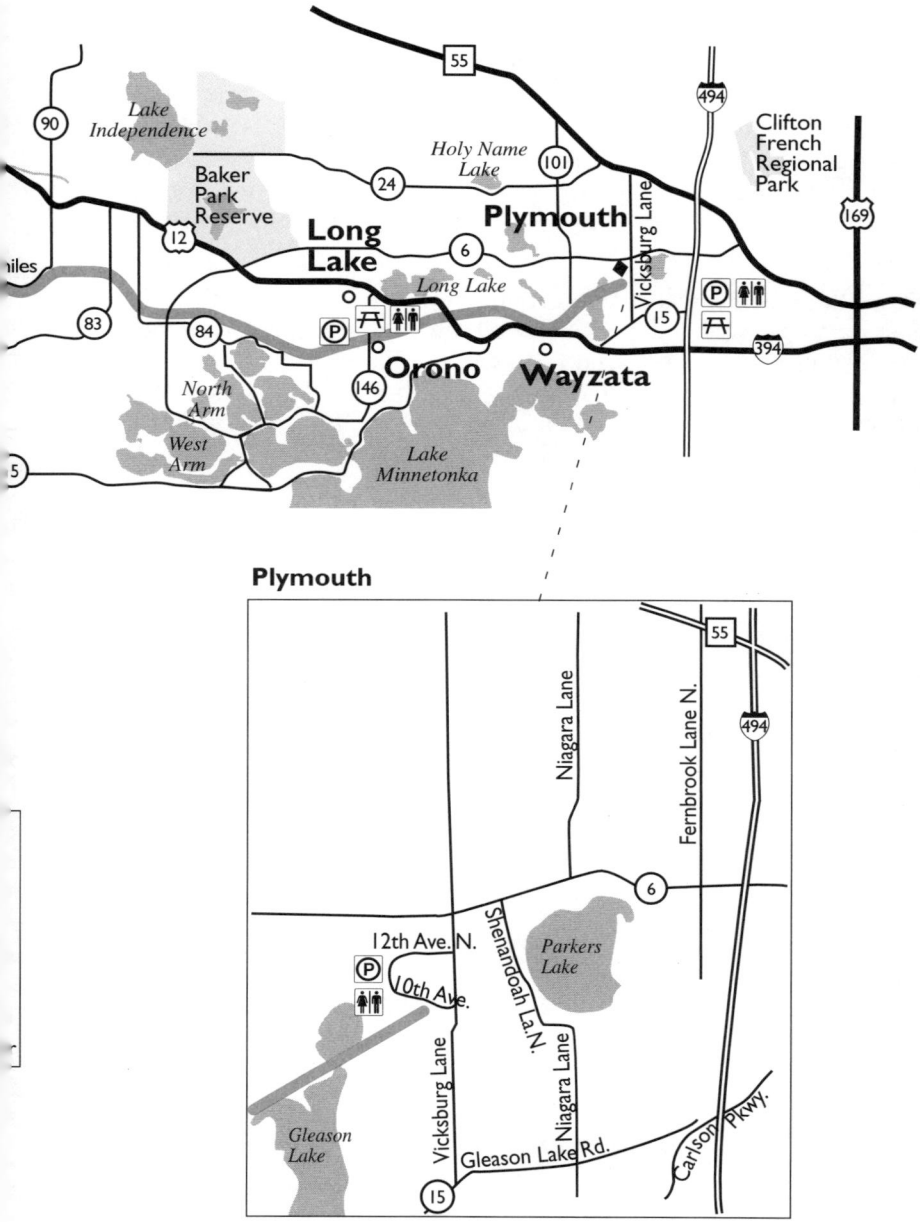
55
494
90
Lake Independence
Holy Name Lake
101
24
Baker Park Reserve
Clifton French Regional Park
169
Plymouth
Vicksburg Lane
12
Long Lake
6
Long Lake
15
83
84
394
Orono
Wayzata
146
North Arm
West Arm
Lake Minnetonka
Plymouth
55
494
Niagara Lane
Fernbrook Lane N.
6
12th Ave. N.
Shenandoah La. N.
Parkers Lake
10th Ave.
Vicksburg Lane
Niagara Lane
Gleason Lake
Gleason Lake Rd.
Carlson Pkwy.
15

MANKATO (CITY)

WHERE: City of Mankato
LENGTH: 7 miles
SURFACE: paved
TRAIL USE: 

The City of Mankato continues to expand its network of paved off-road bike paths within the city limits. Miles of off-road trail are scattered at several locations throughout the city (see map). While connections between paved trails is mostly via street, considerable expansion is in the planning stages.

Of particular note will be construction of a connecting link between the Sakatah Trail and the downtown biking headquarters in the depot on Riverfront and Main Street. It will parallel the east bank of the Minnesota River north to Highway 14, then east to the Sakatah on Lime Valley Road. Funding has been approved for this link, but actual work suspended pending final location of an east-west railway planned for this area.

There is currently a paved off-road link from the depot to the Trailhead North of the 5½ mile Red Jacket Trail (see page 86).

Mankato has many amenities to take advantage of, including the charm of older brick buildings that were built with intricate design appendages. In the Mankato area you'll find the Mankato Civic Center, Blue Earth County Heritage Center, the Judge Lorin P. Cray Mansion, the R.D. Hubbard House, "urban" restaurants and many fun goings on. Nearly 20 parks and nearby Minneopa State Park (complete with waterfall), provide lots of area for outdoor activities. Be on the look-out for officers on bikes, which are a common sight downtown, not because of crime, but for ease of getting around and to have a closer relationship with people.

FOR MORE INFORMATION:

Mankato Chamber and Visitors Bureau
122 S. Riverfront Dr.
Mankato, MN 56002
507-345-4519

Mankato Parks Department
P.O. Box 3368
Mankato, MN 56002
507-387-8650

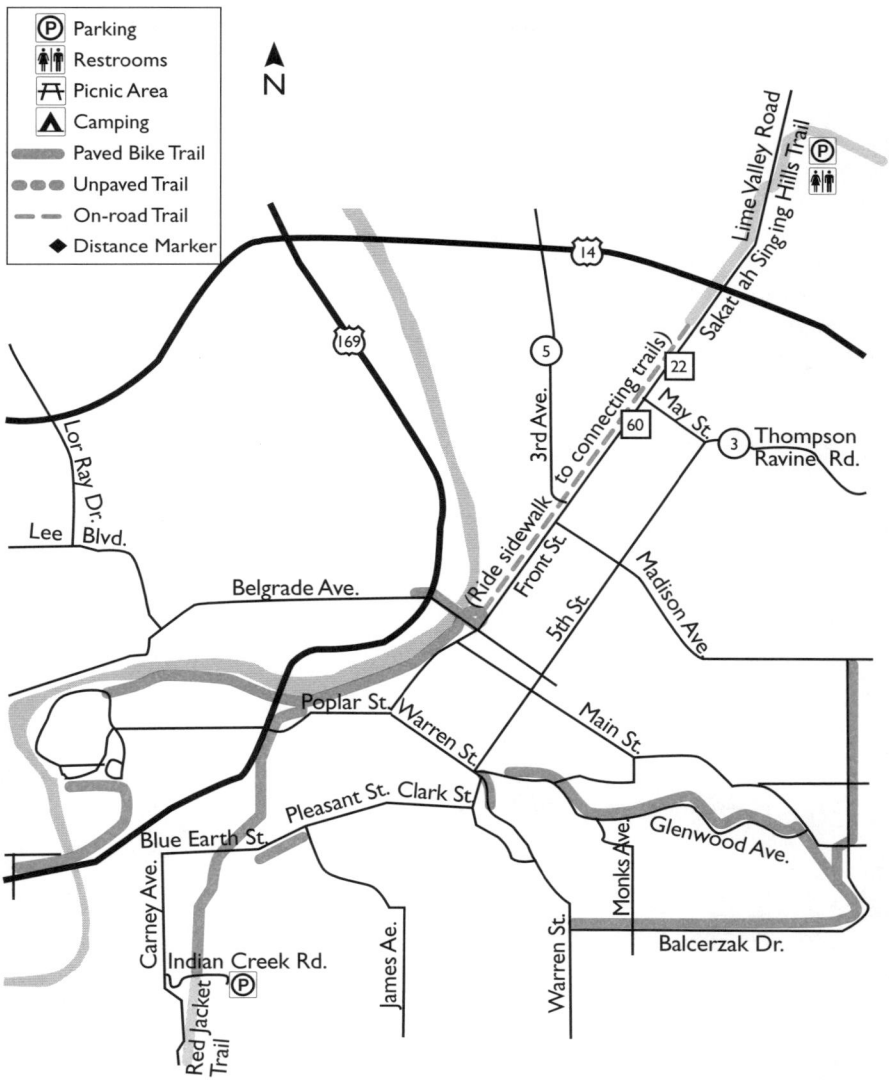
Parking
Restrooms
Picnic Area
Camping
Paved Bike Trail
Unpaved Trail
On-road Trail
Distance Marker
N
Lor Ray Dr.
Lee Blvd.
169
Belgrade Ave.
Poplar St.
Warren St.
Pleasant St.
Clark St.
Blue Earth St.
Carney Ave.
Indian Creek Rd.
Red Jacket Trail
James Ae.
Warren St.
Monks Ave.
Glenwood Ave.
Balcerzak Dr.
Main St.
Madison Ave
5th St.
Front St.
(Ride sidewalk to connecting trails)
3rd Ave.
5
14
60
22
May St.
3
Thompson Ravine Rd.
Lime Valley Road
Sakatah Singing Hills Trail

MARSHALL (CITY)

WHERE: City of Marshall
LENGTH: Several miles
SURFACE: Paved
TRAIL USE:

Marshall's bike trails are not extensive, but the Country Club Drive, Highway 7 and Redwood River diversion channel route make for a great ride.

Several parks with various facilities are also located within the city, including the Marshall Aquatic Center, where you can cool off on those hot summer days, or casually stroll through the rose garden. Jeanne's Gardens, located in Independence Park, is an English garden which community volunteers maintain, creating a beautiful area of garden, landscape and wildlife habitat. Another area park is Camden State Park, just a hop, skip and jump away–10 miles south of Marshall off Highway 23.

Bike Shorts

Wear an approved helmet. This is one of the most important precautions you can take to avoid serious injury.

FOR MORE INFORMATION:

Marshall CVB
P.O. Box 352B
Marshall, MN 56258
507-537-1865
www.marshall-mn.org

Marshall Parks and Recreation
344 Main St. W.
P.O. Box 477
Marshall, MN 56258
507-537-6767

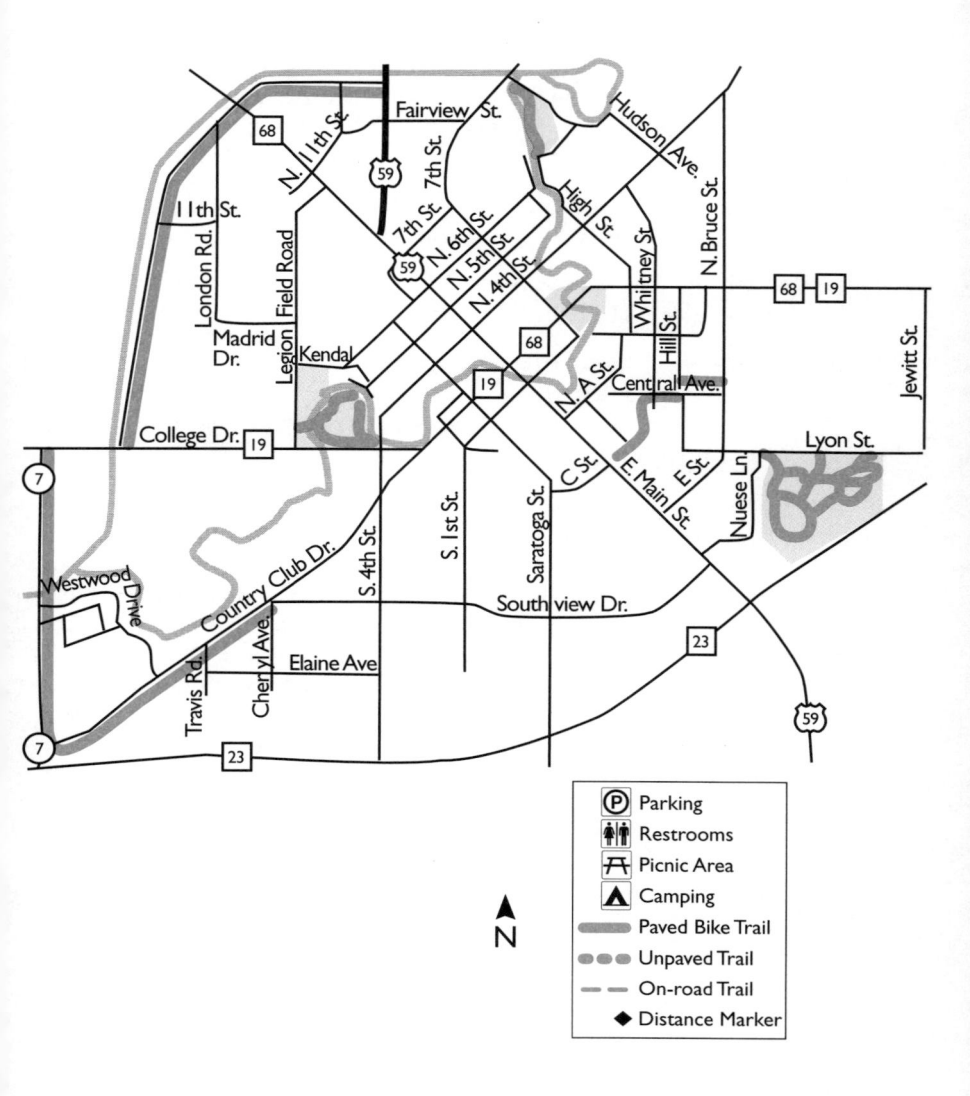
Fairview St.
Hudson Ave.
N. 11th St.
7th St.
11th St.
London Rd.
Field Road
Madrid Dr.
Legion
Kendal
7th St.
N. 6th St.
N. 5th St.
N. 4th St.
High St.
Whitney St.
N. Bruce St.
Hill St.
Central Ave.
Jewitt St.
N. A St.
College Dr.
Lyon St.
C St.
E. Main St.
E St.
Nuese Ln.
S. 4th St.
S. 1st St.
Saratoga St.
Westwood Drive
Country Club Dr.
Southview Dr.
Travis Rd.
Cheryl Ave.
Elaine Ave
68
59
19
7
23
Parking
Restrooms
Picnic Area
Camping
Paved Bike Trail
Unpaved Trail
On-road Trail
Distance Marker
N

RED JACKET

WHERE: Mankato to Rapidan
LENGTH: 5.5 miles
SURFACE: Paved
TRAIL USE:

Trailhead North: At the Indian Creek Road in south Mankato where it connects to a paved city bike trail. There is parking available here. Take the Front Street exit south off Highway 169. The best route to Indian Creek Road is south on Carney Avenue.

Mid Access: At the Red Jacket trestle crossing the Le Sueur River and State Highway 66. There is parking available on east side.

Trailhead South: At the Village of Rapidan, with a paved shoulder continuing west along Highway 9 to the dam on the Blue Earth River.

Although short in length, this is a great two-way ride and can be extended several miles further by utilizing the paved Mankato city off-street trails with which it connects or on paved shoulders along Highway 9, 60 and 69.

You will cross open farm country as well as views of scenic woods and river breaks along the Blue Earth River. Of special note is the Red Jacket trestle where you cross the river. This trestle is the reason why the trail exists and it is a classic. Foresighted individuals from Mankato, and especially Mr. Al Frosberg, thought the trestle worth saving and proceeded to do so. Their effort expanded into a bike trail which is the first rail-trail in Minnesota recovered for public use after years of private ownership by several landowners. This trail was constructed and is administered by Blue Earth County.

The trail includes an interesting tunnel under Highway 66 and an alternate trail adjacent to the main trail for a short distance to take you down to a parking area and across a new bridge over the Le Sueur River before re-connecting with the main trail.

FOR MORE INFORMATION:

Blue Earth County Park Department
35 Map Drive
P.O. Box 3083
Mankato, MN 56002
507-625-3281

Mankato Chamber of Commerce
112 River Front Drive
P.O. Box 999
507-345-4519

Mankato

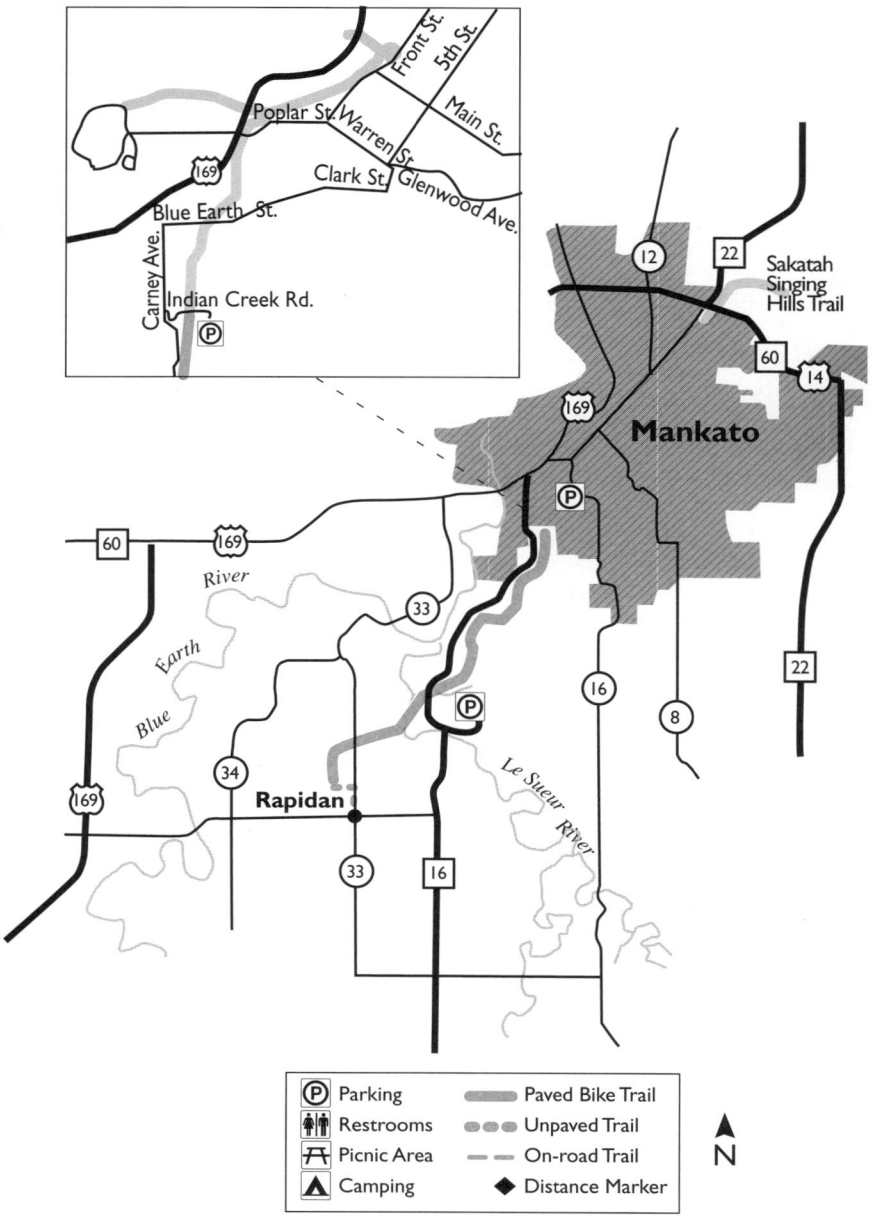
Front St.
5th St.
Main St.
Poplar St.
Warren St.
Clark St.
Glenwood Ave.
Blue Earth St.
Carney Ave.
Indian Creek Rd.
169
12
22
Sakatah Singing Hills Trail
60
14
Mankato
60
169
River
Earth
Blue
33
16
8
22
34
Rapidan
Le Sueur River
169
33
16
Parking
Restrooms
Picnic Area
Camping
Paved Bike Trail
Unpaved Trail
On-road Trail
Distance Marker
N

SAKATAH SINGING HILLS

WHERE: Faribault to Mankato
LENGTH: 39 miles
SURFACE: Paved
TRAIL USE:

Trailhead East: At West Central Faribault, near Highway 21. Parking is available 400 feet northwest of the junction at Highway 21 and the 7th Street stoplight. The trail follows old rail bed west from just south of this parking lot.

Mid Access: Mileages are west to east. At mile 4½ near Eagle Lake, there is parking, but no facilities. At mile 11, off County Road 26, there is parking, but no facilities. At mile 16, Elysian, there is a parking lot with a new building and restrooms. At mile 24, Waterville, just north of Highway 13 & 60 intersection, there is street parking. At mile 25, Sakatah State Park on Cannon Lake, there is parking, picnic tables, restrooms and fresh water. At mile 35, Shager County Park on Cannon Lake, there are picnic tables, parking, shelter, restrooms and fresh water.

Trailhead West: At Mankato, just north of Highway 14 and west of Highway 22, where it ties into the Mankato City bikeway system. Parking is one-quarter mile north of Highway 14 and 22 interchange on Lime Valley Road. There are portable toilets one-quarter mile east of lot along the trail.

A newly paved trail, Sakatah Singing Hills traverses parts of three counties along its 39 miles. This level trail wanders near lush pastures and farmland, along several lakes, through three small towns and a forested state park. There are swimming beaches within a short ride off the trail at Sakatah Lake State Park, Waterville, Elysian, Madison Lake and Cannon Lake. The fish hatchery in Waterville is open to visitors.

FOR MORE INFORMATION:

Trail Office
Box 11
Elysian, MN 56028
507-267-4774

Faribault Chamber of Commerce
530 Wilson Avenue
P.O. Box 434
Faribault, MN 55021
507-334-4381

Mankato Chamber of Commerce
112 River Front Drive
P.O. Box 999
Mankato, MN 56002
507-345-4519

The proposed Mankato connection between the Sakatah trail and the city trails at the downtown depot has not been finished and is currently on hold pending possible railroad relocation in Mankato.

The trail follows city streets through the town of Waterville, but you will find it well marked and on light traffic roads. Along with the completion of paved surfacing, the DNR has improved facilities and parking availability all along this trail. You will also find an occasional picnic table at interim points along your route.

Thirty-nine miles makes a pretty good one day ride so you may want to leave a car at Faribault if the wind is westerly, or at Mankato if the wind is easterly.

If you are campers as well as bikers, Sakatah State Park is 15 miles from the Faribault trailhead. In our group opinion, the east 14 miles is the most scenic as well as the most shaded and would make an excellent two-way ride.

One should consider the lakeside town of Elysian as a starting point for both portions of the trail. It is very near the half-way point and has an excellent parking lot and shelter with restrooms and water.

Located on the banks of the Minnesota River, Mankato is the home of Mankato State University. Minneopa Falls in Minneopa State Park is 5 miles west on Highway 68 and US 169.

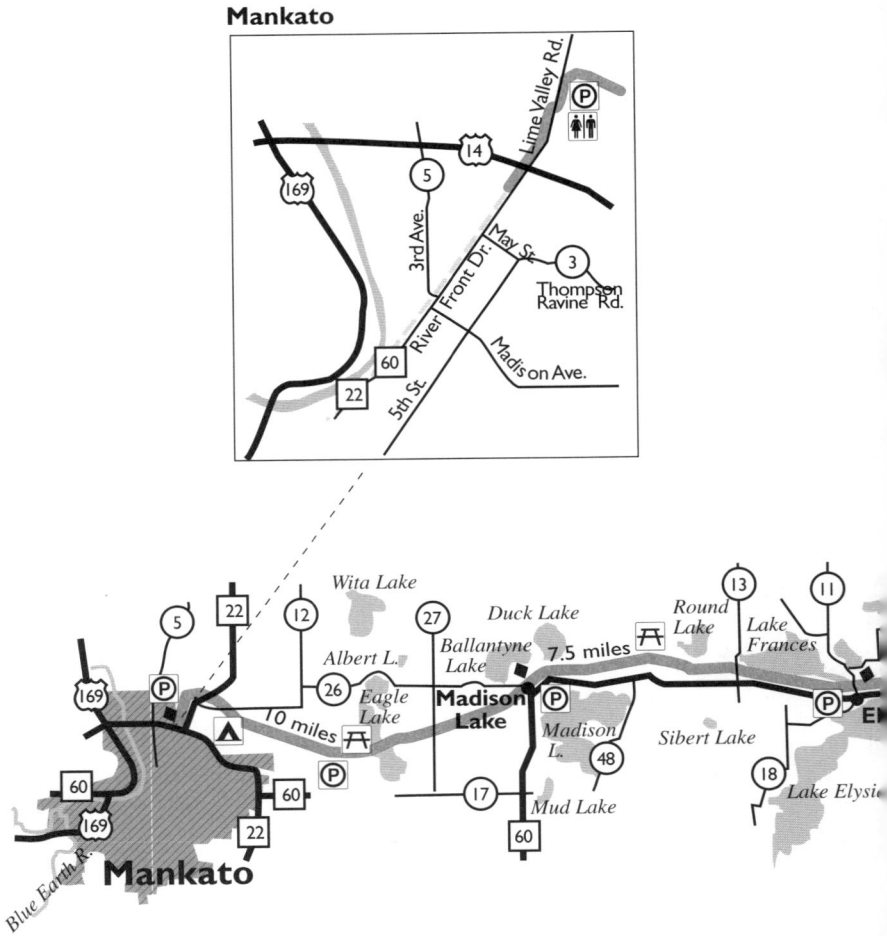

Administered by Minnesota Department of Natural Resources

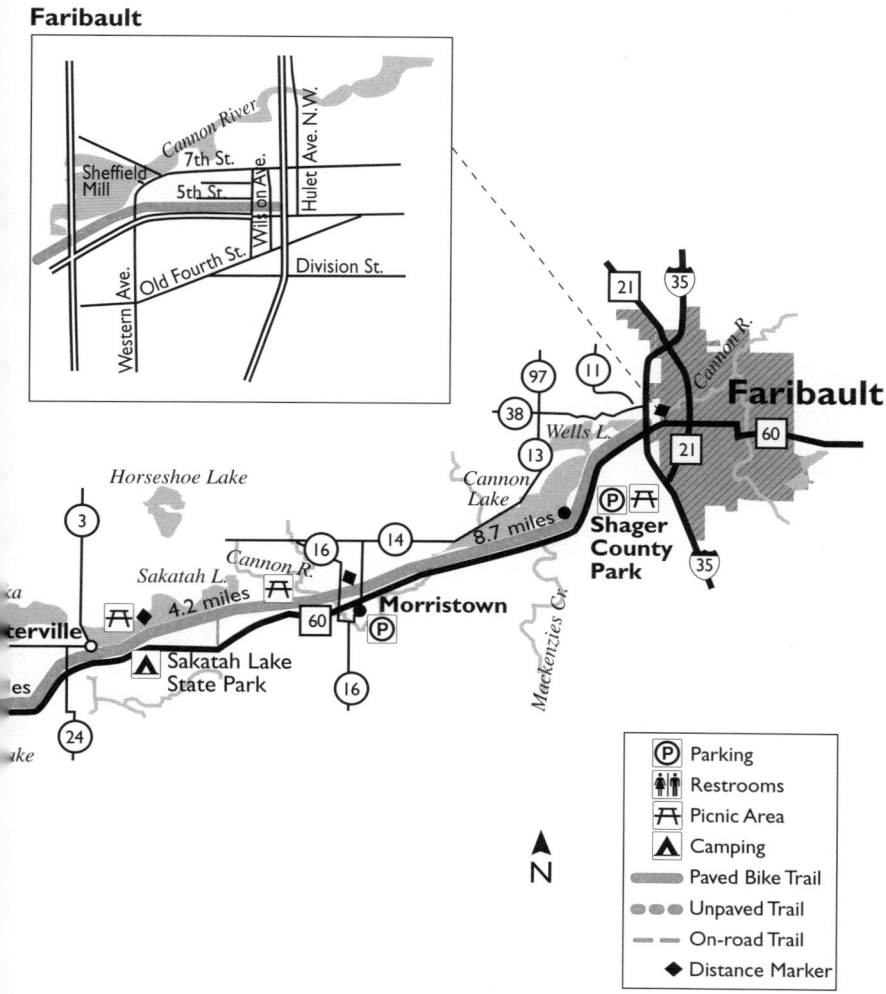
Faribault
Cannon River
7th St.
Sheffield Mill
5th St.
Wilson Ave.
Hulet Ave. N.W.
Old Fourth St.
Division St.
Western Ave.
Faribault
Cannon R.
Wells L.
Horseshoe Lake
Cannon Lake
8.7 miles
Shager County Park
Sakatah L.
Cannon R.
4.2 miles
Morristown
Sakatah Lake State Park
Mackenzies Cr.
Parking
Restrooms
Picnic Area
Camping
Paved Bike Trail
Unpaved Trail
On-road Trail
Distance Marker
N

SAKATAH STATE PARK

WHERE: Waterville
LENGTH: 3 mile portion of Sakatah Singing Hills State Trail traverses through the center of this park
SURFACE: Paved
TRAIL USE:

Access: Park entrance is on Highway 60, east of Waterville.

Sakatah State Park is located on the east edge of Waterville and provides excellent camping and hiking. Biking is pretty much limited to the state trail but restroom facilities are available just off the trail.

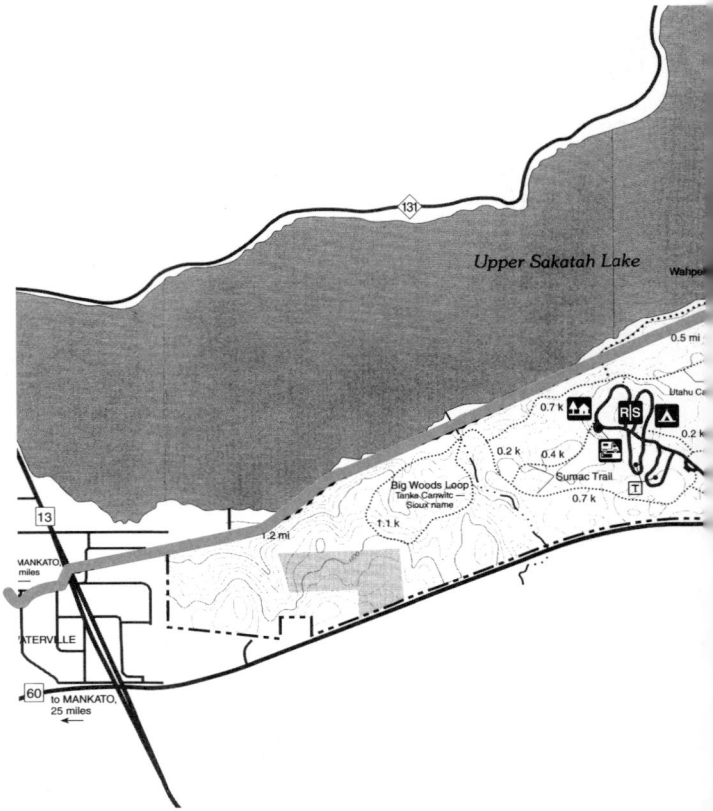

FOR MORE INFORMATION:

Sakatah Lake State Park
R.R.2, Box 19
Waterville, MN 56096
507-362-4438

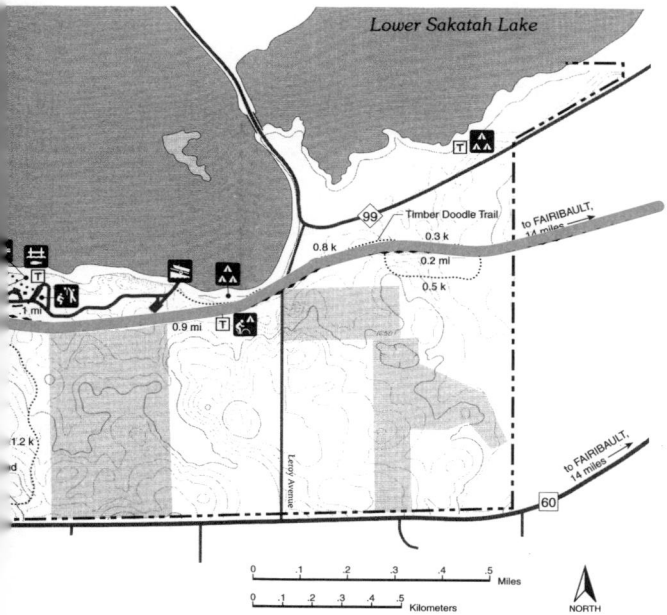

TRAILS

- Hiking Only
- Hiking/Ski
- Snowmobile
- Sakatah Singing Hills Trail
  - Snowmobiling
  - Skiing
  - Hiking
  - Bicycling

FACILITIES

- Information/Office
- Picnic Area
- Interpretive/Trail Center
- Fishing Pier
- Boat Ramp
- Campground
- Primitive Group Camp
- Bicycle Touring Camp
- Trailer Sanitation Station
- Camper Cabin
- Volleyball Court
- Restrooms/Showers
- Private Property
  Public Use Prohibited
  (except on designated trails)
- Toilets

SIBLEY STATE PARK

WHERE: Willmar/New London
LENGTH: 5 miles
SURFACE: Paved
TRAIL USE:

Access: 15 miles north of Willmar on US Highway 48.

Although part of this trail goes along the shore of Lake Andrew, expect some hills elsewhere.

Bike Shorts

Plan your ride so you are off the streets, roads and trails by dusk. Bicycles are best left parked or stored at night, but if you must, be sure you have front, side and rear reflectors, plus lights. Wear or switch to light-colored clothing.

Adults today are very health conscious and bicycling is one of the best forms of exercise. In addition to fitness and family fun, rail-trails provide an important contribution to regional economies.

FOR MORE INFORMATION:

Sibley State Park
800 Sibley Park Road N.E.
New London, MN 56273
320-354-2055

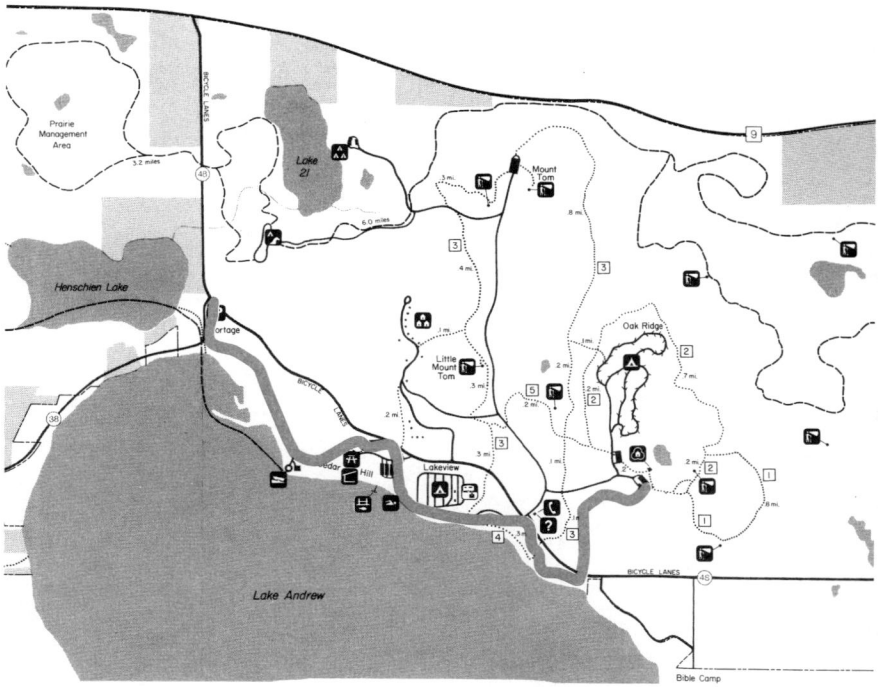

LEGEND

TRAILS

- Hiking
- Horseback / Hiking
- Bicycle / Interpretive
- Canoe Route

TRAIL NAMES

1. Pondview
2. Parker-Fremberg
3. Mount Tom
4. Lakeview
5. Oak Hills

PRIVATE PROPERTY
Public Use Prohibited
(except on designated trails)

FACILITIES

- Information/Office
- Picnic Area
- Swimming
- Boat Ramp
- Overlook
- Interpretive/Trail Center
- Shelter
- Telephone
- Equestrian Area
- Campground
- Group Center
- Primitive Group Camp
- Trailer Sanitation Station
- Parking
- Fishing Pier

SCALE

MILES: 0, .1, .2, .3, .4, .5, 1.0

KILOMETERS: 0, .5, 1.0, 1.5

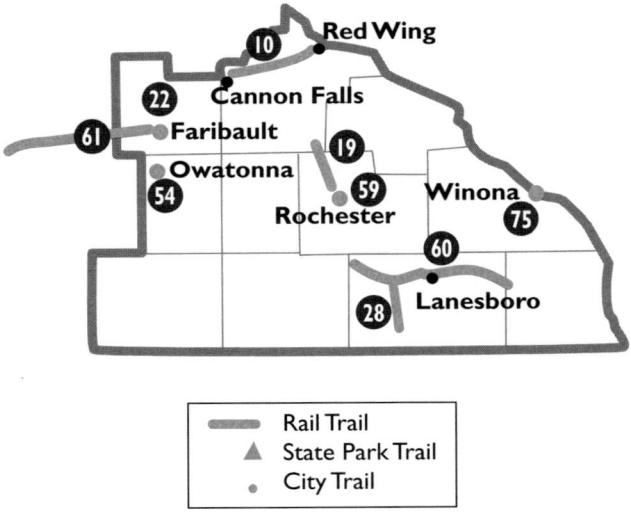
Red Wing
10
22
Cannon Falls
61
Faribault
19
Owatonna
54
59
Winona
Rochester
75
60
Lanesboro
28
Rail Trail
State Park Trail
City Trail

Southeast Minnesota

Trail

10. Cannon Valley Rail-Trail . . . . . .page 98
19. Douglas State Rail-Trail . . . . . .page 102
22. Faribault City Trails . . . . . .page 104
28. Harmony-Preston Valley State Rail-Trail . . . . . .page 113
54. Owatonna City Trails . . . . . .page 106
59. Rochester City Trails . . . . . .page 108
60. Root River State Rail-Trail . . . . . .page 112
61. Sakatah Singing Hills State Rail-Trail
(see Southwest section) . . . . . .page 88
75. Winona City Trails . . . . . .page 116

*** Numbers refer to large map on page 11 and opposite page**

CANNON VALLEY

WHERE: Cannon Falls to Red Wing
LENGTH: 19.7 miles
SURFACE: Blacktop
TRAIL USE:

Trailhead West: Cannon Falls–Exit Highway 52 on County Road 19 into Cannon Falls. Parking lot is on Highway 19 one block west of Main Street.

Mid Access: Highway 19 east from Cannon Falls to County Road 7, north to Welch. Or, Highway 61 east of Miesville to County Road 7 south. There is parking, shelter, picnic tables, restrooms and water here.

Trailhead East: Old West Main Street and Bench Street, one block off Highway 61 in west Red Wing. There is a parking lot with facilities. To downtown Red Wing, you may follow Old West Main along the marked historic route near the Mississippi River.

For a trail with great scenery in all seasons, shelter from the wind and shade from the hot sun, this is the place to be. The trail follows the Cannon River Valley from Cannon Falls to Red Wing. At 19.7 miles, it is a short one-way ride or a quite manageable two-way trip. Although not part of the DNR State Trail system, this is a scenic, well-maintained, paved trail. A daily or seasonal "wheelpass" is required for trail use. This trail suffered some flood damage in 1998, but the trail is open and funds are on hand for permanent repairs.

"Wheelpasses" are for users 18 years or older, and refer to anything with wheels: bicycles, in-line skates, skateboards, etc. They are available at self-purchasing stations at major access points, from merchants in Cannon Falls and Red Wing, or you may encounter an attendant along the trail.

For this gem of a trail, we are indebted to a group of private citizens from Cannon Falls, Welch and Red Wing who saw the recreational value of the area. They secured the property and obtained the grants and assistance to improve it and replace the numerous bridges you will cross. The trail parallels the river along the south side between bluffs and trees with few stretches of open country. The many bridges tell the rider there are a lot of small gorges and feeder steams which empty into the Cannon River.

If you plan to ride both ways on your day, we recommend starting at Red Wing, where there is a parking lot near the beginning of the trail just off old West Main Street. This gives you an opportunity to explore

Red Wing with its old river-town flavor. It also gives you the benefit of the slight downhill grade on the last one-half of the trip, rather than the first half. Along the way, you will find picnic tables about 3½ miles east of Cannon Falls, and portable restrooms at approximately one-third distance intervals. Refreshments in the village of Welch are available if you wish to take a short side trip.

Some local sites in the area include the beautifully restored St. James Hotel in Red Wing, where you also might consider a Mississippi River cruise. Cannon Falls offers canoeing and tubing on the Cannon River.

See map page 100.

Cannon Valley Trail sign

FOR MORE INFORMATION:

Trail Office
306 West Mill St.
Cannon Falls, MN 55009
507-263-0508

Cannon Falls Chamber of Commerce
103 N. 4th St.
P.O. Box 2
Cannon Falls, MN 55009
507-263-2289

Red Wing Area
Chamber of Commerce
420 Levee Street
Red Wing, MN 55066
651-388-4719

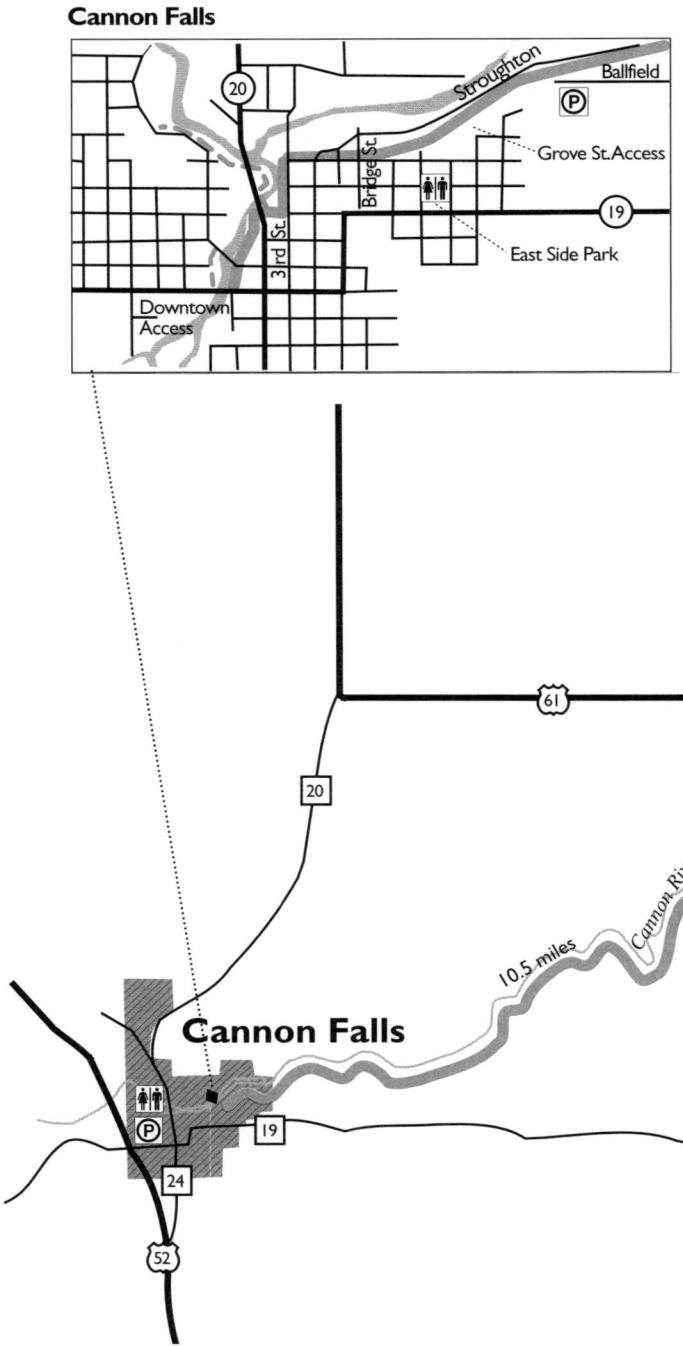
Cannon Falls
20
Stroughton
Ballfield
Grove St.Access
Bridge St.
19
3rd St.
East Side Park
Downtown
Access
61
7
20
Welch
Cannon River
10.5 miles
7
Cannon Falls
19
24
52

Red Wing

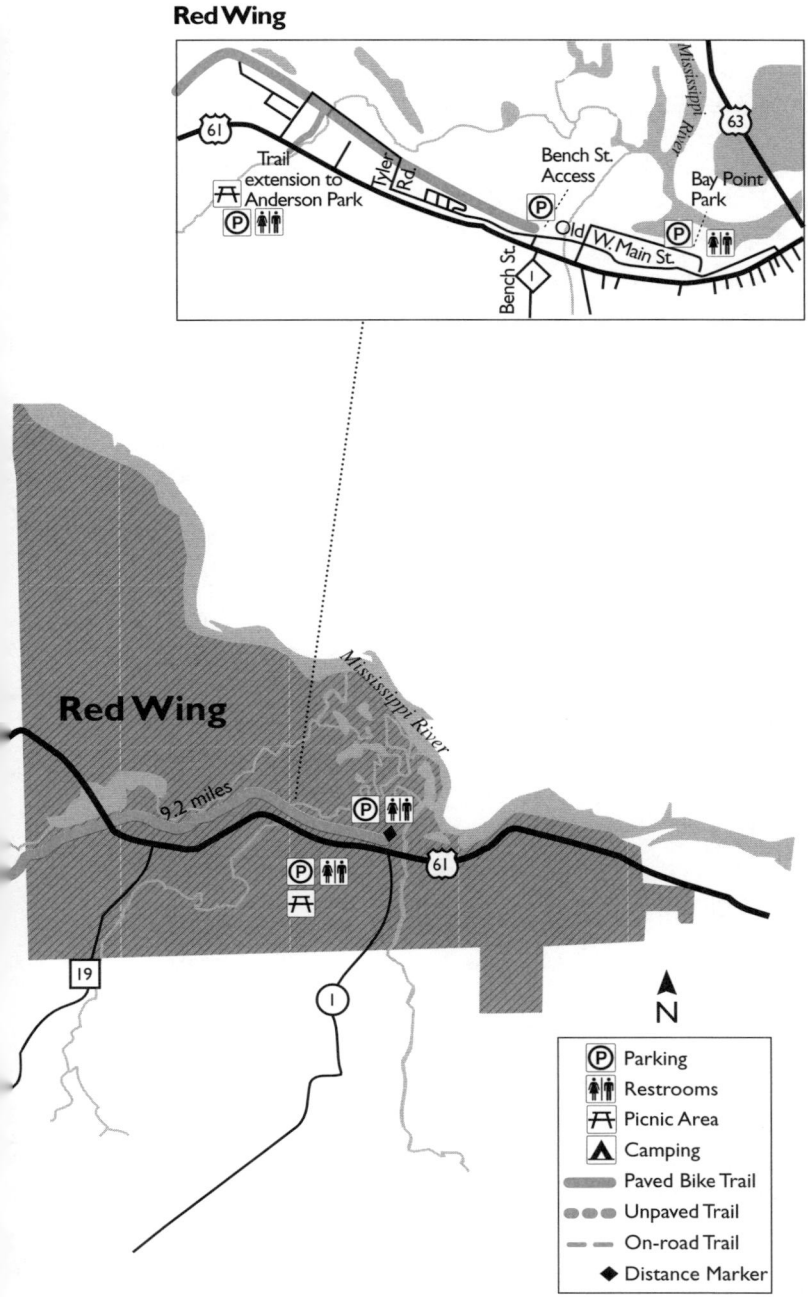
61
Trail extension to Anderson Park
Tyler Rd.
Bench St. Access
Mississippi River
63
Bay Point Park
Old W. Main St.
Bench St.
1
Red Wing
Mississippi River
9.2 miles
61
19
1
N
Parking
Restrooms
Picnic Area
Camping
Paved Bike Trail
Unpaved Trail
On-road Trail
Distance Marker

DOUGLAS STATE

WHERE: Pine Island to Rochester
LENGTH: 12.5 miles
SURFACE: Blacktop
TRAIL USE:

Trailhead North: Pine Island Park on the NE corner of Pine Island just south of exit from Highway 52. You will find parking, restrooms, water and picnic tables here.

Mid Access: Douglas on County Road 14, exit off highway 52. There is a large parking lot, shelter, water and restrooms at milepost 5 from Rochester.

Trailhead South: About 2 miles NW of Rochester on County Road 4, or, if you are driving on Highway 52, take the IBM exit west to County Road 4. There is ample paved parking, shelter and portable restrooms here.

The Douglas Trail is one of the few in the state that can be covered in its entirety, riding both directions, in less than four hours. Its 12½ mile length combined with easy access and adequate parking at both trailheads make this an excellent half-day, one-vehicle trip. Repair and widening of some bad spots have been done with complete widening and resurfacing planned. Benches, tables and a shelter have recently been added along the trail.

This is a good choice for an early or late season ride when that unusually nice day comes along, but we recommend it at any time during the biking season.

En route, you will cross the Zumbro River and Plum Creek on wide, refurbished bridges. The trail itself is wide and in excellent condition, with the only hazard being the need to cross several country gravel roads. The trail winds past a golf course and through fertile farm country. It is not heavily wooded, but there is tree cover much of the way. You may encounter horseback riders as a horse and cross-country ski trail parallel the bike path and the two cross at occasional well-marked points.

Following the recent construction of the Circle Drive road around north and west Rochester, two bike path overpasses have been added. One crosses 41st St. N.W. and one crosses Circle Drive near the golf course. Access to parts of the Rochester City Trail system (page 109) is available at both sites. Rochester has many areas of interest, including the Mayo Clinic and Museum, Mayowood, and the 30,000 giant Canada geese that live at Silver Lake Park. Bring a bag of bread and wear shoes.

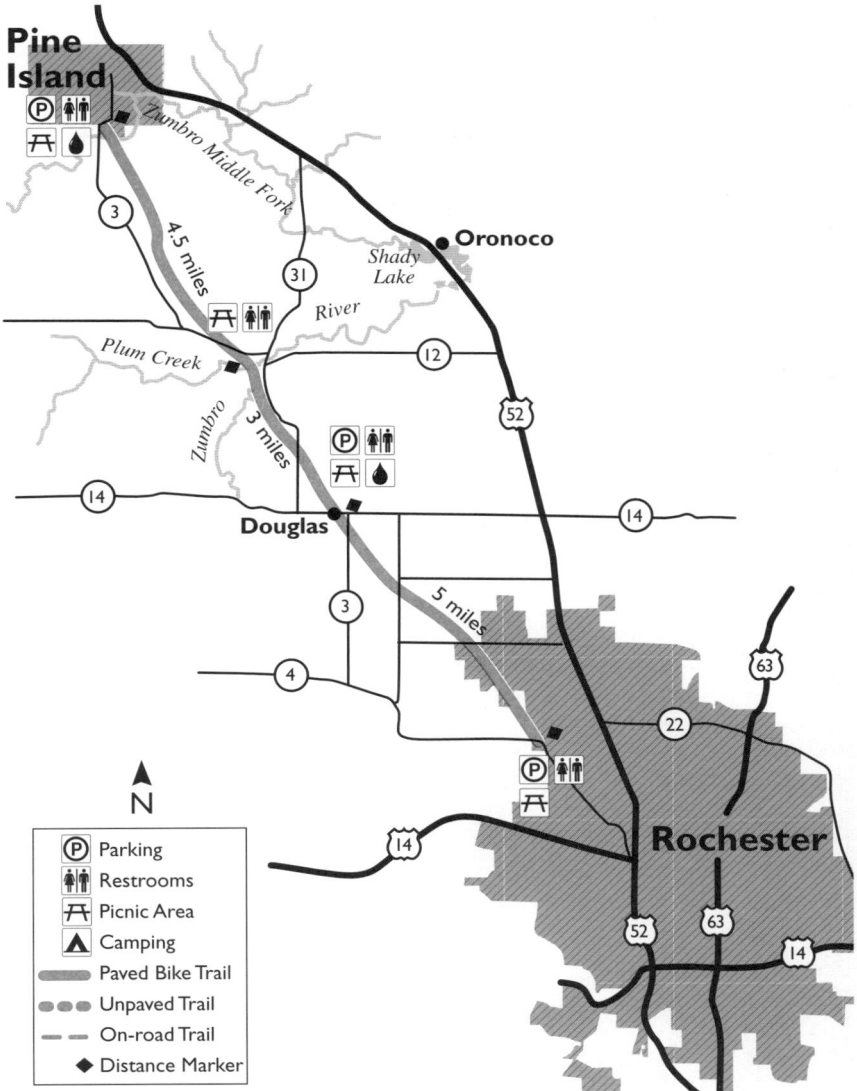

Administered by Minnesota Department of Natural Resources

FOR MORE INFORMATION:

Rochester Visitor Bureau
150 South Broadway Suite A
Rochester, MN 55904
507-288-4331
800-634-8277

Trail Office
2300 Silver Creek Road N.E.
Rochester, MN 55906
507-285-7176

FARIBAULT (CITY)

WHERE: City of Faribault
LENGTH: 4 miles
SURFACE: Paved
TRAIL USE: 

Faribault is located at the east end of Sakatah Singing Hills State Trail, which gives it a direct connection to Mankato 39 miles to the west. The planned connection to Faribault's city trails has not yet been completed. Their paved trail following the Straight River from the north edge of town to the south edge is well worth the time.

The Mill Towns Trail is a paved recreational trail in the works that would link the Cannon Valley Trail (Cannon Falls to Red Wing) and the Sakatah Singing Hills Trail (Faribault to Mankato). This trail will skirt west and north edge of Faribault. Call Northfield Chamber of Commerce (1-507-645-5604) for updated information.

Bike Shorts

Keep your tires inflated to the pressure noted on the side of the tire.

FOR MORE INFORMATION:

Faribault Area Chamber of Commerce
530 Wilson Ave. N.W.
Faribault, MN 55021
507-334-4381

Parks and Recreation
15 West Division St.
City Hall
Faribault, MN 55021
507-332-6112

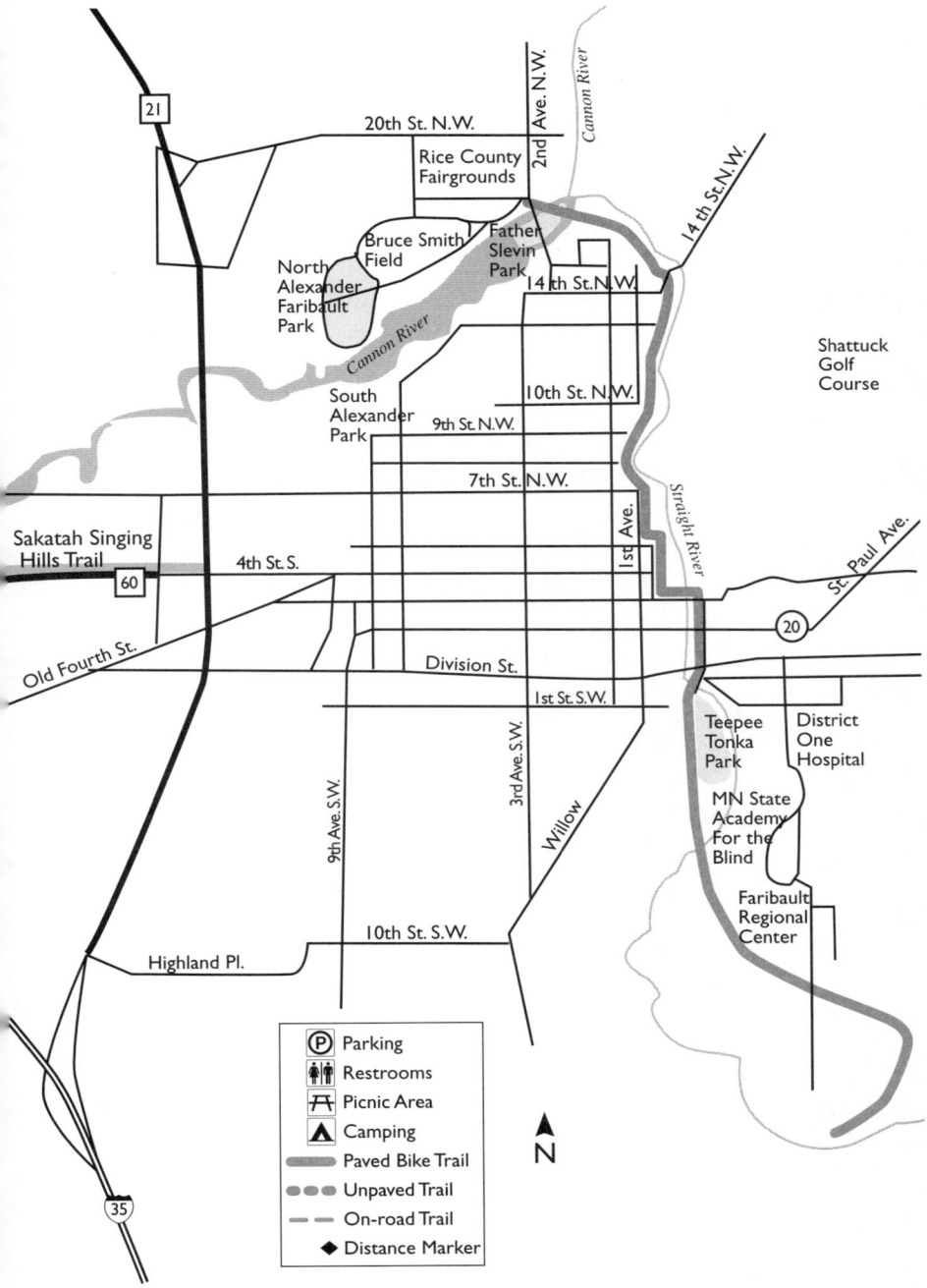
21
20th St. N.W.
2nd Ave. N.W.
Cannon River
Rice County Fairgrounds
14th St. N.W.
Bruce Smith Field
Father Slevin Park
North Alexander Faribault Park
14th St. N.W.
Cannon River
Shattuck Golf Course
South Alexander Park
10th St. N.W.
9th St. N.W.
7th St. N.W.
Straight River
Sakatah Singing Hills Trail
60
4th St. S.
1st Ave.
St. Paul Ave.
20
Old Fourth St.
Division St.
1st St. S.W.
Teepee Tonka Park
District One Hospital
3rd Ave. S.W.
9th Ave. S.W.
Willow
MN State Academy For the Blind
Faribault Regional Center
10th St. S.W.
Highland Pl.
Parking
Restrooms
Picnic Area
Camping
Paved Bike Trail
Unpaved Trail
On-road Trail
Distance Marker
N
35

OWATONNA (CITY)

WHERE: City of Owatonna
LENGTH: 5.75 miles
SURFACE: Paved, 12 feet wide
TRAIL USE:

The Owatonna trail system has been the beneficiary of four substantial contributions by estate or trusts of four entrepreneurial families. Those contributions have resulted in an exceptional trail system traversing the scenic city north to south and east to west.

The total trail system connects three major parks plus the 225 acre Kaplan Woods Parkway. All of the trail is lighted for night recreation use.

Owatonna City Trail

FOR MORE INFORMATION:

Parks and Recreation Department
540 West Hill Circle
Owatonna, MN 55060
507-444-4321

Visitors Bureau and Chamber of Commerce
507-451-7970

Owatonna CVB
320 Hoffman Drive
Owatonna, MN 55060
507-451-7970
1-800-423-6466
www.owatonna.org

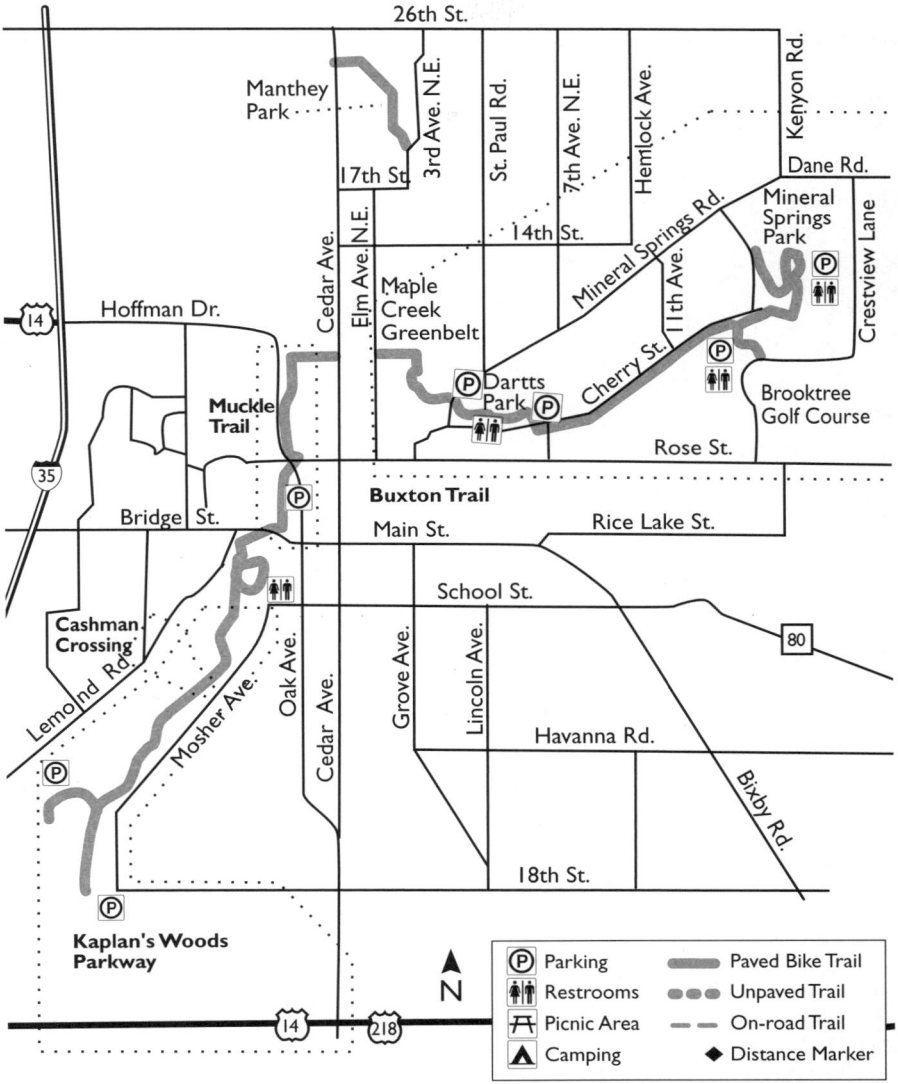
26th St.
Manthey Park
3rd Ave. N.E.
St. Paul Rd.
7th Ave. N.E.
Hemlock Ave.
Kenyon Rd.
Dane Rd.
17th St.
14th St.
Mineral Springs Rd.
Mineral Springs Park
Crestview Lane
Cedar Ave.
Elm Ave. N.E.
Maple Creek Greenbelt
11th Ave.
Cherry St.
Hoffman Dr.
14
Muckle Trail
Dartts Park
Brooktree Golf Course
Rose St.
35
Buxton Trail
Bridge St.
Main St.
Rice Lake St.
School St.
Cashman Crossing
80
Lemond Rd.
Mosher Ave.
Oak Ave.
Cedar Ave.
Grove Ave.
Lincoln Ave.
Havanna Rd.
Bixby Rd.
18th St.
Kaplan's Woods Parkway
N
14
218
Parking
Restrooms
Picnic Area
Camping
Paved Bike Trail
Unpaved Trail
On-road Trail
Distance Marker

ROCHESTER (CITY)

WHERE: City of Rochester
LENGTH: 26 miles
SURFACE: Paved
TRAIL USE:

Rochester has a number of parks with good trails, as well as off-road trails following the Zumbro River and a new connection to the Douglas State Trail northwest of the city. Their routes and paths are well-marked and quite extensive.

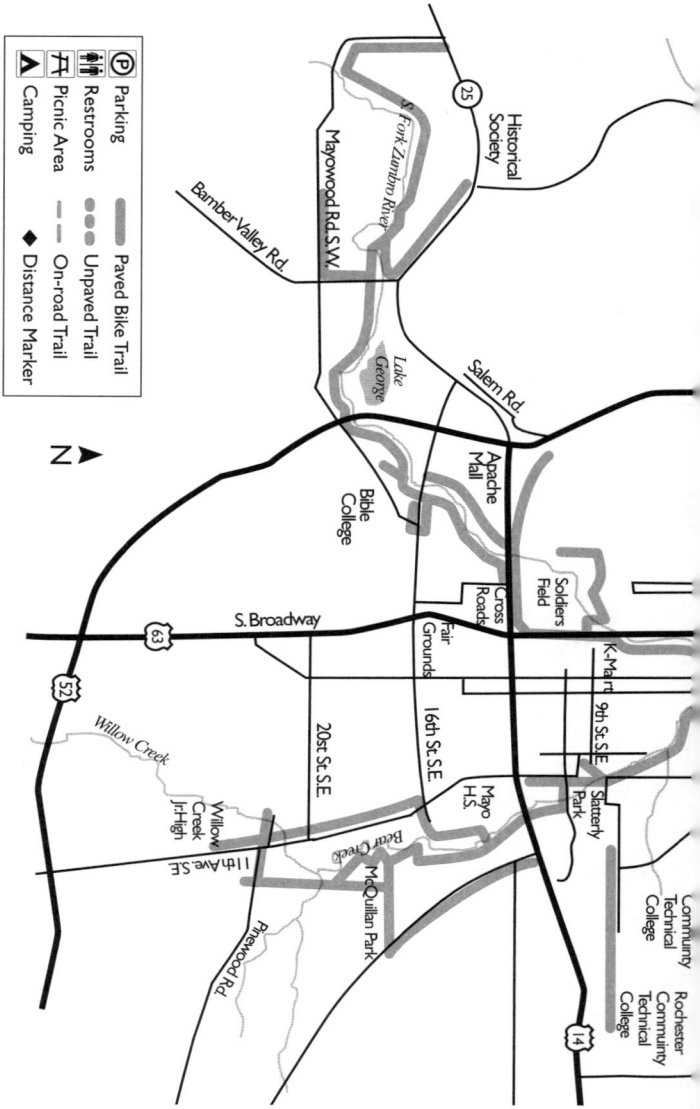

FOR MORE INFORMATION:

Rochester CVB
150 So. Broadway, Suite A
Rochester, MN 55904
507-288-4331, 1-800-634-8277
www.rochestercvb.org

Rochester Parks
201-4th St. S.E.
Rochester, MN 55904
507-281-6160

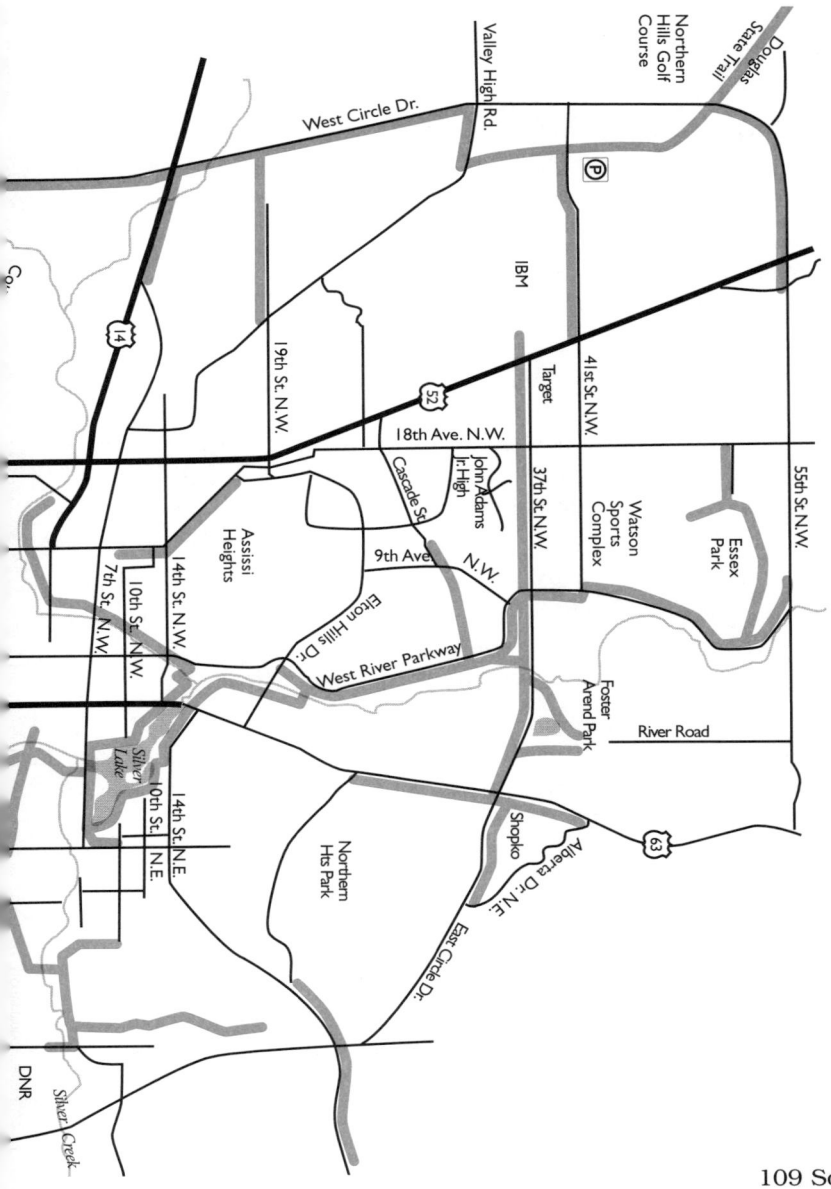

ROOT RIVER

WHERE: Fountain to Houston
LENGTH: 42 miles
SURFACE: Paved
TRAIL USE:

Trailhead West: At the South end of the Main St. in Fountain. There is parking, as well as rest rooms here.

Mid Access: At Whalen, where you will find restrooms and picnic tables. At Lanesboro, the trail passes through the center of town, crossing County Road 250.

There is also access at the Isinours Unit on County Road 17. The parking lot is located about one-quarter mile west of County Road 17 at the Isinours wood lot. This is also the Trailhead North of the Harmony-Preston Valley Trail (see page 113).

Trailhead East: Houston, a new trail center building at 200 West Plum Street where information, full facilities and parking are available.

The Root River Trail now provides 42 paved miles along the Root River Valley and through the hardwood forest and bluffs of this historic region. Consider it for an early or late season ride, but it is great any time of the year. It is one of the more level trails except at the extreme west end and a short adjustment about mid-point between Fountain and Lanesboro.

Trail Headquarters: At the former depot in Rushford, located one block west of Mill Street (which is also Highway 43) and adjacent to the downtown area. The depot is open year-round and is being developed into a railroad and trail museum.

The 42 miles make this a fairly long one-way ride for the casual bicyclist, but the opportunities and attractions of this general area suggest an overnight stay at one of the several bed and breakfasts or motels along or near it.

The Root River State Trail follows the watershed and general route of the south branch of its namesake between Fountain and Lanesboro and joins the main branch just east of Lanesboro. Although the trail is not always adjacent to the river, you will often see trout fishermen, canoeists and other outdoor enthusiasts on your ride. The trail includes 46 bridges with lengths of up to 500 ft. Of course, the towns of Fountain, Lanesboro and Rushford are attractions in themselves, with the entire downtown section of Lanesboro listed on the National Register of Historic Places.

The route will take you through the scenic bluffs and extensive hardwood forest of southern Minnesota. Be alert for wildlife, especially through Lost Lake Game Refuge just west of Lanesboro. Worthwhile side trips include the State Fish Hatchery south of Lanesboro on Highway 16 or the Amish Community and shops at Harmony. Root River Trail towns annually sponsor a bike ride the third week in May called Sykkle Tur.

We prefer to plan this trip for a one-way ride from the Trailhead West at Fountain to Rushford and eventually Houston. The main reason is that it gives you a downhill ride all the way with one exception when the trail leaves the valley to get on top of the bluffs and returns to the rail bed after a short distance.

If your party has chosen a one-way ride, your best bet is to park a vehicle in Fountain and one in Houston. Take Highway 8 from Fountain to Lanesboro and Highway 16 from Lanesboro to Houston.

At Fountain, there is ample parking, a shelter and portable restrooms. From this point, the trail takes an immediate downhill grade for nearly two miles until it reaches the river valley. Three miles further along you will see an old railroad building and another parking lot. This was once the point where the railroad used to put on a second engine to pull the trains up the grade you just came down. It is also the site of the Isinours Demonstration Woodland, where you may want to take a walking side trip and view the many varieties of trees (labeled) with which the foresters are experimenting or are observing.

In Lanesboro you will ride by the dam which provides electricity. Lanesboro has recently constructed a new building along the trail housing both a trail office and the Lanesboro Visitor's Center, including restrooms.

Lanesboro is a picturesque village with antique shops, a winery, campground, a historic inn and bed and breakfast inns. An eatery on the Main St. has live music and wonderful food. There is a resident woodcarver and Amish gift shop, along with many other interesting attractions and eateries.

Heading east, your next stop might be Whalen where they conveniently provide picnic tables and restrooms at trailside. Your next chance for refreshments is Peterson, 9 miles further east. Nearing Rushford is the only part of the trip in open country or paralleling a highway. Once in Rushford, you will find ample parking near the depot, excellent restaurants and accommodations. Since the trail now continues beyond Rushford, you will need to traverse city streets from the Depot to pick up the paved trail on the east side of town. We recommend a route from the depot around and behind the IGA grocery store as the most direct.

See page 114 for map.

Root River Trail

FOR MORE INFORMATION:

Trail Office
Box 376
Lanesboro, MN 55949
507-467-2552

Lanesboro Visitor Center
100 Milwaukee Road
P.O. Box 348
Lanesboro, MN 55948
800-944-2670

HARMONY-PRESTON VALLEY

WHERE: Harmony to Root River State Trail via Preston
LENGTH: 17.8 miles
SURFACE: Paved 10 feet wide
TRAIL USE:

Trailhead North: Isinours demonstration woodlot, just west of County Road 17 intersection with Root River State Trail. Follow County Road 8 east out of Fountain approximately 4 miles, then south 3 miles on County Road 17. You will find parking here.

Mid Access: Preston. One-half mile south of Highway 52 in east Preston adjacent to the fairgrounds. There is ample parking and a trail headquarters building with restrooms and information.

Trailhead South: Harmony on Highway 52 at 4th Street. Parking one-half mile west of Highway 52 with facilities.

A welcome link to one of the most popular trails in the state and one that provides additional bicycle access to the scenic southeastern blufflands. It crosses sparkling trout streams and views range from limestone bluffs to rolling pastoral landscapes. The north half from Preston to the Root River Trail (see page 110) is both level and scenic, while the Preston to Harmony half presents an uphill climb for part of the 12 miles, but an easy ride going north.

Preston has developed a beautiful parking area and trail building, along with many small town facilities and points of interest. The Amish community of Harmony is unique in the offering of Amish crafts and produce shops you will not find elsewhere.

FOR MORE INFORMATION:

Trail Office
Box 376
Lanesboro, MN 55949
507-467-2552

Historic Bluff Country
P.O. Box 609
15-2nd St. N.W.
Harmony, MN 55939
507-886-2230
800-428-2030
FAX 507-886-2934
www.bluffcountry.com

ROOT RIVER AND HARMONY-PRESTON

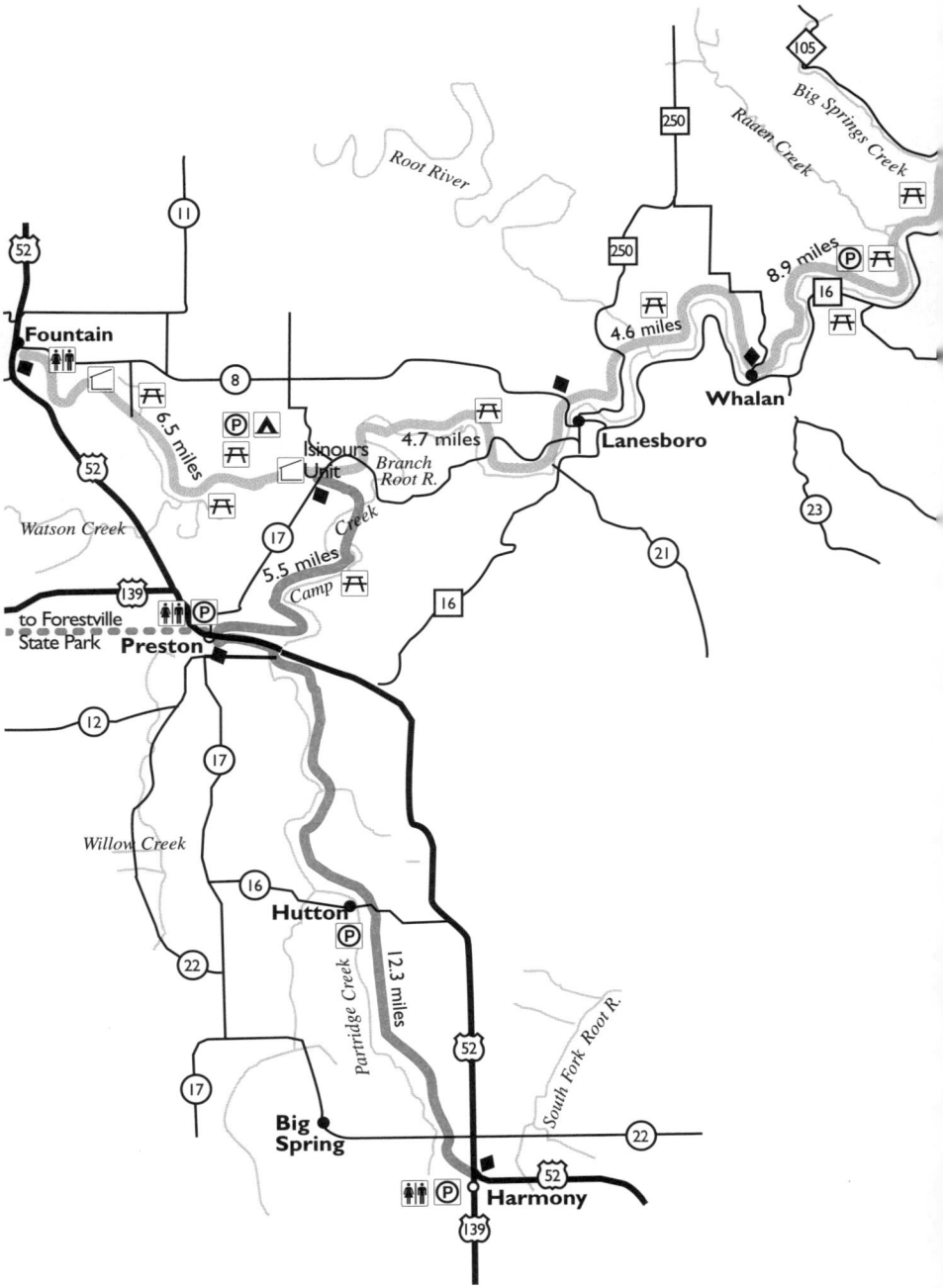

ROOT RIVER AND HARMONY-PRESTON

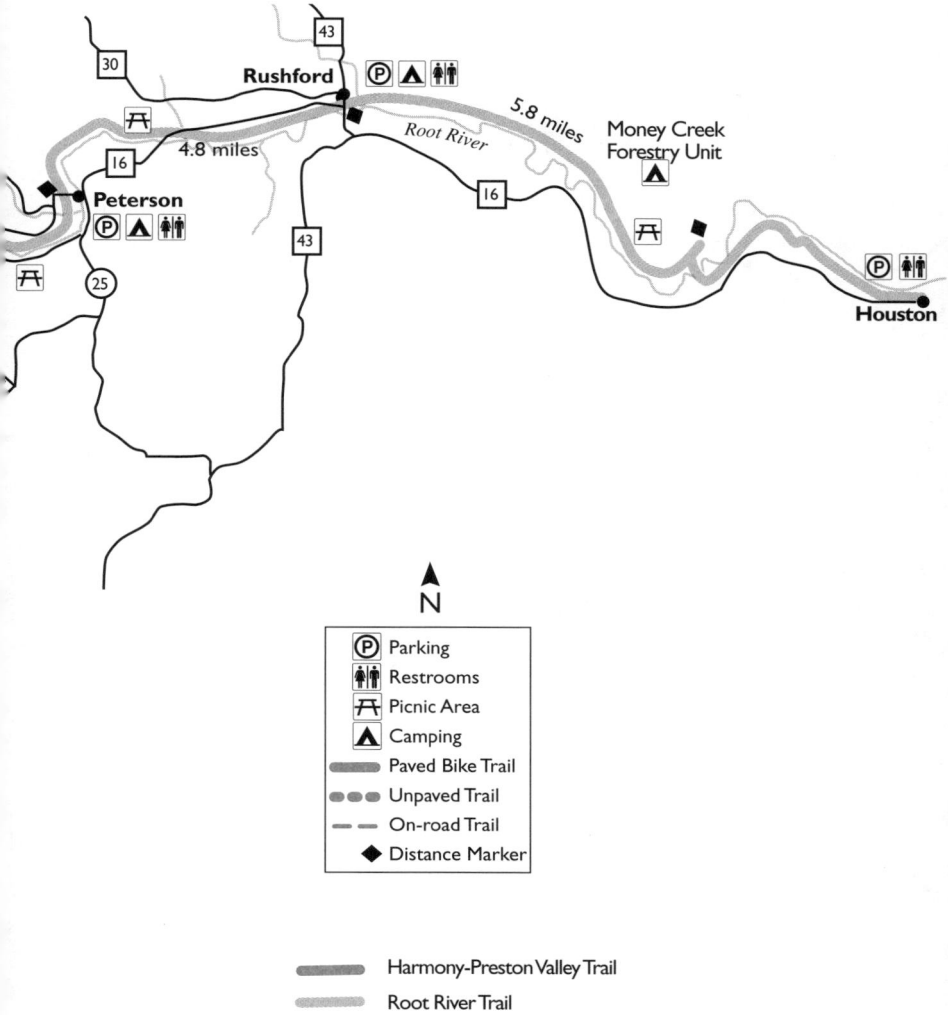

Administered by Minnesota Department of Natural Resources

WINONA (CITY)

WHERE: City of Winona
LENGTH: 5.5 miles
SURFACE: Paved
TRAIL USE:

The city's primary bike trail is a circle route around Lake Winona. Plans are currently underway to construct a bicycle/hiking path on top of their extensive flood dike system. If and when it is finished, it will add several miles of off-road trail.

In addition, most of the required $691,000 cost of a new trail has been raised. The trail will connect the downtown area with the Knopp sub-division on the west near St. Mary's. An underpass under Highway 14 and also under Highway 61 are required to provide a safe bike-hike connection. It is anticipated that work will commence in 1999.

If you want a longer ride, Winona is just a few miles from the Root River Trail (see page 110) and Wisconsin's Great River Trail (see page 212).

This historic area (many buildings on National Register of Historic Places) provides lots of things to do and see while you're in Winona, complete with magnificent views of the river valley.

Bike Shorts

Go with the traffic flow, signal your turns and lane changes and be especially alert for pedestrians or car doors opening when passing a line of parked cars or other roadside obstructions. Stay as close to the right side of the road as possible.

FOR MORE INFORMATION:

Winona CVB
67 Main Street
Winona, MN 55987-0870
507-452-2272
1-800-657-4972
www.visitwinona.com

Winona Park and Recreation
207 Lafayette
P.O. Box 378
Winona, MN 55987

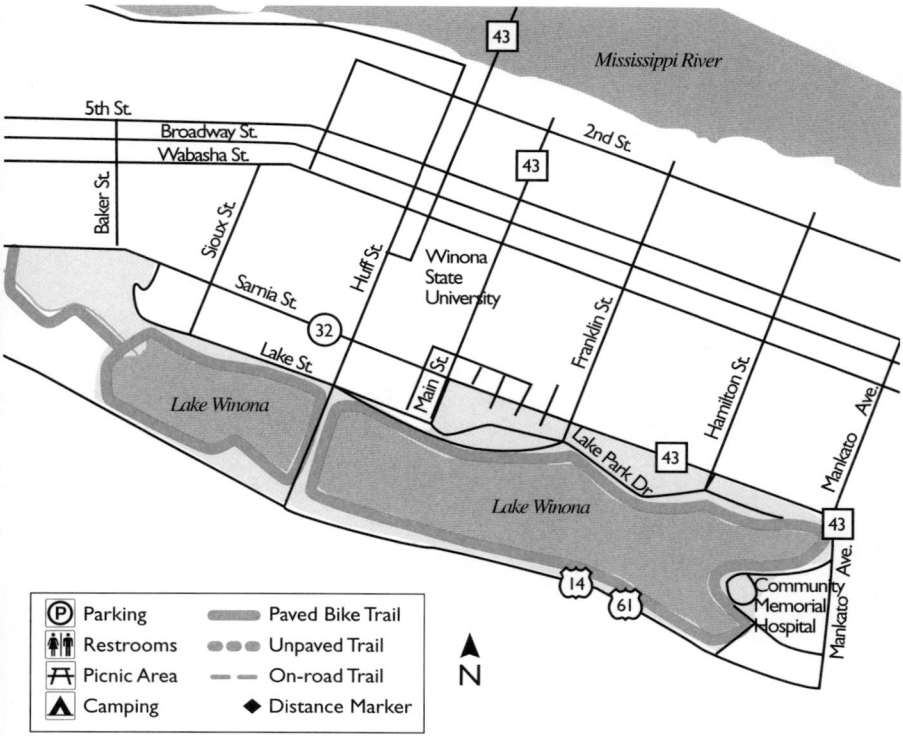
Mississippi River
43
5th St.
Broadway St.
Wabasha St.
2nd St.
43
Baker St.
Sioux St.
Huff St.
Winona State University
Sarnia St.
32
Lake St.
Main St.
Franklin St.
Hamilton St.
Mankato Ave.
Lake Winona
Lake Park Dr.
43
Lake Winona
43
14
61
Community Memorial Hospital
Mankato Ave.
Parking
Restrooms
Picnic Area
Camping
Paved Bike Trail
Unpaved Trail
On-road Trail
Distance Marker
N

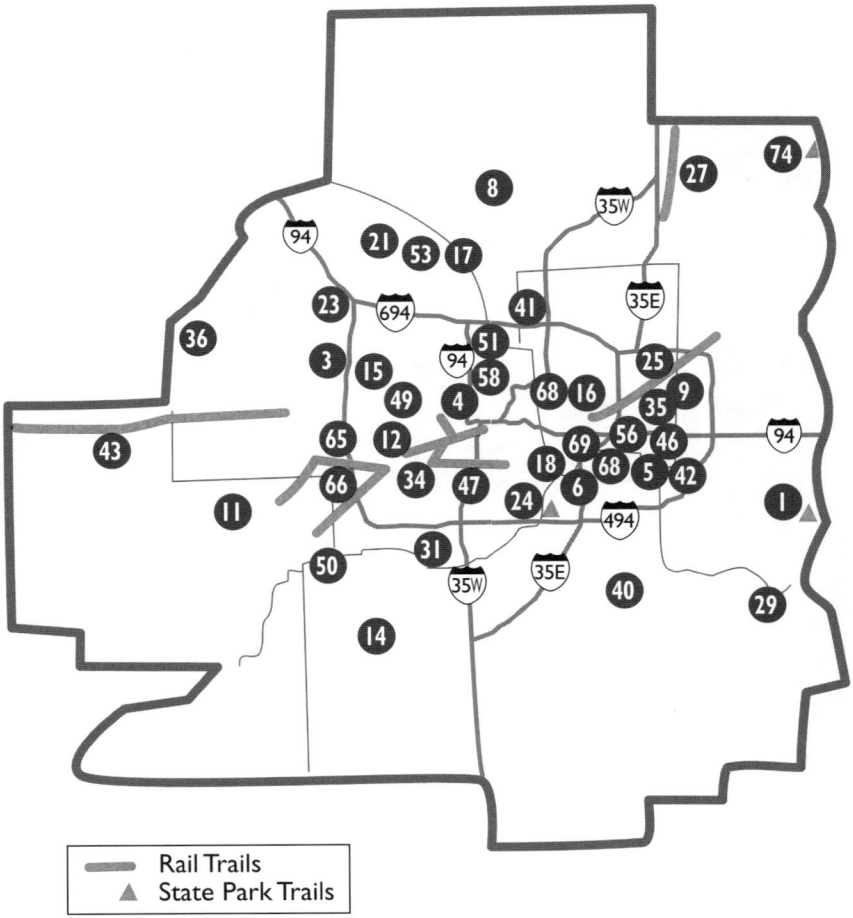
74
27
8
35W
94
21
53
17
23
694
41
35E
36
51
94
25
3
15
58
68
16
9
49
4
35
65
12
69
56
46
94
43
18
68
5
42
66
34
47
6
24
494
1
11
31
50
35W
35E
40
29
14
Rail Trails
State Park Trails

Metro Minnesota

Trail

1. Afton State . . . . . .page 124
3. Baker Park Reserve . . . . . .page 126
4. Bassets Creek . . . . . .page 128
5. Battle Creek Regional . . . . . .page 134
6. Big River Trail . . . . . .page 135
8. Bunker Hills Regional . . . . . .page 136
9. Burlington Northern Regional . . . . . .page 138
11. Carver Park Reserve . . . . . .page 140
12. Cedar Lake Trail . . . . . .page 129
14. Cleary Lake Regional Park . . . . . .page 141
15. Clifton E. French Park Reserve . . . . . .page 142
16. Como Park . . . . . .page 143
17. Coon Rapids Dam Regional Park . . . . . .page 144
18. Crosby Farm/Hidden Falls Regional Park . . . . . .page 145
21. Elm Creek Park Reserve . . . . . .page 146
23. Fish Lake Park Reserve . . . . . .page 147
24. Fort Snelling State Park . . . . . .page 148
25. Gateway Segment-Willard Munger State Trail . . . .page 150
27. Hardwood Creek (see Central section) . . . . . .page 65
29. Hastings . . . . . .page 154
31. Hyland Lake Park Reserve . . . . . .page 155
34. Kenilworth . . . . . .page 138
35. Lake Phalen Regional Park . . . . . .page 156
36. Lake Rebecca Park Reserve . . . . . .page 157
40. Lebanon Hills Regional . . . . . .page 158
41. Long Lake Regional Park-New Brighton . . . . . .page 159
42. Lower Afton Road . . . . . .page 160
43. Luce Line (see Metro section) . . . . . .page 78
46. McKnight Road . . . . . .page 162
47. Midtown Greenway . . . . . .page 131
49. Minneapolis Grand Rounds . . . . . .page 164
50. Minnesota Valley State Park . . . . . .page 170
51. Mississippi Regional Trail Corridor . . . . . .page 172
53. North Hennepin Trail Corridor . . . . . .page 176
56. Phalen Creek Regional . . . . . .page 178
58. Rice Creek West Regional . . . . . .page 179
65. Southwest Region LRT-No. Corridor . . . . . .page 180
66. Southwest Region LRT-So. Corridor . . . . . .page 181
68. St. Paul Grand Rounds . . . . . .page 184
69. Summit Avenue Trail . . . . . .page 188
74. William O'Brien State Park . . . . . .page 190

*** Numbers refer to large map on page 11 and opposite page**

URBAN BIKE TRAILS

Bicycling continues to grow in popularity with most communities recognizing the need to plan for safe bicycle routes. There are miles of urban bicycle paths in Minnesota, with many now under construction or in the planning stages. The emphasis in this book is on trails and paths separate from the auto roads, although many on-street lanes are included.

Consider taking the precaution of registering your bicycle with the State of Minnesota. It costs $10.00 for three years. Stickers can be purchased at some local bike shops, Hennepin County Service Centers or at a bike registration office at the Sears store on Rice Street in St. Paul.

Some metro suburbs may not be included in this section because information was either not provided, or designated bicycle paths are minimal or non-existent.

MINNEAPOLIS AND ST. PAUL METRO TRAILS

Included in this section are several bike trails in a variety of locations across the metro area. In addition to providing trails for recreation, both cities, along with their respective park boards, continue to expand the cities' commuter bike trails and encourage this efficient means of transportation by providing numerous bicycle racks and lockers that accomodate your entire bicycle. While Minneapolis has miles of well-marked, on-street bike lanes, St. Paul has not yet developed comparable commuter bicycle routes.

In Minneapolis, bicycles are now banned from Nicollet Mall weekdays from 6AM to 6PM but the city has added new lanes and striping on alternate downtown routes on both Marquette and 2nd Ave. and has recently added three new commuter trails to its system (some still in process). For information on commuter routes, locker locations, etc. for both Minneapolis and St. Paul, call Metro Commuter Services at 651-602-1602.

Following are some agencies that may be helpful in providing more information on urban trails.

Minneapolis Department of Public Works Transportation Trails
In addition to trails administered by the Parks Department, Minneapolis Public Works initiates and administers several urban trails. Probably the most notable among them to date is the Cedar Lake Trail into downtown Minneapolis (see page 129).

Hennepin County Parks
Several Hennepin County Parks have paved bike trails. These trails are open to the public from 5 AM until sunset. There is also an enforced speed limit of 15 miles per hour. For trail information, contact Hennepin County Parks, 12615 County Road 9, Plymouth, MN 55441-1248, 612-559-9000.

Ramsey County Parks
Ramsey County Parks are open one-half hour before sunrise and close one-half hour after sunset While the county parks generally do not offer paved trails, the regional parks do. For trail information, contact Ramsey County Parks and Recreation, 2015 N. Van Dyke St., Maplewood, MN 55109, 651-745-2500.

CITIES WITH ADDITIONAL BIKING OPPORTUNITIES

The following cities have at least some biking opportunities. For more information about biking opportunities in these communities, be sure to contact their Chamber of Commerces and Tourist offices.

Apple Valley 612-953-2300
You can tour much of Apple Valley on paved off-road trails. This would include the Minnesota Zoo and into Lebanon Hills Regional Park. (see page 158)

Bloomington 612-948-8877
The city of Bloomington provides many miles of off-road paved bicycle paths, especially in the Bush Lake, Hyland Lake and Normandale Lake areas.

Brooklyn Center 612-569-3382
This is the site of several very scenic off-road trails in the Palmer Lake area, paralleling Shingle Creek. Ride all the way from Brooklyn Park city limits to Minneapolis city limits safe from vehicle traffic.

Brooklyn Park 612-493-8350
Brooklyn Park has some excellent asphalt trails, especially in Brookdale, Palmer Lake Park, and along the Edinbrook drainage channel. The city also includes most of the North Hennepin Trail Corridor. (See page 176)

Burnsville 612-895-4504
Limited off-road trails but several miles of marked street shoulder.

Champlin 612-421-2820/8100
The city of Champlin has limited off-road bicycle trails but has plans for expansion.

Chaska 612-448-5633 ext. 105
This city has made major strides in providing both off-road and street-side bicycle paths. It also has access to, or is close to three regional rail-trails, the North and South Corridors of the LRT to Hopkins and back to Victoria and the Minnesota Valley State Trail to Shakopee.

Eagan 651-681-4660
Another community with extensive off-road trails, offering 17.6 miles of 8' paved north-south trails and 15½ miles of east-west trails.

Eden Prairie 612-949-8441
Eden Prairie has one of the most extensive bicycle trail systems in the area.

Fridley 612-572-3570
Fridley combines road shoulder trails with several miles of off-road stretches.

Hastings 651-437-4127
Although Hastings off-road trails are not extensive, you will find some very attractive ones. They are augmented by several miles of marked road shoulder.

Inver Grove Heights 651-450-2587
Excellent off-road trails throughout the urban area.

Lakeville 612-985-4600
The city paved trails are excellent and easy.

Maple Grove 612-494-6500
Maple Grove is continuing to expand its trail system.

Mendota Heights 651-452-1850
The city provides an extensive network of off-road paved trails. It also includes the 4.2 mile Big Rivers Regional Trail in Mendota (see page 135). Via the Mendota Bridge, this will also provide another link with the Minneapolis Trails.

Minnetonka 612-939-8203
Minnetonka is part of the Minnetonka Loop Trail System and connections are available to both the north corridor of the LRT and the Luce Line State Trail, on the north.

Plymouth 612-509-5200
Although a lot of Plymouth's bicycle paths are road shoulder and sidewalk, several miles of off-road are dispersed throughout the area.

Robbinsdale 612-531-1278
To date, Robbinsdale has relatively limited off-road bikeways.

Rosemount 612-888-0957
Rosemount trails are concentrated in the western edge of the city with paved trails being somewhat limited.

Roseville 651-415-2100
Roseville has expanded its off-road trail system. A north-south ride paralleling Lexington Avenue and east-west along County Road C are especially fine urban rides.

Shoreview 651-490-4600
Shoreview has over 15 miles of paved, mostly roadside, but well-marked trails. Snail Lake Park provides some excellent off-road rides.

Woodbury 651-714-3583
Woodbury has done a great job of trail construction within its urban area. You will find their trails paved and well-marked with most parallel, but separate, from roads and streets.

AFTON STATE PARK

WHERE: Hastings
LENGTH: 4 miles
SURFACE: Paved
TRAIL USE:

Access: From St. Paul, go 9 miles east on I-94 then 7 miles south on County Road 15, 3 miles east on County Road 20.

Four miles of paving in a scenic setting along the St. Croix River and near Afton Alps ski area make this park well worth bringing your bicycle. Other park trails are quite rugged, offering a challenging hike or cross-country ski. The park offers hiking, swimming, fishing, boating, volleyball court, horseshoe pit, picnicing, golfing, winter skiing (downhill at nearby Afton Alps) and snowmobiling.

The native prairie is being restored in several areas in the park. A fun hike can start at the Interpretive Center, follow a self-guided interpretive trail, climb the bluff, stop at scenic overlooks eventually circling back to swimming beach and picnic area. The leaves are spectacular in the fall and the river is a great place to watch hawks and eagles.

Bike Shorts

Be alert to changing conditions. Rain will muffle the sound of approaching vehicles and generate slippery conditions, especially after a long period without rain. (Roadway oil and grime can be hazardous until the rain washes them away).

FOR MORE INFORMATION:

Afton State Park
6959 Peller Avenue South
Hastings, MN 55033
651-436-5391

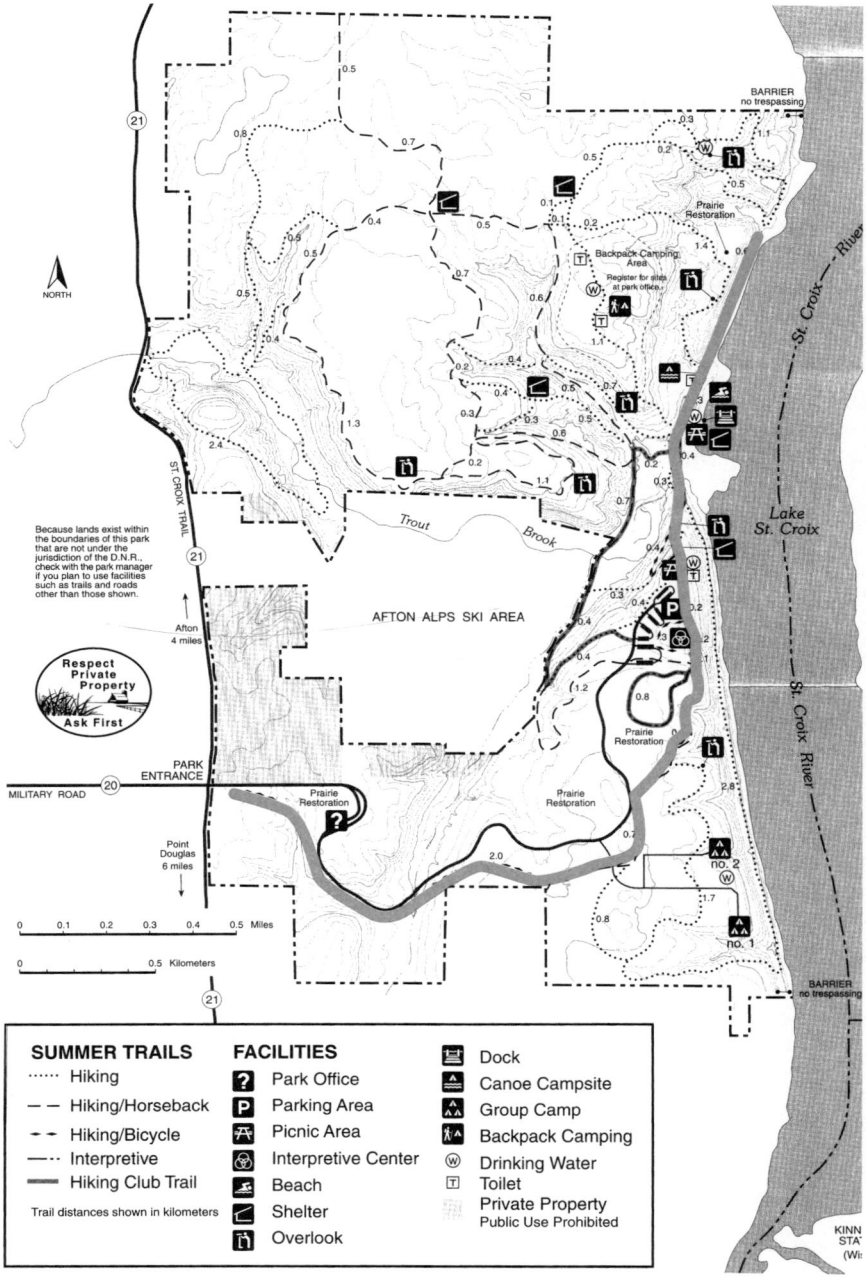
NORTH
BARRIER
no trespassing
Prairie Restoration
Backpack Camping Area
Register for sites at park office.
St. Croix River
Lake St. Croix
Trout Brook
ST. CROIX TRAIL
21
Because lands exist within the boundaries of this park that are not under the jurisdiction of the D.N.R., check with the park manager if you plan to use facilities such as trails and roads other than those shown.
Afton 4 miles
AFTON ALPS SKI AREA
Respect Private Property
Ask First
PARK ENTRANCE
MILITARY ROAD
20
Point Douglas 6 miles
no. 2
no. 1
0 0.1 0.2 0.3 0.4 0.5 Miles
0 0.5 Kilometers
SUMMER TRAILS
Hiking
Hiking/Horseback
Hiking/Bicycle
Interpretive
Hiking Club Trail
Trail distances shown in kilometers
FACILITIES
Park Office
Parking Area
Picnic Area
Interpretive Center
Beach
Shelter
Overlook
Dock
Canoe Campsite
Group Camp
Backpack Camping
Drinking Water
Toilet
Private Property
Public Use Prohibited

BAKER PARK RESERVE

WHERE: Approx. 20 miles west of downtown Minneapolis on County Road 19, between Highway 12 and Highway 55
LENGTH: 6.2 miles
SURFACE: Paved
TRAIL USE:

Access: From Highway 12, take County Road 19 north and follow 19 to the main park entrance. From Highway 55, take County Road 24 west to County Road 19, turn south and follow 19 to the main park entrance, or take Highway 55 to county Road 19, turn south and follow 19 to the main entrance.

Terrain is somewhat rolling and the trail goes through woods as well as meadows. The park includes three lakes offering swimming, boating, fishing and golf in addition to its paved trails.

Bike Shorts

When planning a trip, be aware of your own capabilities as well as the limitations and health of your friends. A ride which tests one's outer limits is best left to those conditioned to do so.

FOR MORE INFORMATION:

Baker Park Reserve
Phone: 479-2258 (Gate)
476-466 (Office)

Hennepin Parks
12615 County Road 9
Plymouth, MN 55441
612-559-9000

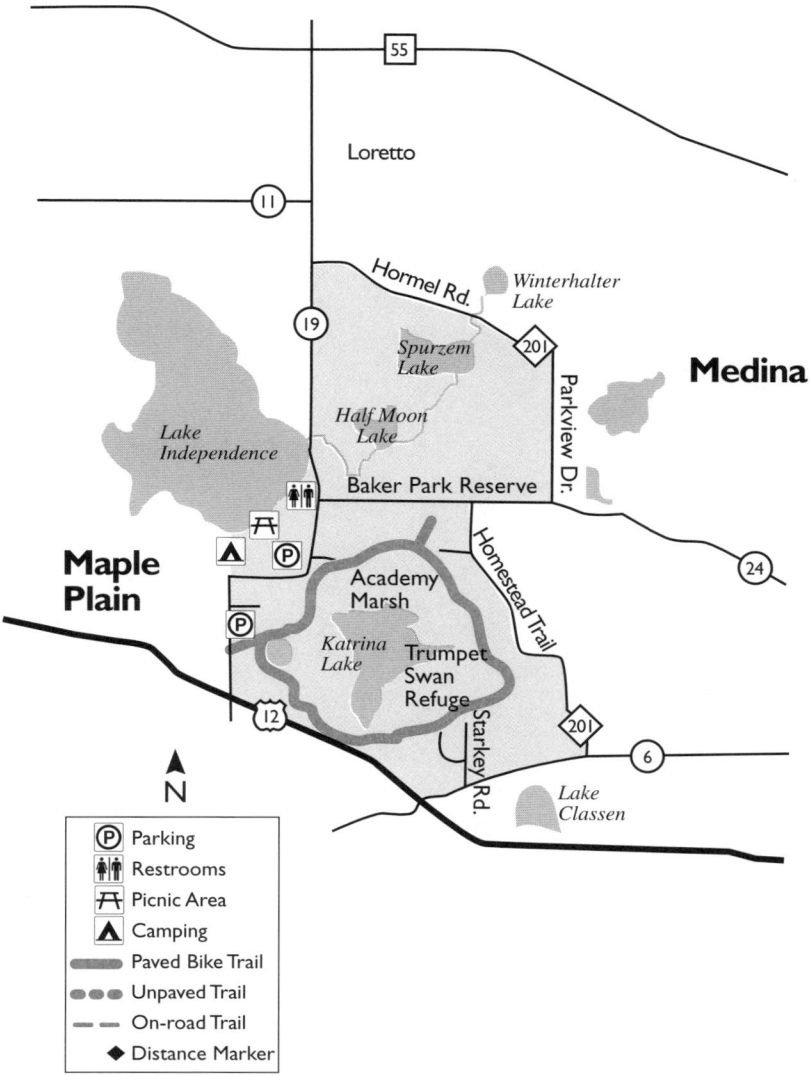
55
Loretto
11
Hormel Rd.
Winterhalter Lake
19
Spurzem Lake
201
Medina
Parkview Dr.
Half Moon Lake
Lake Independence
Baker Park Reserve
Maple Plain
Academy Marsh
Homestead Trail
24
Katrina Lake
Trumpet Swan Refuge
12
201
6
Starkey Rd.
Lake Classen
N
Parking
Restrooms
Picnic Area
Camping
Paved Bike Trail
Unpaved Trail
On-road Trail
Distance Marker

BASSETS CREEK

WHERE: Minneapolis
LENGTH: .3 miles
SURFACE: Paved, bicycle lanes minimum 14 ft. wide with parallel pedestrian lane minimum of 6 ft. wide.
TRAIL USE: 

Trailhead North: Wirth Parkway, north of Highway 55.

Trailhead South: Connects with Cedar Lake Trail just west of the point where Cedar Lake Trail goes under I-394. Best parking is near Target Center, the Ice Arena, or the Sculpture Garden at the Walker Art Center.

Another new commuter trail administered by the Hennepin County Park Board provides a route from the northwest into the loop area. Plans include eventually extending it west to connect with the Luce Line DNR rail-trail. (See page 132.)

Bike Shorts

Good water bottles are inexpensive and readily available. Be sure you carry ample water for your trip and use it often. Dehydration can sap your strength and may even cause more serious problems.

FOR MORE INFORMATION:

Department of Public Works
Minneapolis City Hall, Room 233
Transportation Division
350 S. 5th St.
Minneapolis, MN 55415
612-673-2352

WHERE: Minneapolis
LENGTH: 5 miles
SURFACE: Paved, 10' wide, with separate paved walking trail
TRAIL USE: 

Trailhead West: At Highway 100 and Cedar Lake Road, southbound on Highway 100, take Stephen Drive, exit right, and drive south to Minnetonka Boulevard, then back on frontage road to trail access, where there is minimal parking. If you are headed northbound on Highway 100, take the Cedar Lake Road exit.

Mid Access: At numerous locations, see map.

Trailhead East: In downtown Minneapolis, at 12th and Glenwood, just west of the Target Center. There is parking available at the 7th Street Garage.

This is the first route in the state constructed especially for non-motorized commuting. This trail is administered by the Minneapolis Department of Public Works, Transportation and Special Projects Division.

Utilizing federal transportation funds, this trail has a higher speed limit and includes a separate paved trail for skaters, runners and walkers to facilitate its basic purpose of commuting. It is now the most heavily-used trail in the entire Metro Area.

The separation of bicycles from foot traffic is not unique, but it is the first case where the entire trail is so designed. Efforts toward building dual trails in congested areas is becoming a reality, and would certainly be a safety improvement. (See page 132.)

FOR MORE INFORMATION:

Department of Public Works
Minneapolis City Hall, Room 233
Transportation Division
350 S. 5th St.
Minneapolis, MN 55415
612-673-2352

KENILWORTH

WHERE: Minneapolis
LENGTH: 1.5 miles
SURFACE: Paved, bicycle lanes minimum 14 ft. wide with paralleled pedestrian minimum of 6 ft. wide
TRAIL USE: 

South Trailhead: There is a small parking lot southeast of 28th Street but this trail terminates where it joins the Midtown Greenway Trail. There is no direct access at this point.

North Trailhead: This trail connects the Cedar Lake Trail and the Midtown Greenway Trail with no direct access where it joins the Cedar Lake Trail (see east access for Cedar Lake Trail as closest access point).

Another commuter trail located on a route leased from the Regional Railroad Authority. It provides a direct link between the Cedar Lake commuter trail and Midtown Greenway. (See page 132.)

Bike Shorts

The old Irish prayer "May the wind blow always at your back" is only partially true for bicyclists. Be prepared for the vacuum effect of passing vehicles, sudden gusts or sudden absences when passing roadside buildings, trees or other shelter.

FOR MORE INFORMATION:

Department of Public Works
Minneapolis City Hall, Room 233
Transportation Division
350 S. 5th St.
Minneapolis, MN 55415
612-673-2352

MIDTOWN GREENWAY

WHERE: Minneapolis
LENGTH: 5.6 miles (when completed)
SURFACE: Paved–bicycle lanes minimum 14 ft. wide with parallel pedestrian lane minimum of 6 ft. wide
TRAIL USE:

West Trailhead: Trail joins the Kenilworth Trail near 31st and Chowen Avenue (no designated parking).

Mid Access: Dean Avenue west of Lake of the Isles. Southeast corner of Lake of the Isles where it connects to the Lake trail system. At James, Irving and Humboldt there are grade level entrances but the trail drops below grade for the next several blocks with access only at Bryant Avenue South and Nicollet Avenue Street parking.

East Trailhead: Currently at Nicollet Avenue When Phase II is implemented, additional access will be included. Street parking.

A new multi-use trail paralleling the 29th Street rail corridor in south Minneapolis. As yet, there are limited public facilities and parking except at Lake of the Isles. The right of the way is leased from the Regional Authority and will be administered by the City of Minneapolis. It will provide a non-stop corridor from Chowen Avenue to Nicollet, continuing east to Hiawatha Avenue when Phase II is completed. Phase III, extending all the way to the Mississippi River is planned for the future. (See page 132.)

FOR MORE INFORMATION:

Department of Public Works
Minneapolis City Hall, Room 233
Transportation Division
350 S. 5th St.
Minneapolis, MN 55415
612-673-2352

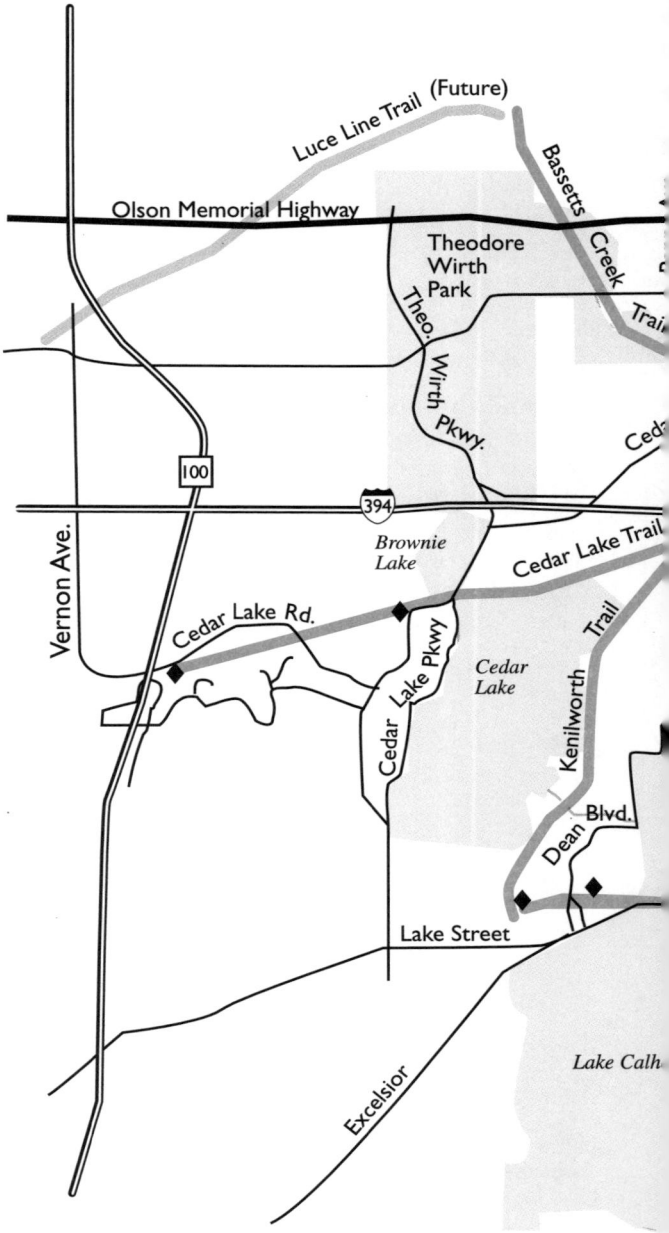
Luce Line Trail (Future)
Olson Memorial Highway
Bassetts Creek
Theodore Wirth Park
Theo. Wirth Pkwy.
100
394
Brownie Lake
Cedar Lake Trail
Vernon Ave.
Cedar Lake Rd.
Cedar Lake Pkwy
Cedar Lake
Kenilworth Trail
Dean Blvd.
Lake Street
Excelsior

Broadway
Washington Ave.
rth
neapolis
55
Target
Center
ood Ave.
Bassetts Creek
Linden Ave.
Hennepin Ave.
Downtown
Minneapolis
Parade
Ice
Garden
Douglas Ave.
94
Hennepin Ave.
Bryant Ave. S.
Nicollet Ave.
35W
5th Ave. S.
Midtown Greenway
(Phase II-to Hiawatha)
Lagoon Ave.
29th St.
Parking
Restrooms
Picnic Area
Camping
Paved Bike Trail
Unpaved Trail
On-road Trail
Trail Access
N

BATTLE CREEK REGIONAL PARK

WHERE: Maplewood
LENGTH: 1.75 miles
SURFACE: Paved, 12' wide
TRAIL USE:

Trailhead West: At the Point Douglas Road Bikeway/Battle Creek Park Entrance Road. You will find a large parking lot here.

Trailhead East: At Battle Creek Park, east of the McKnight Road Bike Path. There is a parking lot here.

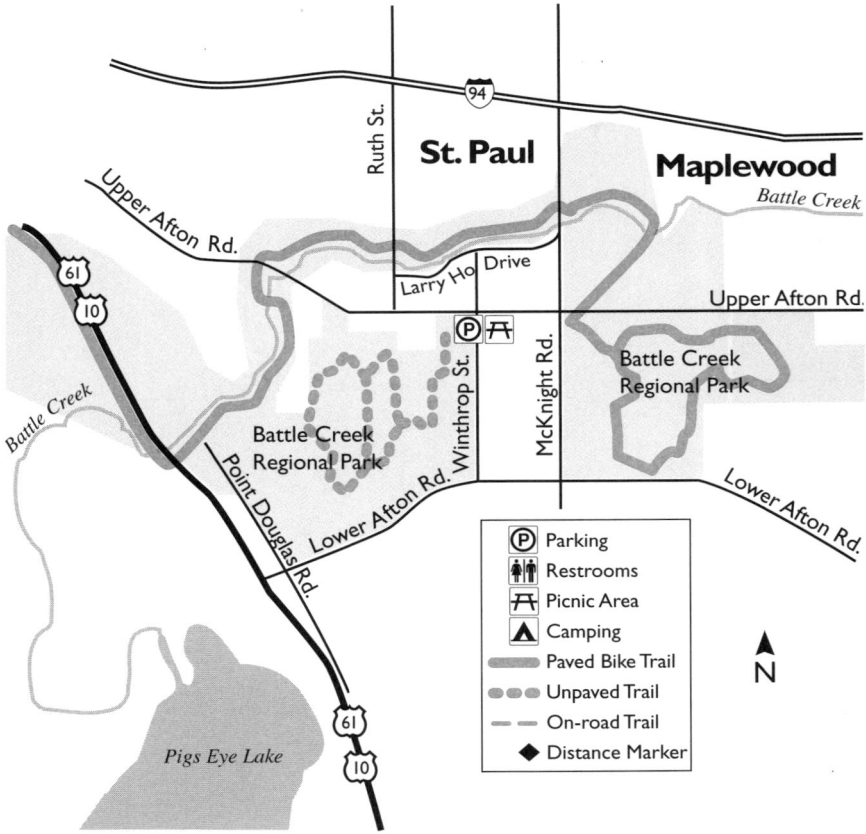

FOR MORE INFORMATION:

Ramsey County Parks & Recreation
2015 Van Dyke St.
Maplewood, Minnesota 55109
651-748-2500

WHERE: Lilydale, Mendota and Mendota Heights
LENGTH: 4.2 miles
SURFACE: Asphalt, 10' wide
TRAIL USE:

Trailhead North: The trail begins at Lilydale Park, just where it crosses under I-35E. Parking and facilities are available here.

Trailhead South: At Pilot Knob Road and Trunk Highway 13 in Mendota Heights. Limited parking here.

The Big River Trail was constructed by Dakota County and opened in the late fall of 1995. It is also administered by Dakota County and has rapidly become a very popular addition to the urban trail system. It follows the old Soo line rail bed and is surprisingly scenic.

Of special interest is an overlook just off Old Trunk Highway 13 which is difficult to get to except by this trail. Parking is available where Mendota Heights Road ends on the Sibley Memorial Highway. There is a paved connection from this lot to the main trail. Parking is also provided in Mendota near the historical marker just below St. Peter Church.

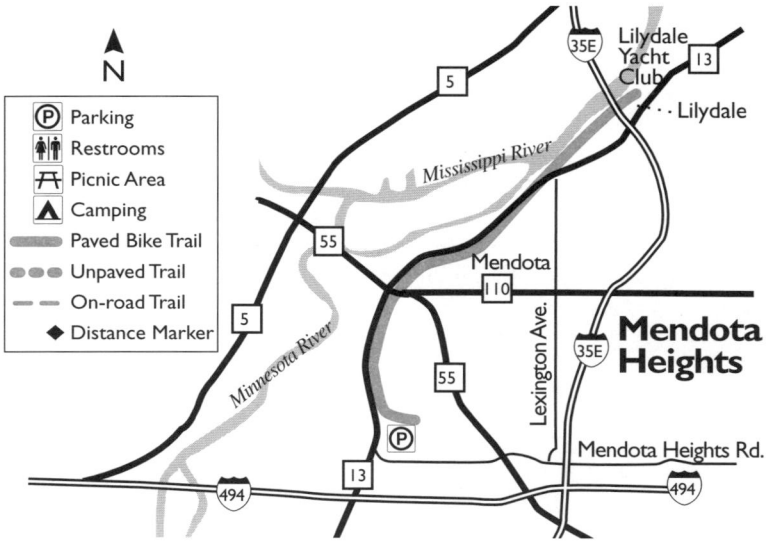

FOR MORE INFORMATION:

Mendota Heights City Hall
1101 Victoria Curve
Mendota Heights, MN 55118
651-452-1850

BUNKER HILL REGIONAL PARK

WHERE: Anoka County-Coon Rapids
LENGTH: 5.5 miles
SURFACE: Paved
TRAIL USE:

Access: Park entrance off County Roads A, B and D.

The park includes a variety of activities including archery and the Bunker Hills Stables complete with guided horse trail riding and hay and sleigh rides. The Bunker Hills Golf Course is here as well as picnic pavilions and sites for camping. A very popular summer feature is the Wave Pool with its air-generated waves, the first of its kind in the state. Bunker Hills was one of the first parks in the regional system.

Bike Shorts

Obey traffic laws and obey traffic signs. Most serious accidents involve motor vehicles. Drivers are conditioned to expect you to do as another motor vehicle would.

FOR MORE INFORMATION:

Anoka County Parks
550 N.W. Bunker Lake Blvd.
Anoka, MN 55304
612-757-3920

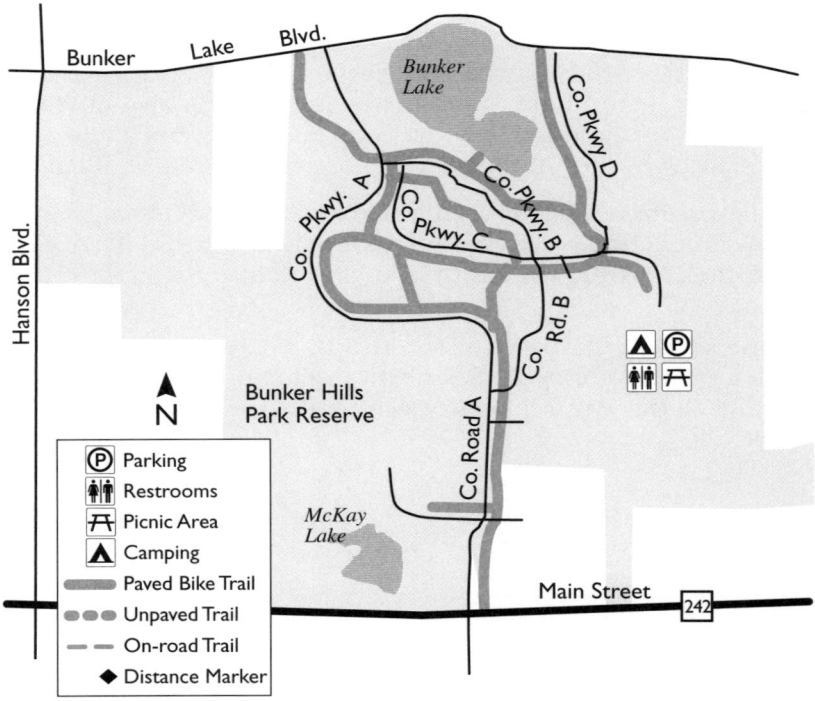
Bunker Lake Blvd.
Bunker Lake
Co. Pkwy D
Co. Pkwy. A
Co. Pkwy. C
Co. Pkwy. B
Hanson Blvd.
Co. Rd. B
N
Bunker Hills Park Reserve
Co. Road A
McKay Lake
Main Street
242
Parking
Restrooms
Picnic Area
Camping
Paved Bike Trail
Unpaved Trail
On-road Trail
Distance Marker

BURLINGTON NORTHERN REGIONAL

WHERE: St. Paul
LENGTH: 6 miles
SURFACE: 12 feet paved
TRAIL USE:

This is a new trail with the southern 6 miles at or near completion. The northern section (to downtown White Bear Lake) is funded and right-of-way negotiations are in progress.

The Burlington Northern Trail connects to the Phalen Creek Trail just south of Lake Phalen at the intersection of Wheelock Parkway, Johnson Parkway and East Shore Drive. The latter is also built on the Burlington Northern rail bed and combining both trails into one ride permits a 10½ mile off-road ride through residential St. Paul.

There are plans to surface the 1½ miles from Johnson Parkway north to Frost Avenue. The 2½ miles from Frost Avenue to Beam Avenue is already complete, with the north end presently terminating near Maplewood Mall.

This is an excellent off-road trail in an urban setting. It provides a connection to the Gateway DNR Trail and will eventually become an off-road trail all the way from downtown St. Paul to downtown White Bear Lake.

FOR MORE INFORMATION:

Ramsey County Parks and Recreation Department
2015 North VanDyke Street
Maplewood, MN 55109
651-748-2500

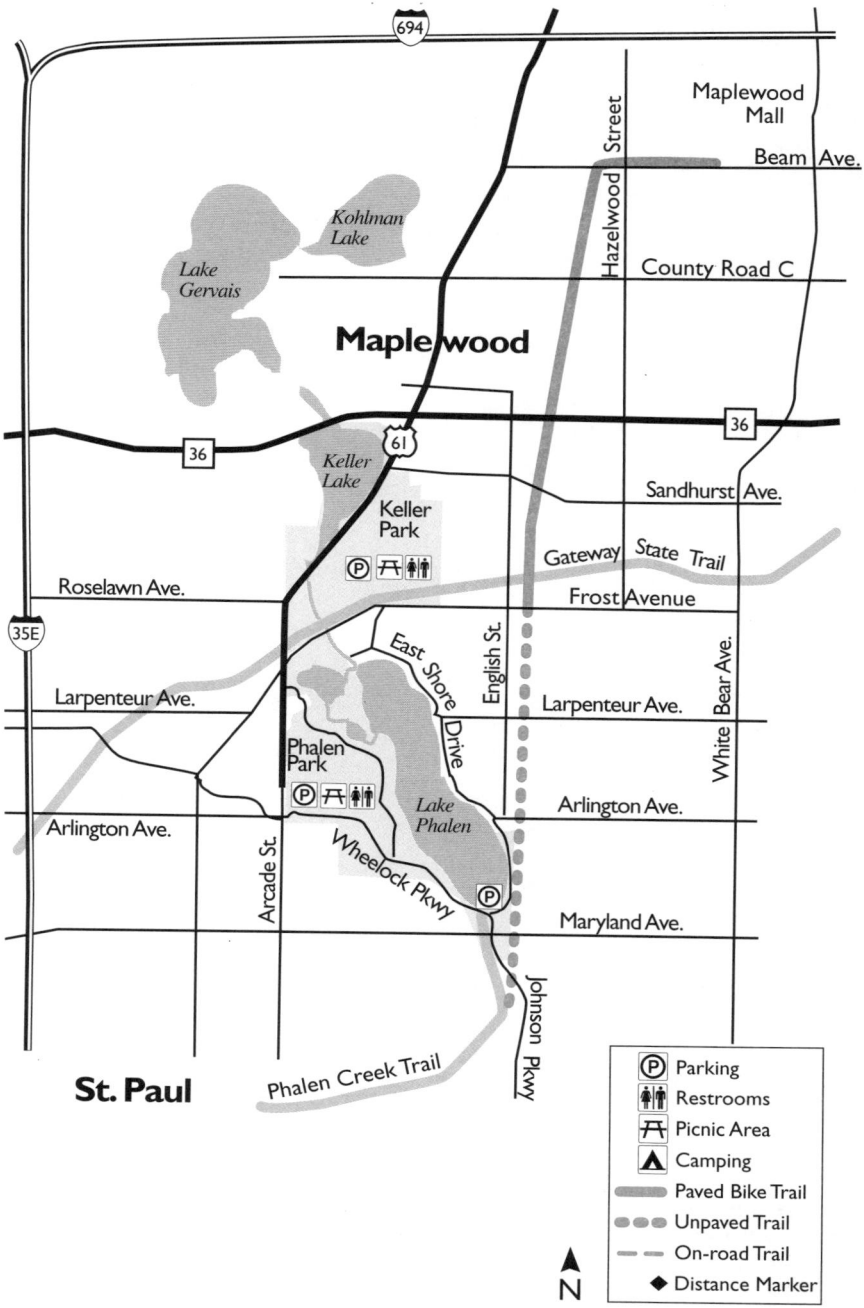
694
Maplewood Mall
Beam Ave.
Hazelwood Street
Kohlman Lake
Lake Gervais
County Road C
Maplewood
36
61
Keller Lake
Keller Park
Sandhurst Ave.
Gateway State Trail
Roselawn Ave.
Frost Avenue
35E
East Shore Drive
English St.
Bear Ave.
White
Larpenteur Ave.
Phalen Park
Lake Phalen
Arlington Ave.
Arcade St.
Wheelock Pkwy
Maryland Ave.
Johnson Pkwy
St. Paul
Phalen Creek Trail
Parking
Restrooms
Picnic Area
Camping
Paved Bike Trail
Unpaved Trail
On-road Trail
Distance Marker
N

CARVER PARK RESERVE

WHERE: Victoria
LENGTH: 7.65 miles
SURFACE: Paved
TRAIL USE:

Access: Located in Victoria, on Carver County Road 11. Take Highway 7 west from Minneapolis and turn left on County Road 11. Or take Highway 5 west from Minneapolis and turn right on County Road 11.

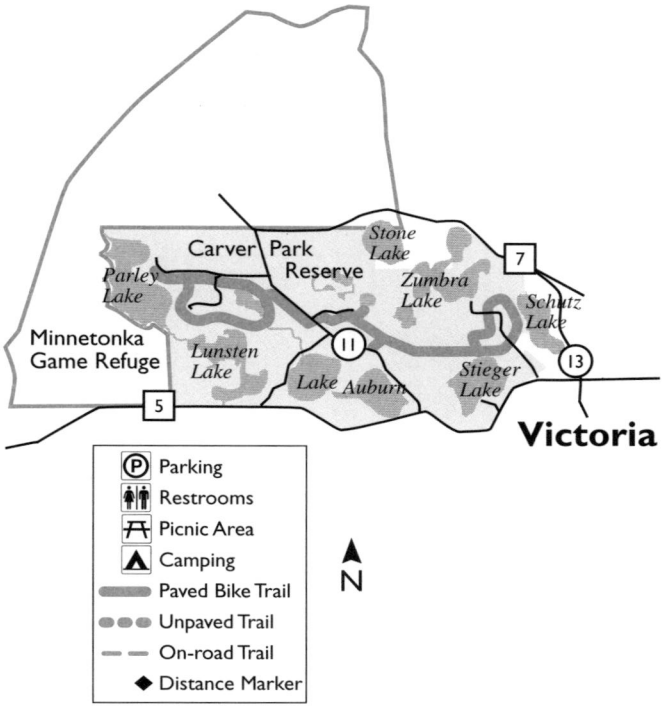

FOR MORE INFORMATION:

Hennepin Parks
12615 County Road 9
Plymouth, MN 55441
612-559-9000

Nature Center
612-472-4911
Gate
612-446-9474

WHERE: Prior Lake
LENGTH: 3.5 miles
SURFACE: Paved
TRAIL USE:

Access: Located near Prior Lake on Scott County Road 27. From I-35W, go west on County Road 42, then south on County Road 27. Or take I-494 to County Road 18, go south on 18 to Highway. 101, then east to Highway 13, south on 13 to County Road 42, east on 42 to County Road 27, and south on 27 to the park entrance.

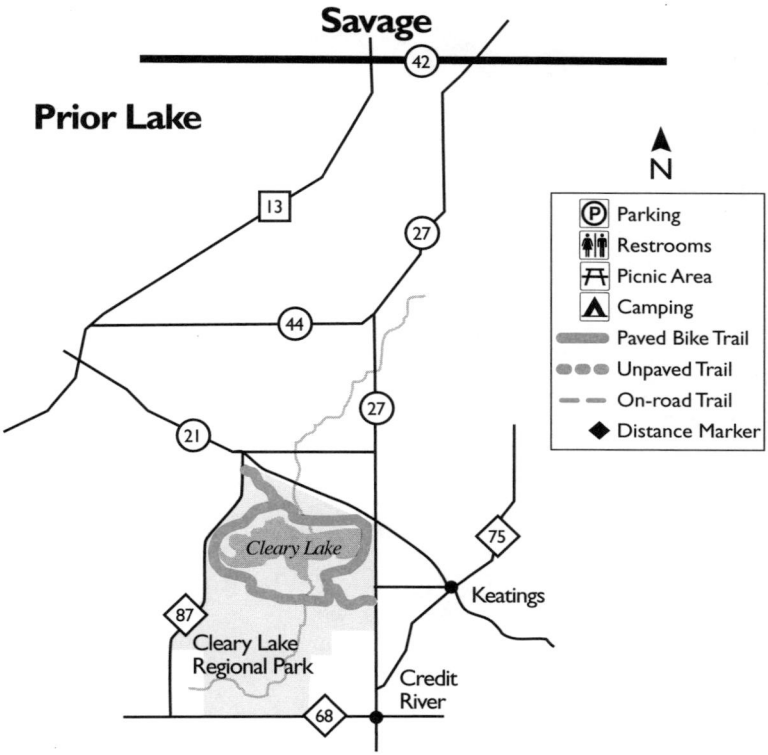

FOR MORE INFORMATION:

Hennepin Parks
12615 County Road 9
Plymouth, MN 55441
612-559-9000

Visitor Center
612-447-2171

CLIFTON E. FRENCH PARK RESERVE

WHERE: Medicine Lake
LENGTH: 2 miles
SURFACE: Paved
TRAIL USE:

Access: Take exit 22 east off I-494 (at County Road 9) in Plymouth to park entrance.

Although limited trail distance now, plans include expanding a connection east to Theodore Wirth Park where links will eventually connect to the several metro area trails.

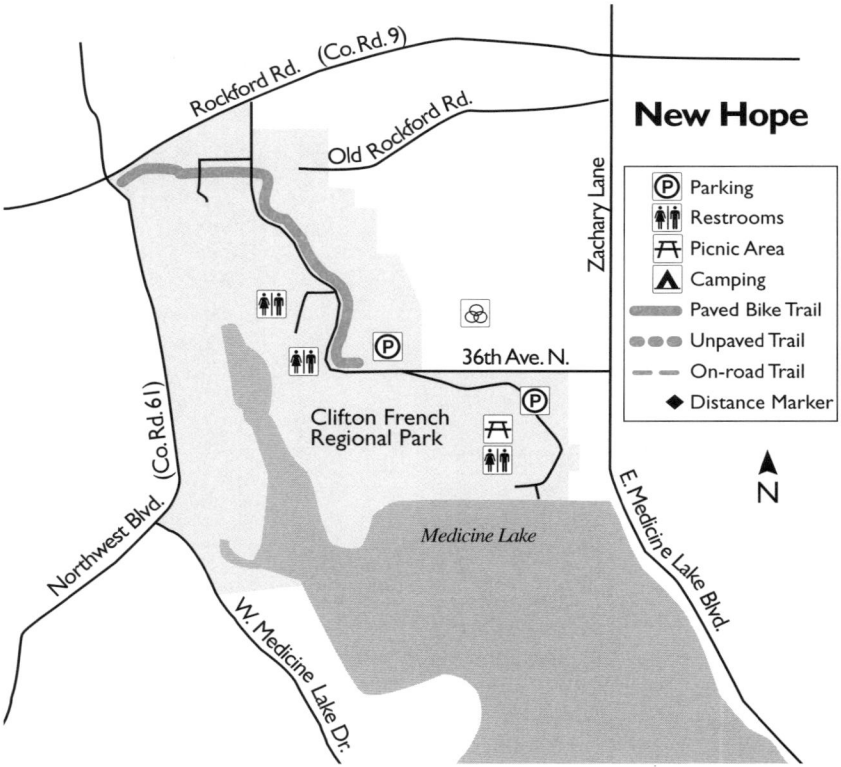

FOR MORE INFORMATION:

Hennepin Parks
12615 County Road 9
Plymouth, MN 55441
612-559-9000

Clifton E. French Park
612-559-9000

WHERE: St. Paul
LENGTH: 1.8 miles
SURFACE: Paved
TRAIL USE:

Access: Off Como Avenue or Lexington Parkway.

FOR MORE INFORMATION:

St. Paul Parks & Recreation
300 City Hall Annex
St. Paul, MN 55102
651-266-6400

COON RAPIDS DAM REGIONAL PARK

WHERE: Coon Rapids
LENGTH: 3 miles
SURFACE: Asphalt, 8' wide
TRAIL USE:

Access: Use the main entrance off Egret Boulevard.

Ample parking and facilities are available in this Anoka County Park.

This is a multi-use park, with one of its main features being the Coon Rapids Dam which terminates near the Visitor Center. A biking/walking path across the bridge will connect with the North Hennepin Regional Trail in Brooklyn Park. At the southern end of the trail, you will connect directly to the 8 miles of the Mississippi Regional Trail Corridor traversing Fridley and Columbia Heights.

FOR MORE INFORMATION:

Anoka County Parks
550 N.W. Bunker Lake Blvd.
Anoka, MN 55304
612-757-3920

CROSBY FARM / HIDDEN FALLS REGIONAL PARK

WHERE: St. Paul
LENGTH: 6.7 miles
SURFACE: Paved, 10' wide
TRAIL USE:

Trailhead North: At Mississippi River Boulevard and Hidden Falls Drive. There are large parking lots along Hidden Falls Drive and along Crosby Farm Road.

Trailhead East: At Shepherd Road and Crosby Lake Road. There is a small parking lot here.

St. Paul
Hidden Falls Park
Crosby Lake Rd.
Crosby Lake
Crosby Park
Shepard Rd.
Mississippi River
Mississippi River Blvd.
Mendota
Pike Island
5
35
13
56
110
N
Parking
Restrooms
Picnic Area
Camping
Paved Bike Trail
Unpaved Trail
On-road Trail
Distance Marker

FOR MORE INFORMATION:

St. Paul Parks & Recreation
300 City Hall Annex
St. Paul, MN 55102
651-266-6400

ELM CREEK PARK RESERVE

WHERE: Osseo
LENGTH: 9.3 miles, paved (Also a 6.5 mile paved North Hennepin Trail corridor connects the Elm Creek trails with the Coon Rapids Dam.)
SURFACE: Paved
TRAIL USE:

Access: Located northwest of Osseo, between the communities of Champlin, Dayton and Maple Grove. For the recreation area, take County Road 81 to Territorial Road. Turn right and follow to the park entrance.

A 5-mile turf trail is open for mountain biking; the designated mountain bike trail is the only turf trail in the reserve where bikes are permitted.

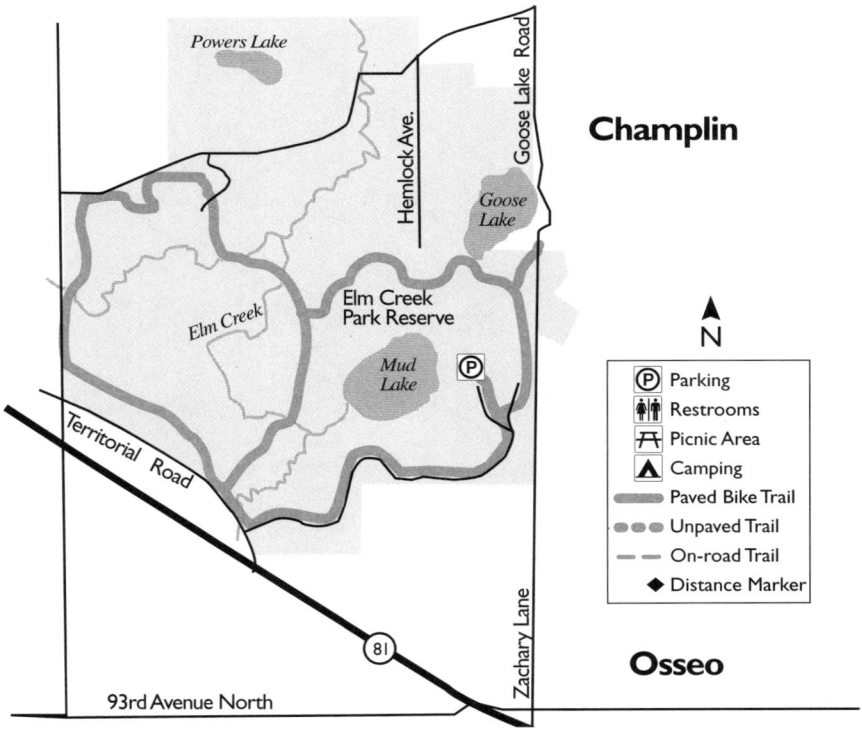

FOR MORE INFORMATION:

Hennepin Parks
12615 County Road 9
Plymouth, MN 55441
612-559-9000

Visitor Center
612-424-5511

FISH LAKE REGIONAL PARK

WHERE: Maple Grove
LENGTH: 1.9 mile
SURFACE: Paved
TRAIL USE:

Access: Exit Highway I-494 west at Bass Lake Road in Maple Grove.

Weaver Lake Rd.
94
Maple Grove
Fish Lake
694
494
Fish Lake Regional Park
Bass Lake Rd.
N
Parking
Restrooms
Picnic Area
Camping
Paved Bike Trail
Unpaved Trail
On-road Trail
Distance Marker

FOR MORE INFORMATION:

Hennepin Parks
12615 County Road 9
Plymouth, MN 55441
612-559-9000

Visitor Center
612-420-3423

FORT SNELLING STATE PARK

WHERE: Highway 5 and Post Road near Minneapolis/ St.Paul Airport
LENGTH: 5 miles
SURFACE: Paved
TRAIL USE:

Trailhead North: Connects to the Minneapolis trail system via the Minnehaha trail access from the parking lot at the Bishop Whipple Building on the north side of Highway 55 across from Fort Snelling itself. Facilities during open hours.

Trailhead South: At the Park entrance. Take the Post Road exit east off Highway 5. A State Park is fee required to park. You will find full park facilities here.

A short but scenic ride which can be combined with the Minnehaha Trail for a longer river valley ride. Eventually, the Minnesota Valley State Park Trail is planned to connect with this one.

Bike Shorts

Watch for road debris or loose rocks or gravel. Slow down if there is excessive debris or broken road surface. Learn to guide your bike very straight and vertical through loose sand or rocks. If you find a short stretch of loose sand it would even pay to practice riding through it a few times to give you needed confidence when it surprises you along the way.

FOR MORE INFORMATION:

Fort Snelling State Park
Highway 5 and Post Road
St. Paul, MN 55111
651-725-2390

St. Paul
Minneapolis
Mendota
55
62
5
13
110
494
Shepard Road
Hidden Falls/ Crosby Park Trail
Mississippi River
Pike Island
Bloomington Road
International Airport
Snelling Lake
Minnesota River
Post Road
Fort Snelling National Cemetary
Park Entrance
Gun Club Lake
Fort Snelling State Park
N
Parking
Restrooms
Picnic Area
Camping
Paved Bike Trail
Unpaved Trail
On-road Trail
Distance Marker

GATEWAY SEGMENT-WILLARD MUNGER STATE TRAIL

WHERE: St. Paul to Pine Point Park
LENGTH: 18 miles
SURFACE: Paved
TRAIL USE:

Trailhead West: Take the Maryland exit off I-35E just north of downtown St. Paul. Go east one block to Westminster Avenue, turn north to Arlington Avenue. It is about one-half block west on Arlington to a paved parking lot on the south side of the street. Vandalism has not permitted portable toilets.

Note: The trail actually dead ends 1.1 mile west on Cayuga Avenue after crossing over I-35E, but with street parking only in residential area.

Mid Access: The trail is accessible from a number of streets and city parks. Phalen-Keller Regional Park has parking available and you can add 2.9 miles of paved trail. See map, page 178. In Maplewood, Flicek Park on Frost Avenue has parking available. Near the junction of Highway 36 and I-694 in Oakdale, there is a paved parking lot and portable restrooms. From Highway 36 go south one-quarter block on Hadley Avenue to 55th Street North. Go east on 55th Street one-half mile to parking area on right. In Pine Springs, from Highway 36 go north on Hilton Avenue, and take first right onto High Trail Avenue North. Parking is available in the cul-de-sac. There is a parking lot on the south side of Highway 96 just west of the intersection of Highway 96 and Kimbro Avenue North.

Trailhead East: Although the trail continues a short distance east (not paved), the best access and parking is at Pine Point Park. Approximately five miles north of Stillwater on Highway 55 (Norell Avenue North) on the west side of the road. Washington County charges a fee for parking. There are portable restrooms here.

The Gateway Trail's wide surface, easy access and excellent parking facilities provide a first-class trail with more side trip options than most. The metropolitan location, especially the west 8.3 miles, make it one of the more popular multi-use trails. Expect more than the usual amount of foot, skater and wheelchair traffic on the western half. With the cooperation of MN DOT, an overpass over I-35E was recently completed especially for this trail. This made possible a 1.1 mile extension and opens the way to link with the St. Paul Grand Rounds Trail and Capitol Complex.

You will find this to be a ride of contrasts. The west half winds through concentrated residential sections, along or through city parks and golf courses and crosses some busy streets. The eastern half passes through more open country, light traffic roads and lighter trail use. You may encounter horseback riders as the DNR has included a riding path paralleling the bike trail on the section north of I-694.

At just under 17 miles, this is a good trail for a ride both ways in one day. There are many opportunities for side trips to lengthen your ride. Phalen-Keller Regional Park has 2.9 miles of paved trail. You can ride either west to Mahtomedi or east to Stillwater on the paved Washington County trail that intersects with the Gateway at Washington County #12. When you reach Pine Point Park you will see a Washington County paved trail along #55 (Norell Avenue) both north and south for several miles.

Excellent bridges with no more than a 5% grade take you up and over two of the busiest streets (McKnight and White Bear). Expect to cross numerous city streets and a few county roads. Also, note a darker than usual surface on sections of this trail. The DNR is experimenting with a surface of shredded junk tires and pulverized shingles as aggregate mix rather than gravel in the bituminous. Both the DOT and the DNR are still evaluating its possibilities.

FOR MORE INFORMATION:

DNR Trail Office
1200 Warner Road
St. Paul, MN 55106
651-772-7935

St. Paul Chamber of Commerce
332 Minnesota St.
#N-205
St. Paul, MN 55101
651-223-5000

White Bear Lake
White Bear Lake
Birchwood Village
12
Willer
35E
61
694
10
Pin
Spr
694
35E
10
Little Canada
Maplewood
3.7 miles
36
N. Saint Paul
Keller Lake
4.6 miles
Phalen-Keller Regional Park
Lake Phalen
West minster Ave
Arlington Ave.
White Bear Ave.
McKnight Road

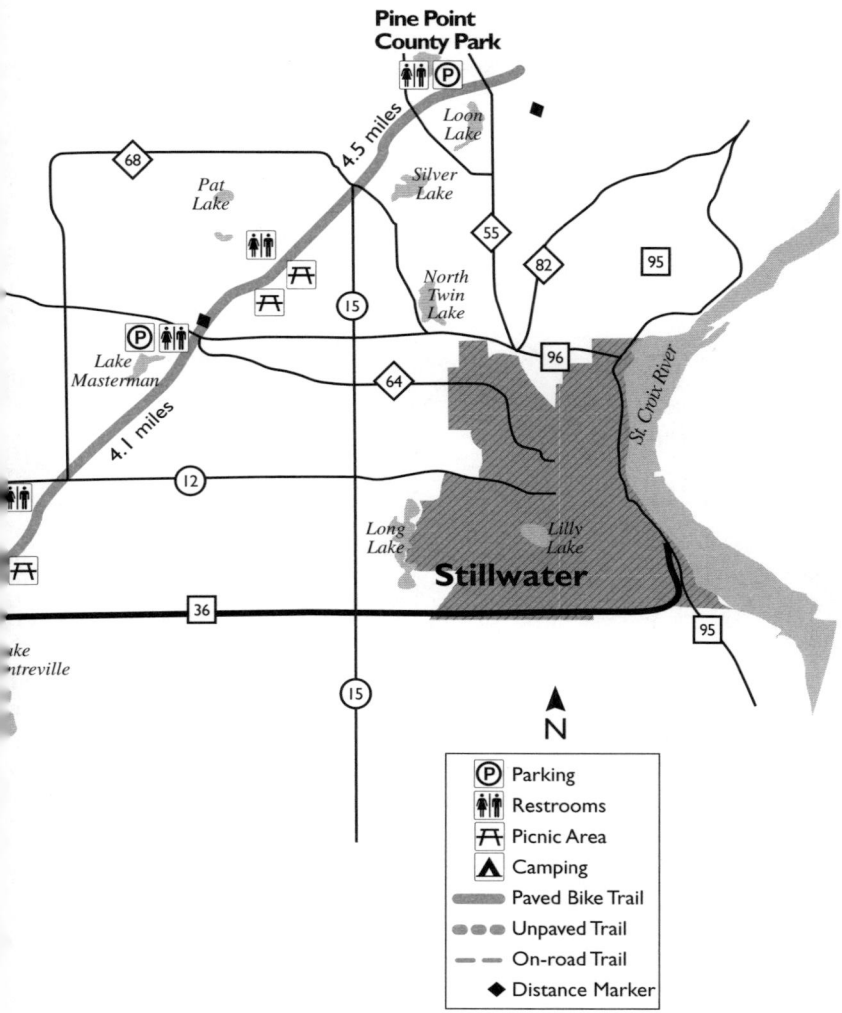

Administered by Minnesota Department of Natural Resources

HASTINGS (CITY)

WHERE: City of Hastings
LENGTH: 3 miles
SURFACE: Paved
TRAIL USE:

Access: Various city streets (see map below).

Although Hasting's off-road trails are not extensive, you will find some very attractive ones. They are augmented by several miles of marked road shoulder.

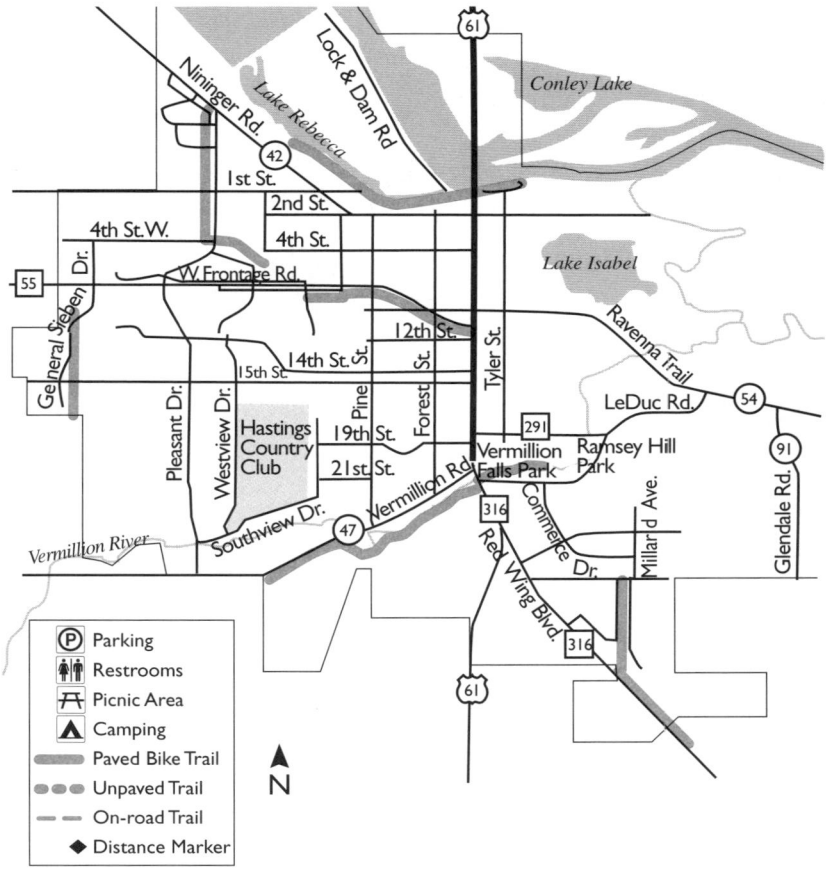

FOR MORE INFORMATION:

Hastings Chamber of Commerce
651-437-6775

Hastings City Hall
651-437-4127

HYLAND LAKE PARK RESERVE

WHERE: Bloomington
LENGTH: 5.5 miles
SURFACE: Paved
TRAIL USE:

Access: Located on East Bush Lake Road in Bloomington. From I-494, go south on Normandale Boulevard (Highway 100) to 84th Street. Turn right and follow 84th Street to East Bush Lake Road. Go south on East Bush Lake Road and follow the signs to Richardson Nature Center and Hyland Visitor Center.

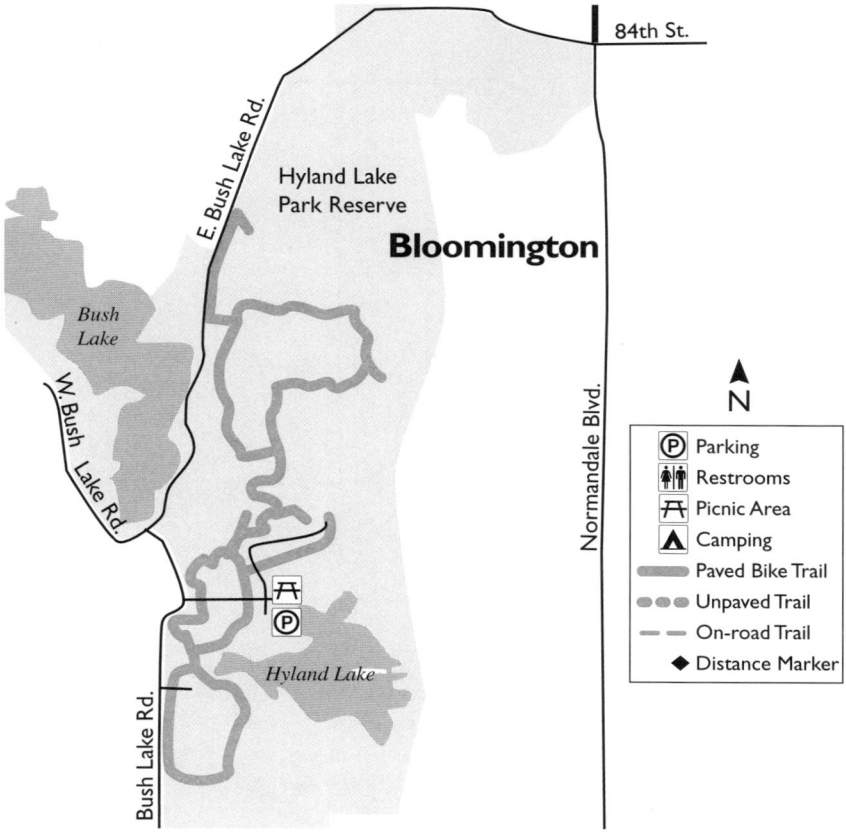

FOR MORE INFORMATION:

Hyland Park Office
612-941-4362

Hennepin Parks
12615 County Rd. 9
Plymouth, MN 55441
612-559-9000

LAKE PHALEN REGIONAL PARK

WHERE: St. Paul
LENGTH: 3 miles
SURFACE: Paved, 8' wide
TRAIL USE:

Trailhead North: At Keller Park there are parking lots on both sides of Highway 61, just north of the Munger Gateway State Trail.

Trailhead South: At the intersection of Wheelock Parkway, Johnson Parkway, and East Shore Drive, at the south end of Lake Phalen, where there is a small parking lot. There are also four large parking lots along Phalen Drive, north of Wheelock Parkway, in Phalen Park.

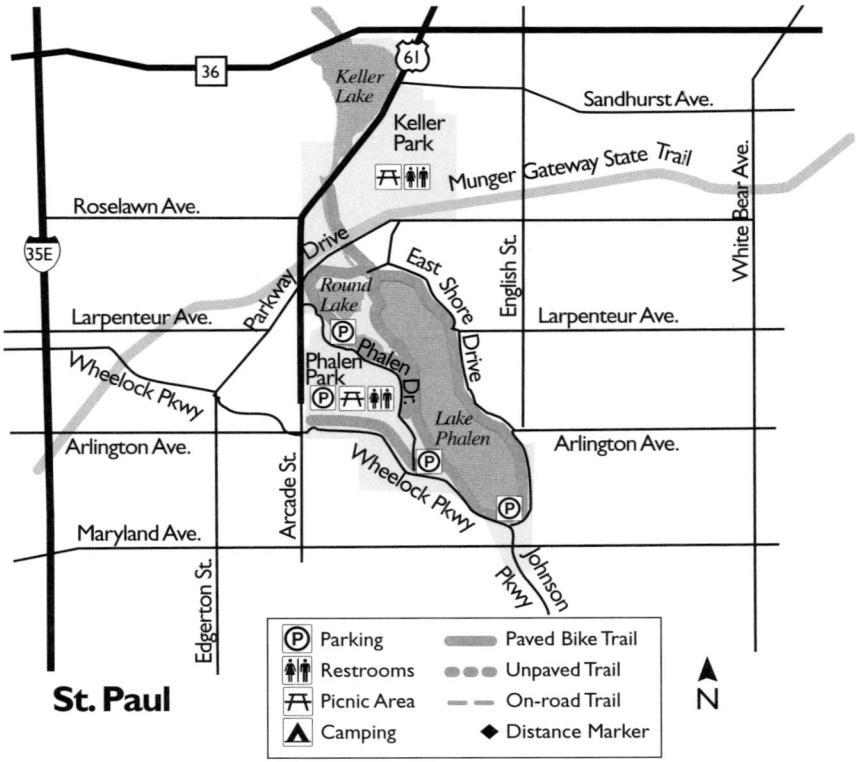

FOR MORE INFORMATION:

Phalen Center
1000 E. Wheelock Parkway
St. Paul, MN 55106
651-298-5721

St. Paul Parks & Recreation
300 City Hall Annex
St. Paul, MN 55102
651-266-6400

LAKE REBECCA PARK RESERVE

WHERE: West Minneapolis
LENGTH: 6.5 miles
SURFACE: Paved
TRAIL USE:

Access: Located approximately 30 miles west of Minneapolis on County Road 50. Take Highway 55 west to County Road 50, turn left and follow to the park entrance.

Rockford
50
55
Lake Rebecca
E. Lake Rebecca Rd.
Lake Sarah
Lake Sarah Dr.
Lake Sarah Regional Park
Dogwood St.
Lake Rebecca Park Reserve
11
92
Lake Sarah Rd.
Delano
Houghey Lake
Robina Lake
Fogelman Rd.
12
Parking
Restrooms
Picnic Area
Camping
Paved Bike Trail
Unpaved Trail
On-road Trail
Distance Marker
N

FOR MORE INFORMATION:

612-475-4666

Hennepin Parks
12615 County Rd. 9
Plymouth, MN 55441
612-559-9000

LEBANON HILLS REGIONAL PARK

WHERE: Eagan, west section; Apple Valley, east section
LENGTH: 4.2 miles in west section, 6.5 miles in east section
SURFACE: Paved
TRAIL USE:

Access: Parking and facilities are available off Johnny Cake Ridge Road, Pilot Knob Road and Cliff Road.

The two sections of this park are popular for hiking, horseback riding and camping, so expect some traffic on the trails. The west section of the park is adjacent to the Minnesota Zoo.

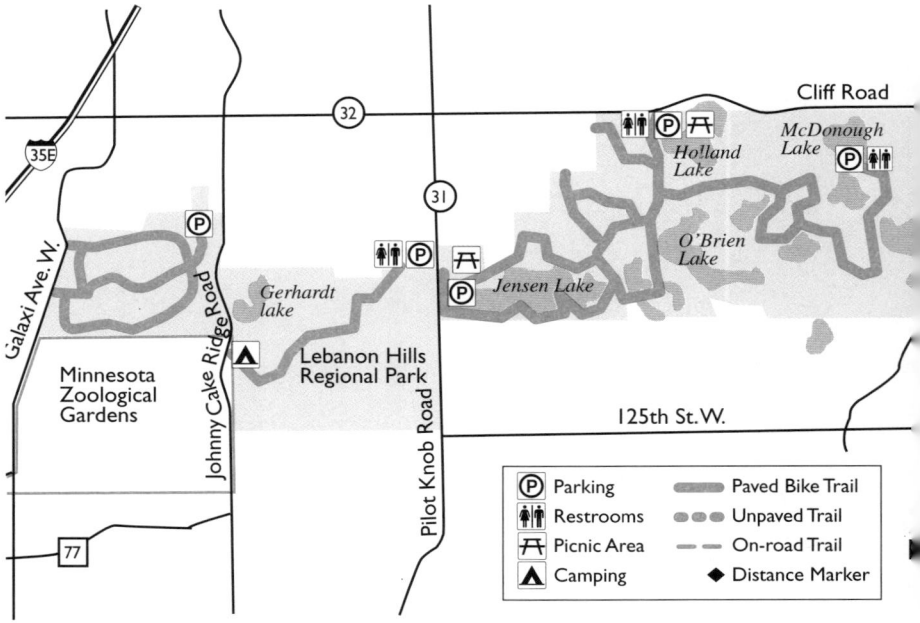

FOR MORE INFORMATION:

Lebanon Hills
12100 Johnny Cake Ridge Road
Apple Valley, MN 55124
612-454-9211

LONG LAKE REGIONAL PARK

WHERE: New Brighton
LENGTH: Approximately 3 miles
SURFACE: Paved 8' wide
TRAIL USE:

Trailhead West: At the park entrance off Long Lake Road. Take the Long Lake Road exit off I-694. You will find parking and facilities here.

Trailhead East: At Highway 96 and old Highway 8. There is limited parking here, in addition to an interesting off-road trail which can be extended northwest to Long Lake Road.

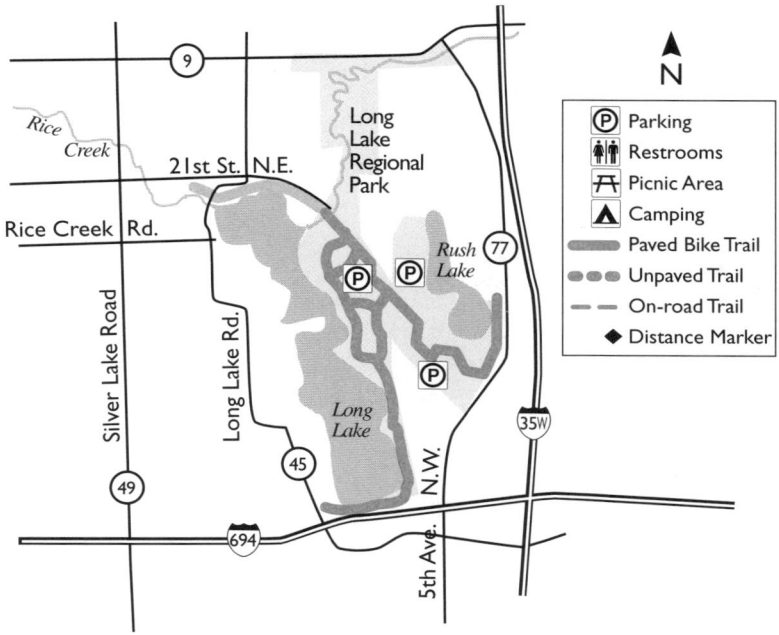

FOR MORE INFORMATION:

New Brighton Parks
400-10th Street N.W.
New Brighton, MN 55112
651-638-2120

LOWER AFTON ROAD

WHERE: St. Paul-Maplewood
LENGTH: 5 miles
SURFACE: On-street bike lanes from the Point Douglas Road Bikeway (near Highway 61) on the west to I-494 and from I-494 to Tower Road in Woodbury.
TRAIL USE:

Trailhead West: At Lower Afton and the Point Douglas Road Bikeway section of the Mississippi River Trail. There is a parking lot at the north end of Point Douglas Road at Battle Creek.

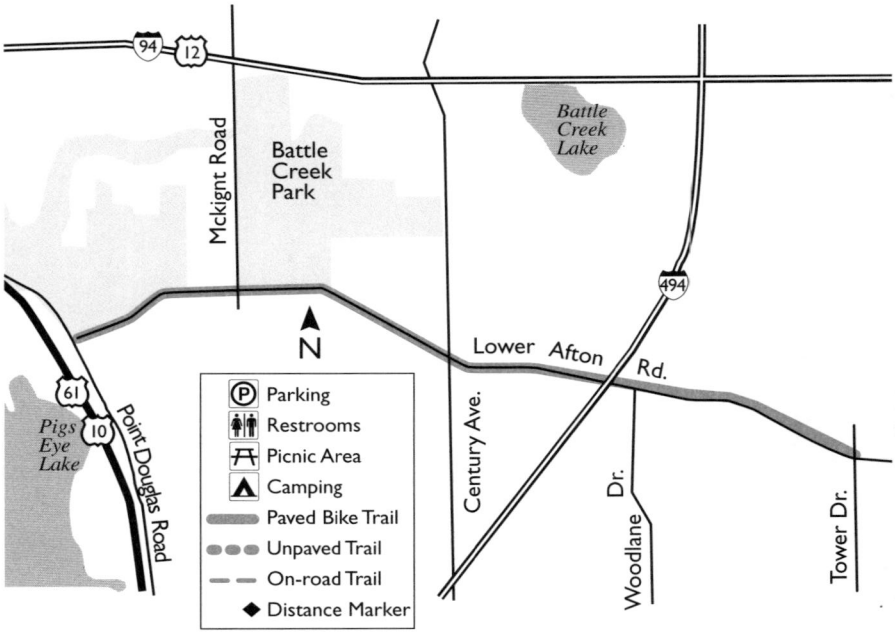

FOR MORE INFORMATION:

Maplewood City Hall
1830 E. Co. Road B
Maplewood, MN 55109
651-770-4500

Accessories

Realizing there are a multitude of accessories available, we will confine our comments to a very few which we have found to be most beneficial to our biking safety and pleasure. Of course, the most important is a good helmet but we also suggest the following to increase your comfort and enjoyment.

1) Seat pads filled with gel provide multiple return on the investment in the form of added comfort.

2) Padded bike shorts reduce chafing, absorb moisture and provide additional padding.

3) A rear view mirror (either helmet or handle bar mounted) is primarily a safety accessory but it also saves neck strain.

4) Padded gloves help reduce discomfort of weight and tension on the hands when subject to long periods in the same position.

5) Frame-mounted water bottle should be translucent to keep track of supply.

MCKNIGHT ROAD

WHERE: St. Paul
LENGTH: 4 miles
SURFACE: Paved 10' wide
TRAIL USE:

Trailhead South: At McKnight and Lower Afton Road. There are parking lots in Battle Creek Park. This trail connects to the Battle Creek Regional Trail (see page 134) and Lower Afton Trail (see page 160).

Trailhead North: At McKnight and Larpenteur.

The McKnight Road Bike Path has few problems with cross traffic because it follows the west edge of Battle creek Park, the west edge of the 3M complex, the east edge of Beaver Lake Park, and the east edge of Hillcrest Golf Course (the 14th tee at Hillcrest, at 1070 feet above sea level, is the highest point in St. Paul). Following the Mississippi River Trail south from the Minnesota Fish Hatchery to the Battle Creek Trail, and then east to the McKnight Road Bike Path, continue north to Larpenteur. Follow the striped/signed on-street bike lanes on Larpenteur west to Lake Phalen. The Lake Phalen Park Trail south to Wheelock Parkway can provide a longer alternative to the Johnson Parkway section of the St. Paul Grand Rounds Bikeway System.

FOR MORE INFORMATION:

St. Paul Parks & Recreation
300 City Hall Annex
St. Paul, MN 55102
651-266-6400

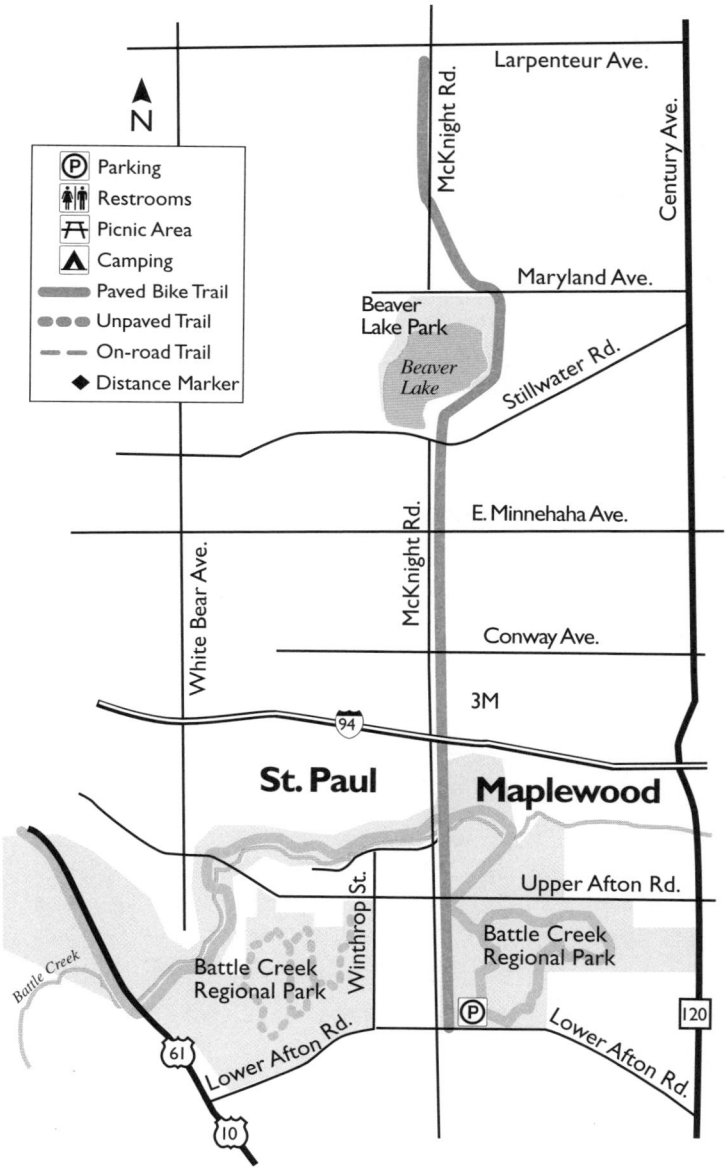
N
Parking
Restrooms
Picnic Area
Camping
Paved Bike Trail
Unpaved Trail
On-road Trail
Distance Marker
Larpenteur Ave.
McKnight Rd.
Century Ave.
Maryland Ave.
Beaver Lake Park
Beaver Lake
Stillwater Rd.
E. Minnehaha Ave.
White Bear Ave.
McKnight Rd.
Conway Ave.
3M
94
St. Paul
Maplewood
Upper Afton Rd.
Winthrop St.
Battle Creek Regional Park
Battle Creek Regional Park
Battle Creek
61
Lower Afton Rd.
Lower Afton Rd.
120
10

MINNEAPOLIS GRAND ROUNDS

WHERE: Minneapolis
LENGTH: 37.9 miles
SURFACE: Asphalt
TRAIL USE:

Biking The Grand Rounds
Submitted by Mary Lynn Pulscher, Minneapolis Parks Planning

The Grand Rounds of the Minneapolis parkway system offers a multitude of diverse amenities and beautiful scenery, including the Mississippi River, the Chain of Lakes and Minnehaha Falls. The Grand Rounds can provide you with a unique tour of one of America's finest urban park systems.

This is a recreational bike path system - the speed limit is 10 mph. Bike paths around Lakes Harriet, Calhoun and Isles are one direction. All other paths in the Grand Rounds are two-directional. Please stay to the right when riding and pass only on the left. You are allowed to bike on the parkways where the speed limit is 25 mph. The bike paths run in close proximity to the parkways, so where gaps exist in the path system it is possible to make connections using the road.

Bikes and in-line skate rentals are available along Lake Street in the Uptown area on the east side of Lake Calhoun.

Bike paths are accessible from any section of the Grand Rounds. There is a small daily fee to use the parking lots at Minnehaha Park, Boom Island and Lakes Nokomis, Harriet, Calhoun and Cedar. Free parking is available in these locations along the parkways in 'bays' and on nearby city streets. Locations not listed here have free parking in general.

During the summer, concessions are available at Minnehaha Park, Lake Nokomis, Lake Harriet, Lake Calhoun and at the Wirth Chalet. Drinking fountains and restrooms are also available at these sites. Because this trail system is located in an urban area you are never really far away from restaurants, restrooms or phones.

The Chain of Lakes - Harriet, Calhoun, Isles and Cedar

Lake Harriet Segment
Length: 2.9 miles
The amenities here include beaches, fishing and sailing docks, playgrounds, tennis courts, picnic areas and concessions. While riding along the east shore, take time to visit the second oldest rose garden in the U.S. with its two historic water display fountains as well as adjacent perennial garden, rock garden and Roberts Bird Sanctuary. If you're out riding on a summer evening stop by the Lake Harriet street-

car or take a boat ride on the Queen of the Lakes. Come back in the winter for ice-fishing, ice skating and cross country skiing.

Lake Calhoun Segment
Length: 3.1 miles
Tired of biking? Rent a canoe at the refectory on the east side and explore Calhoun, Isles, Cedar and Brownie Lakes. Or take in a volleyball game at Thomas Beach on the southwest side.

Lake of the Isles Segment
Length: 2.9 miles
Come for a leisurely ride to view some of the grand historic homes in Minneapolis - when this neighborhood was built in the 1880s no house could cost less then $3000.

Cedar Lake Segment
Length: 1.68 miles
The west side of Cedar Lake has a paved bicycle path that will connect you with Wirth Park. However, if you have a mountain bike it is possible to navigate around the entire lake using dirt trails on the north side (yield to pedestrians!) and maintenance trails along railroad tracks on the east side. This is an excellent lake for swimming and picnicing.

Theodore Wirth Parkway Segment
Length: 6 miles
This is the largest park in the Minneapolis park system with an internal six-mile loop for both pedestrians and bicyclists. This park includes an 18 hole golf course, a par 3 course, concessions at the Wirth Chalet (at the golf course), picnic facilities, swimming beach, the Eloise Butler Wildflower Garden and Bird Sanctuary, the J.D. Rivers Children's Garden and a remnant of a Quaking Tamarack Bog, all of which are surrounded by natural woodlands, ponds and creeks. Be on the look out for wildlife, especially deer. During the winter, Wirth park offers cross-country and downhill skiing and tubing.

Victory Memorial Parkway Segment
Length: 2.84 miles
Victory Memorial Drive is a three mile parkway lined with trees and plaques memorializing the servicemen from Hennepin County who died in World War 1. Stop and visit the Grand Army Circle and War Shrine located along the Drive.

Central River Front Segment
Length: 1.4 miles
This is a relatively new development along the Central Riverfront that includes promenades, walking and biking trails, woodlands, picnic

areas and easy access to the waters edge–bring your fishing gear! This is also the annual site of fireworks for the 4th of July. Two regional amenities not to be missed while visiting the Mississippi Mile are Nicollet Island and Boom Island, both located on the east side of the river. You gain access by taking either the Hennepin Avenue or Plymouth Avenue bridges across the river.

James J. Hill Stone Arch Bridge
This hundred year old railroad bridge was recently reopened as a bicycle and pedestrian facility–no cars allowed! This bridge offers a spectacular view of St. Anthony Falls (the only falls on the entire length of the Mississippi River) and connects Central River Front Trail to the on-road route near the University. Watch barges and pleasure boats work their way through the locks (Lock and Dam #1) on the west side of the bridge.

Nicollet Island Segment
Length: less than 1 mile
Nicollet Island has picnic tables, a large pavilion (with restrooms), an amphitheater and sweeping views of the Mississippi River and Downtown Minneapolis. Nicollet Island is also home to De La Salle–the only high school in the continental United States located on an island. If you have time, bike through the residential north end of the island to enjoy a couple dozen beautifully restored historic homes. Take the crushed limestone trail along the northeastern edge of the island to connect with Boom Island. Boom Island is the largest riverfront park in Minneapolis and includes a boat launch, docks, promenades, picnic areas, open fields, restrooms, drinking fountains and a playground. Also a great place to fly a kite. Have time for a riverboat cruise? Then jump aboard the Anson Northrup for a different view of the river.

Great River Road Segment (a.k.a. West River Road)
Length: 5.4 miles
This scenic connection between the Central Riverfront and Minnehaha park beautiful during autumn. This section of river includes scenic overlooks, picnic tables and scattered benches for resting. The east side of the river includes extensive sand dunes for sun-bathing and some trails for mountain biking (but yield to pedestrians!). [A bike loop can also be made along the river; start at Minnehaha Park, cross the Ford Parkway Bridge to the east side of the river; follow the bike path up the river a few miles to the Franklin Avenue bridge, cross it and rejoin the path on the west side to get back down to Minnehaha Park].

Minnehaha Park Segment
Length: .5 miles
The crowning jewel of the Minneapolis park system includes the stun-

ning Minnehaha Falls, extensive picnic facilities, hiking trails to the Mississippi River, a large refectory, gift shop, playgrounds, several historic statues and the Princess Depot. You may also wish to explore the Stevens House, the first frame dwelling erected west of the Mississippi.

Also near the park is the newly relocated Longfellow House Interpretive Center, a project of the City of Minneapolis and the Minneapolis Park and Recreation. It is located between Hiawatha Ave. and Minnehaha Ave. just south of Minnehaha Parkway.

Minnehaha State Park has become the focus of a critical link for bicycle trails between the cities of St. Paul, Minneapolis, Bloomington, Richfield, Mendota Heights, Ft. Snelling and several government agencies. Although funds have not yet been made available to enable the Longfellow House to reach its full potential, the strategic location at the intersection of pedestrian and bicycle pathways will permit it to serve as an ideal environmental/information/interpretive center when the city and park boards elect to fund it.

The restoration of the House is a rare example of a cooperative effort between intergovernmental agencies and private citizens to effect the preservation and reuse of a historic landmark. Upon final completion of the connecting bikeways, Minnehaha State Park will link the Minneapolis and St. Paul Grand Rounds, as well as the suburban Snelling bike trails. The Mendota Bridge and the Ford Parkway Bridge will also connect to the Longfellow House.

Minnehaha Parkway Segment
Length: 5 miles (from Minnehaha Park to Lake Harriet)
This winding scenic trail takes you along the wooded area of Minnehaha Creek. In the springtime be on the lookout for large stands of daffodils planted by volunteers from People for Parks, a non- profit organization.

Lake Nokomis Segment
Length: 2.7 miles
This regional amenity includes a swimming beach, large playing fields, concession, walking and biking paths and a community center with a gym. During the Aquatennial (held in late July) Lake Nokomis plays host to an annual triathalon and the "famous" milk-carton boat races.

FOR MORE INFORMATION:

For more information, call 612-661-4800 or write:
The Minneapolis Park and Recreation Board
200 Grain Exchange Building
400 S. 4th Street
Minneapolis, Minnesota 55415-1400

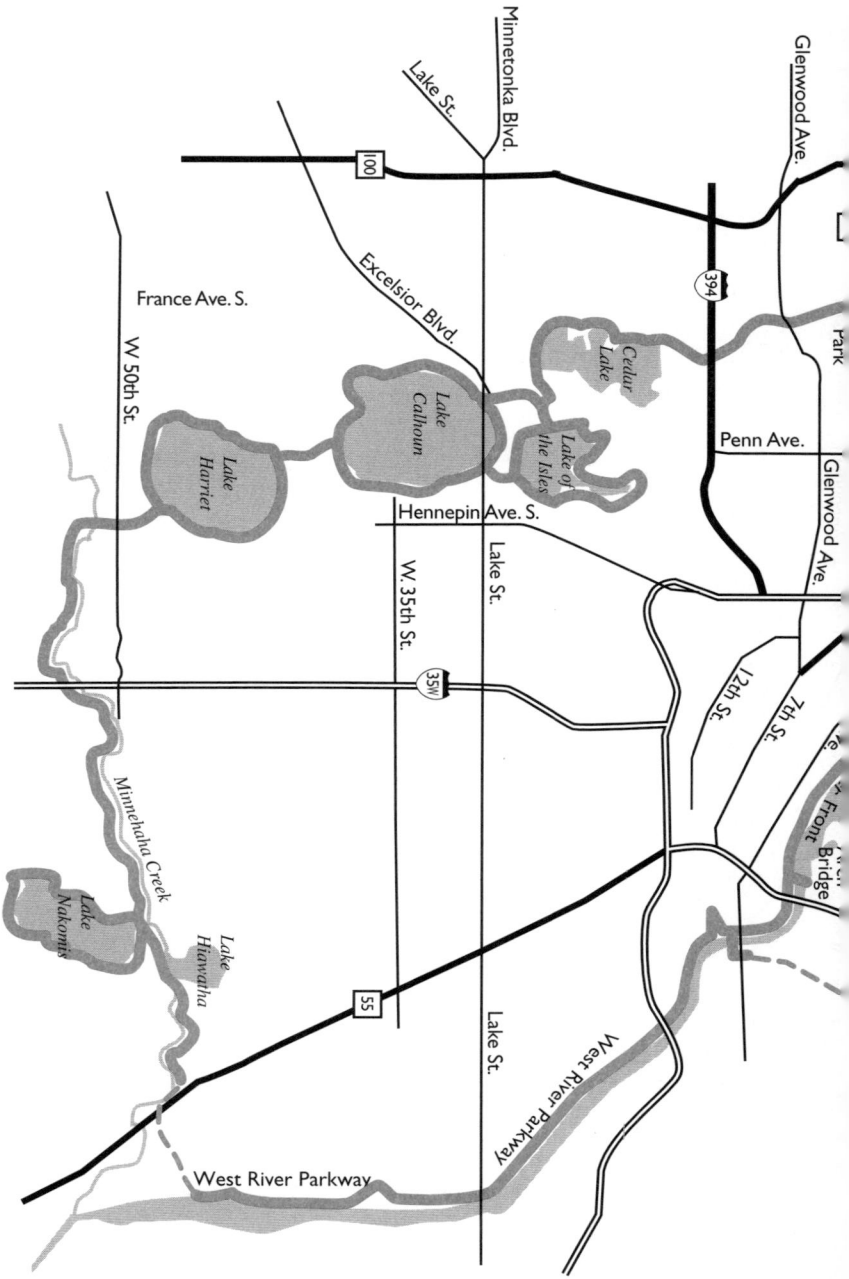
Glenwood Ave.
Minnetonka Blvd.
Lake St.
100
394
Excelsior Blvd.
France Ave. S.
W 50th St.
Cedar Lake
Lake of the Isles
Lake Calhoun
Lake Harriet
Penn Ave.
Glenwood Ave.
Hennepin Ave. S.
Lake St.
W. 35th St.
35W
12th St.
7th St.
Front
Bridge
Minnehaha Creek
Lake Nakomis
Lake Hiawatha
55
Lake St.
West River Parkway
West River Parkway

Crystal
Brooklyn Blvd.
Osseo Rd.
Memorial Pkwy.
Robbinsdale
42nd Ave. N.
Crystal Lake
Memorial Pkwy.
Penn Ave.
W. Broadway
Minneapolis
Plymouth Ave.
Mississippi River
St. Anthony Pkwy.
37th Ave. N.E.
Stinson Blvd.
94
694
252
100
N
Parking
Restrooms
Picnic Area
Camping
Paved Bike Trail
Unpaved Trail
On-road Trail
Distance Marker

MINNESOTA VALLEY STATE PARK

WHERE: Shakopee-Chaska
LENGTH: 6.5 miles completed to date
SURFACE: Paved
TRAIL USE: 

Trailhead East: At Murphy's Landing, two miles east of Shakopee. However, flooding washed out part of the trail, so the best bet is to start in Shakopee. The best access is in the Veteran's Memorial Park, between Shakopee and Murphy's Landing, where you will find parking, water and restrooms.

Mid Access: At Huber Park, near downtown Shakopee and the City Hall, a short block north of the stop light, where Highway 169 turns north to cross the river. Free parking, food and restrooms are available here.

Trailhead West: At Courthouse Lake, near the Carver County Courthouse, in southeast Chaska. Parking is available here.

Some 24,000 acres of parks, wildlife areas and trails comprise the Minnesota Valley system within which a 86-mile bicycle and hiking trail will be located. The area is managed for multiple purposes and trail construction is progressing as funds become available. The majority of the trail is presently open to only horseback, some mountain biking and winter recreation. Recent floods have further delayed improvements.

The trail will traverse both public and private lands and connect five counties and numerous communities along the south side of the Minnesota River. As yet, the only paved trail portion extends from Murphy's Landing 2 miles east of Shakopee to the Chaska city limits.

Because of its short distance, this is a popular hiking and in-line skating trail, in addition to bicycling. It is quite level and sheltered, following an old rail bed. The DNR has provided benches at intervals and a highlight is crossing the Minnesota River on the original railroad swing bridge

FOR MORE INFORMATION:

Minnesota Valley State Park
19825 Park Boulevard
Jordan, MN 55352
612-492-6400

Minnesota River Valley
Headquarters
County Road 57
Jordan, MN 55352
612-492-6400

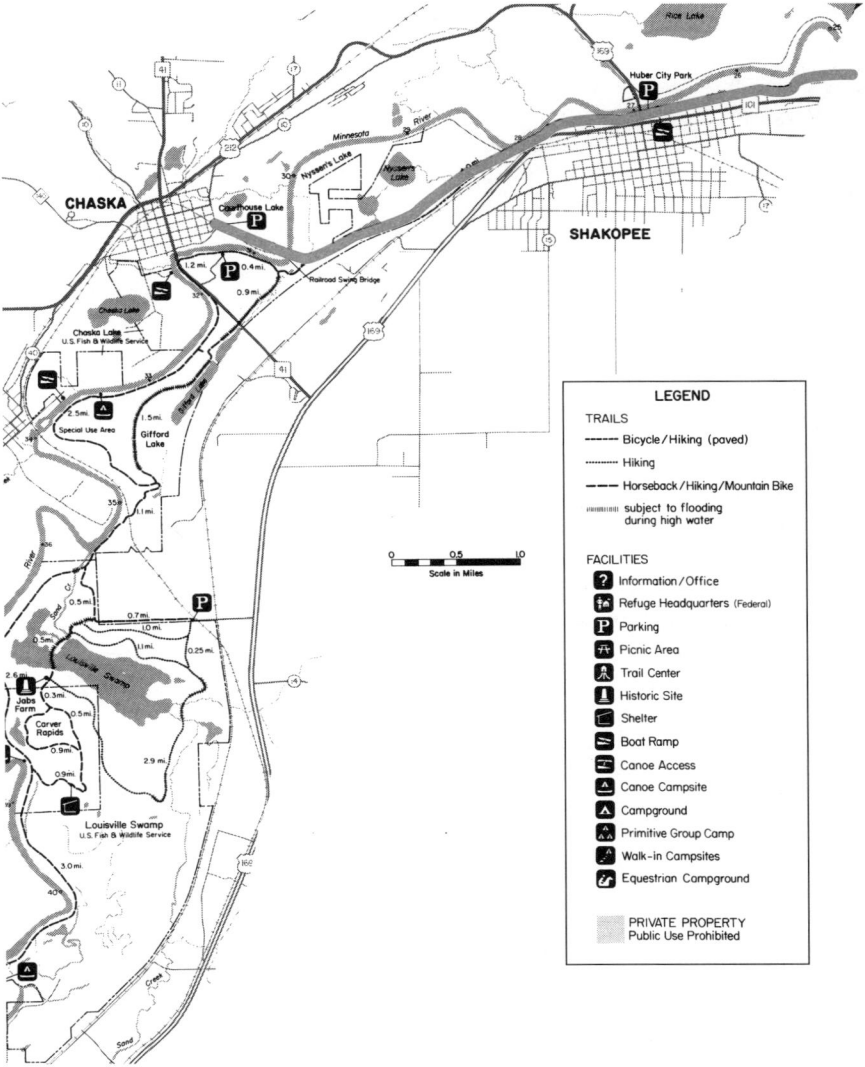
Rice Lake
Huber City Park
Minnesota River
Nyssen's Lake
Courthouse Lake
CHASKA
SHAKOPEE
Railroad Swing Bridge
Chaska Lake
Chaska Lake
U.S. Fish & Wildlife Service
Special Use Area
Gifford Lake
Sand Creek
River
Louisville Swamp
Jabs Farm
Carver Rapids
Louisville Swamp
U.S. Fish & Wildlife Service
Sand Creek
Scale in Miles
LEGEND
TRAILS
Bicycle/Hiking (paved)
Hiking
Horseback/Hiking/Mountain Bike
subject to flooding during high water
FACILITIES
Information/Office
Refuge Headquarters (Federal)
Parking
Picnic Area
Trail Center
Historic Site
Shelter
Boat Ramp
Canoe Access
Canoe Campsite
Campground
Primitive Group Camp
Walk-in Campsites
Equestrian Campground
PRIVATE PROPERTY
Public Use Prohibited

MISSISSIPPI REGIONAL CORRIDOR

WHERE: Coon Rapids Dam to Camden Bridge
LENGTH: 10.5 miles
SURFACE: Paved, 8' wide
TRAIL USE:

Access: Available from numerous streets in Coon Rapids, Fridley and Columbia Heights. However, we highly recommend one of the Anoka County Parks. Islands of Peace, Manomin, Riverfront Regional Park, Riverview Heights, and the Coon Rapids Dam all have ample parking and restrooms.

Scenic river overlooks, the Springbrook Nature Center and Banfill-Locke Arts Center in Manomin Park are some of the attractions along this trail, which makes for an excellent short ride, or a part of a longer ride, through the metro biking system. Although some of it is along city streets, it is well-marked and most is off-road.

Anoka County has a terrific park system and has connected many of them with a super bike route. This trail parallels the river, and passes through or near the Coon Rapids Dam Park, Riverview Heights Park, Manomin, Islands of Peace and Riverfront Regional Park, in addition to connecting with the Minneapolis Trail System.

From 86th Avenue, a striped and signed bike lane continues south on Mississippi Blvd. until reaching Broad Avenue. From Broad Avenue South, the trail alternates from off-road to marked roadside until crossing East River Road where it becomes off-road all the way to St. Anthony Parkway.

FOR MORE INFORMATION:

Anoka County Parks
550 N.W. Bunker Lake Blvd.
Anoka, MN 55304
612-757-3920

Phil and Marlys Mickelson near Lake Kohlmeier

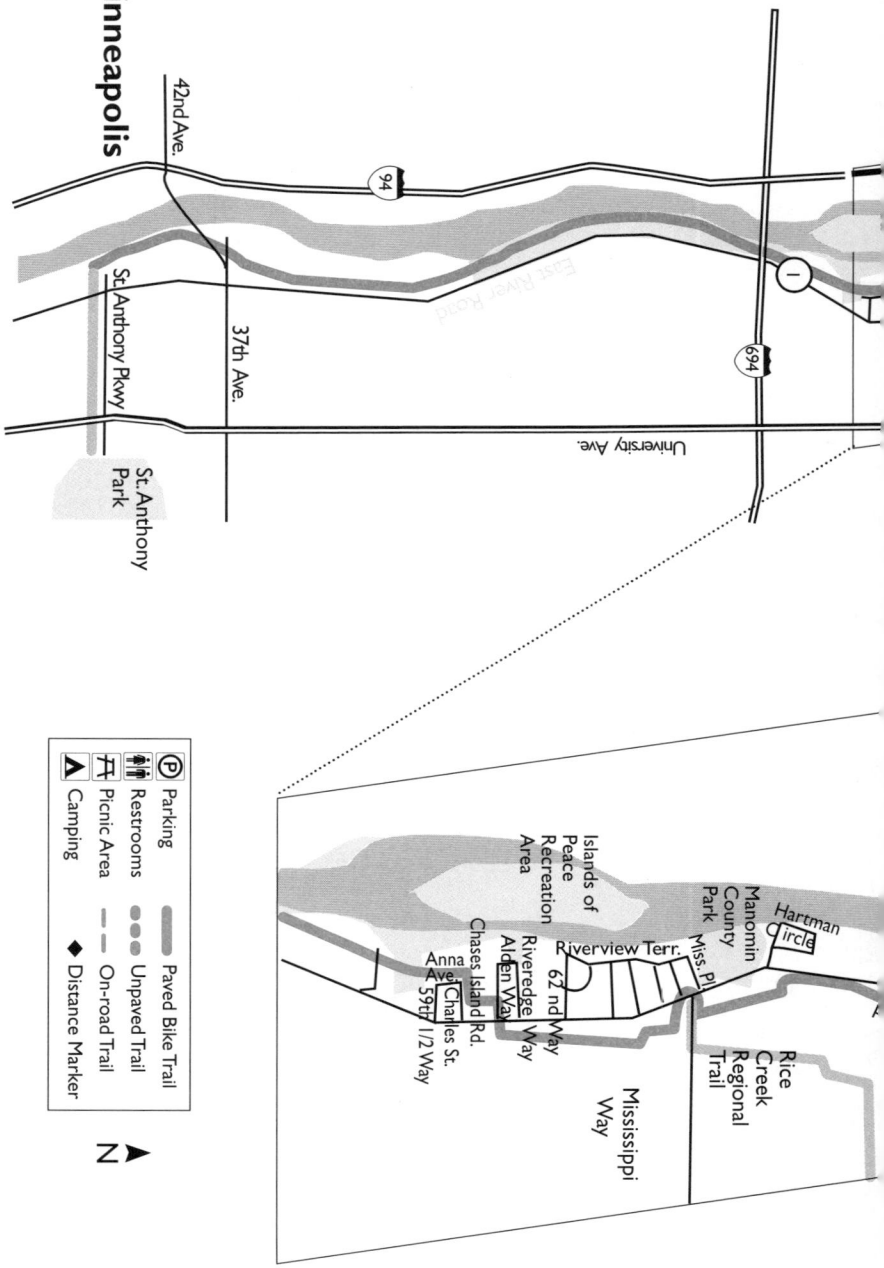
Minneapolis
42nd Ave.
St. Anthony Pkwy
St. Anthony Park
37th Ave.
94
East River Road
694
University Ave.
Hartman Circle
Manomin County Park
Miss. Pl.
Rice Creek Regional Trail
Mississippi Way
Riverview Terr.
62 nd Way
Riveredge Way
Alden Way
Islands of Peace Recreation Area
Chases Island Rd.
Anna Ave.
Charles St.
59th 1/2 Way
Parking
Restrooms
Picnic Area
Camping
Paved Bike Trail
Unpaved Trail
On-road Trail
Distance Marker
N

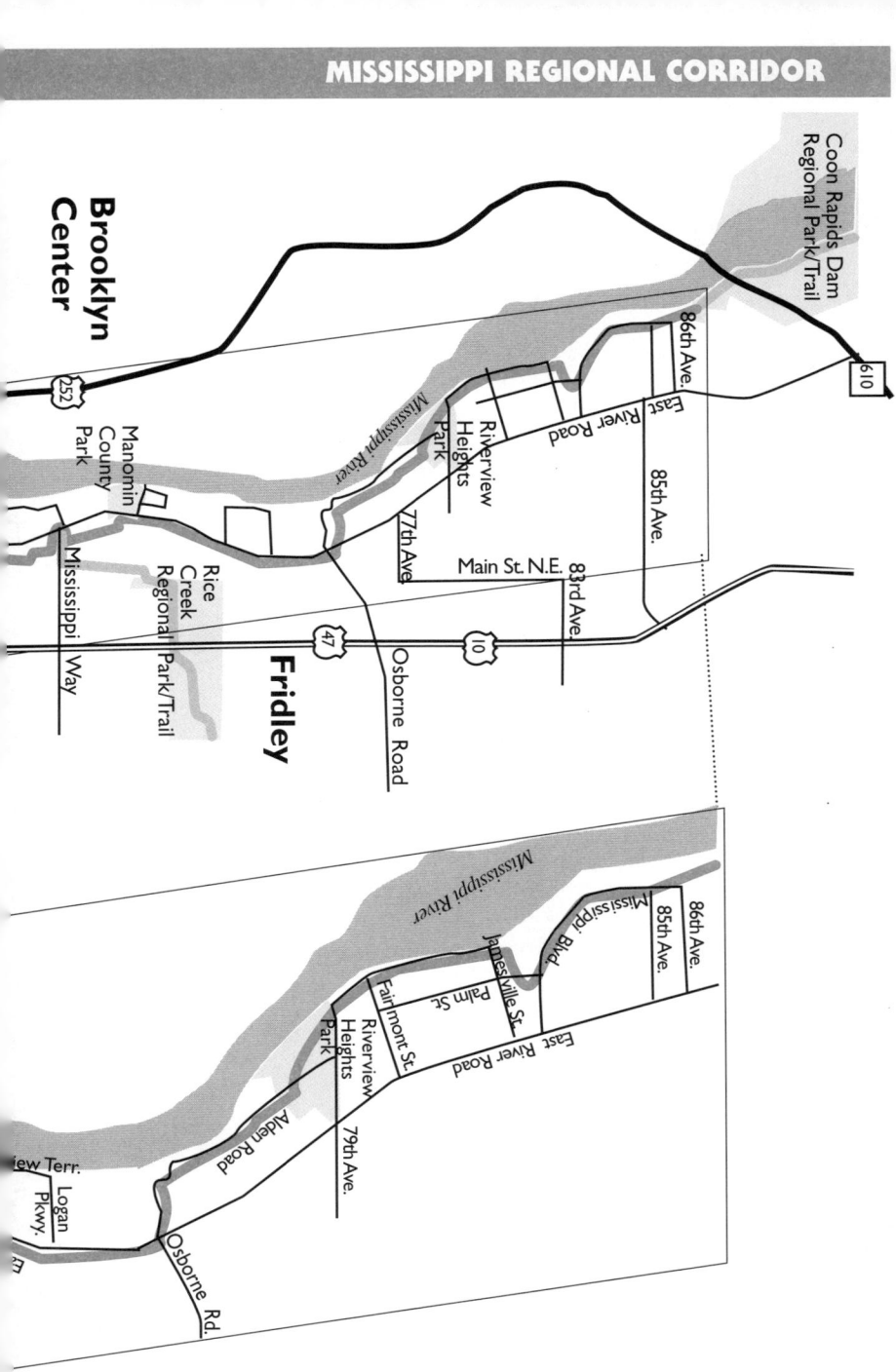
Coon Rapids Dam Regional Park/Trail
610
86th Ave.
East River Road
85th Ave.
Riverview Heights Park
Mississippi River
77th Ave
Main St. N.E.
83rd Ave.
10
47
Osborne Road
Fridley
Rice Creek Regional Park/Trail
Manomin County Park
Mississippi Way
252
Brooklyn Center
Mississippi River
86th Ave.
85th Ave.
Mississippi Blvd.
Jamesville St.
Palm St.
Fairmont St.
East River Road
Riverview Heights Park
79th Ave.
Allen Road
Logan Pkwy.
Osborne Rd.

NORTH HENNEPIN CORRIDOR

WHERE: Brooklyn Park
LENGTH: 7.2 miles (also connects to 9.3 mile Elm Creek Trail)
SURFACE: Paved
TRAIL USE:

Access: Available at several locations along the trail.

This is a very flat trail connecting the Elm Creek Park Reserve and the Coon Rapids Dam Regional Park.

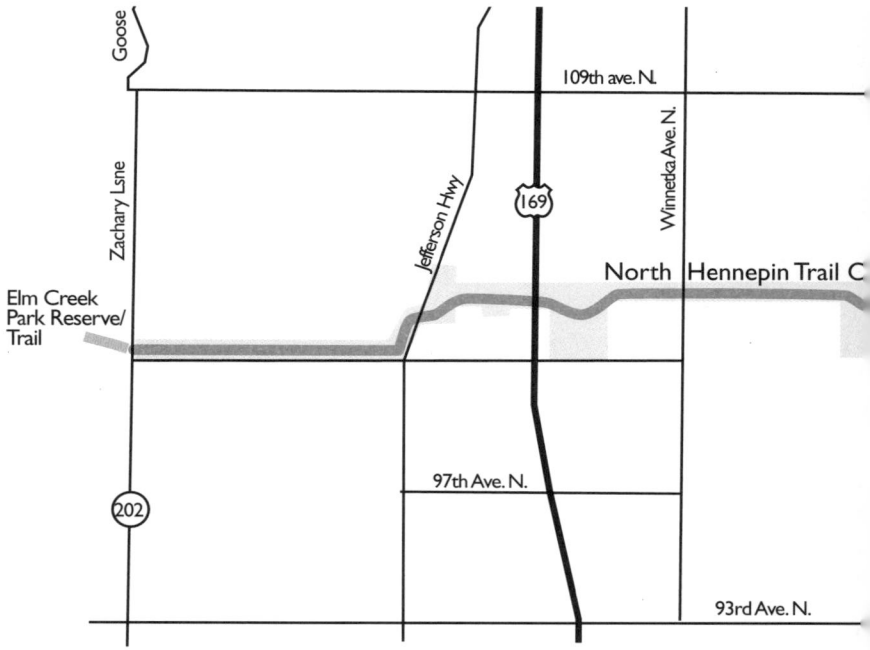

FOR MORE INFORMATION:

Hennepin Parks
12615 County Rd. 9
Plymouth, MN 55441
612-559-9000

This is one of the few trails in the metro area with a parallel trail open to horses, snowmobiles and cross-country skiing. Crossing the Mississippi River at Coon Rapids will connect you with the Anoka County Trail system.

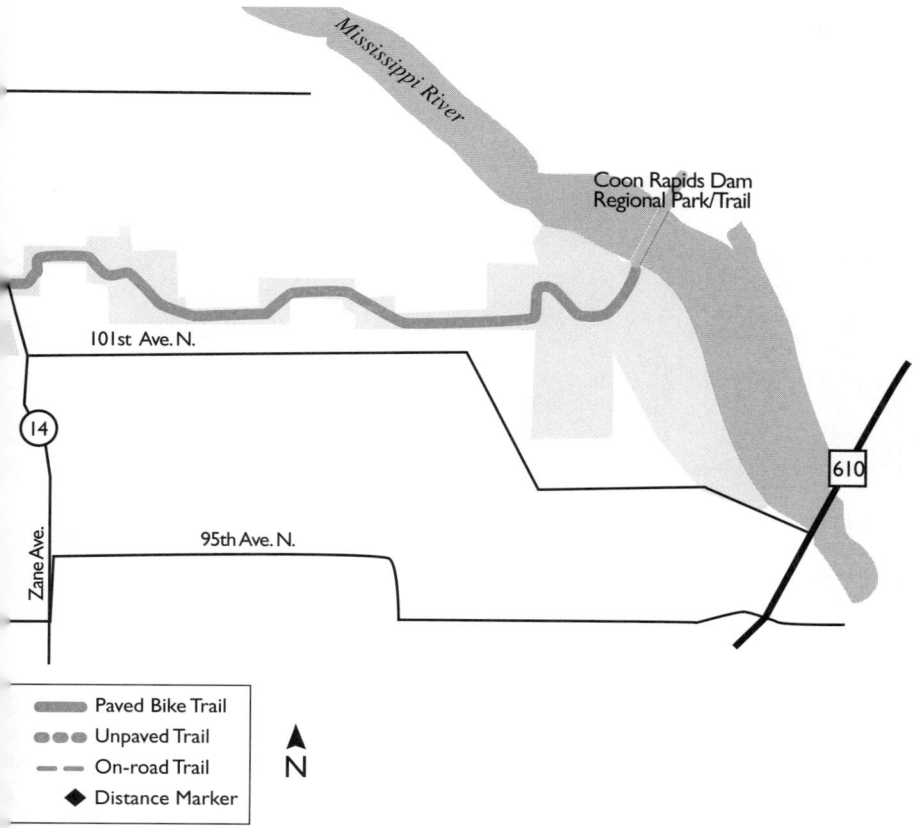

PHALEN CREEK REGIONAL

WHERE: St. Paul
LENGTH: 4.5 miles
SURFACE: Paved, 10' wide
TRAIL USE:

Trailhead North: At the intersection of Wheelock Parkway, Johnson Parkway and East Shore Drive, at the south end of Lake Phalen, where there is a small parking lot.

Trailhead South: At east 7th St. in Swede Hallow Park.

This is a new trail that takes advantage of the Phalen Creek waterway, which will provide safe hiking, biking and skating in a heavily populated area near downtown St. Paul. There is on-road parking only along most of this trail.

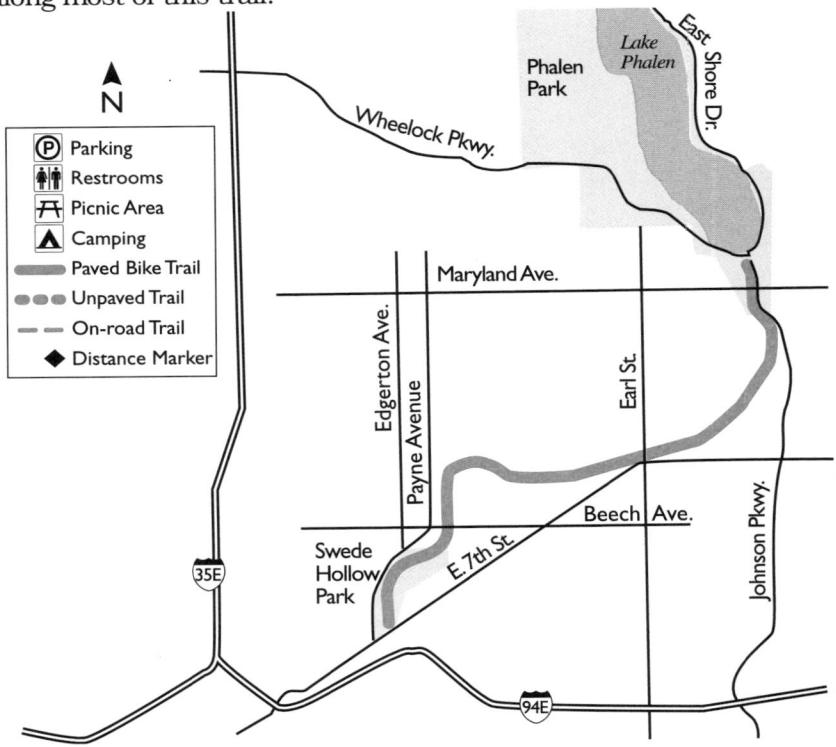

FOR MORE INFORMATION:

Phalen Center
1000 E. Wheelock Parkway
St. Paul, MN 55106
651-298-5721

St. Paul Parks & Recreation
300 City Hall Annex
St. Paul, MN 55102
651-266-6400

WHERE: Fridley
LENGTH: 4.25 miles
SURFACE: Paved, 8' wide
TRAIL USE:

Access: The best parking and facilities are located in the park south of 69th Avenue at the east end just inside the park at the south side of the Target Northern Distribution Center, near the Columbia Arena, east of University Avenue. There is also a trail branch which leads to the dead end of Monroe Street if you enter the park from the south.

This is an excellent short trail through a scenic area. Expect foot and in-line skate traffic throughout.

Connecting bikeways: The trail hooks up with the Trailhead West of the North Mississippi Trail at the junction of Mississippi Street and East River Road. This permits access off Stinson Blvd. At Stinson Boulevard (Ramsey County line), the trail follows the east side of road to the southeast corner of Rice Creek Park. It also connects with Ramsey County Trail system at 69th Avenue and Stinson.

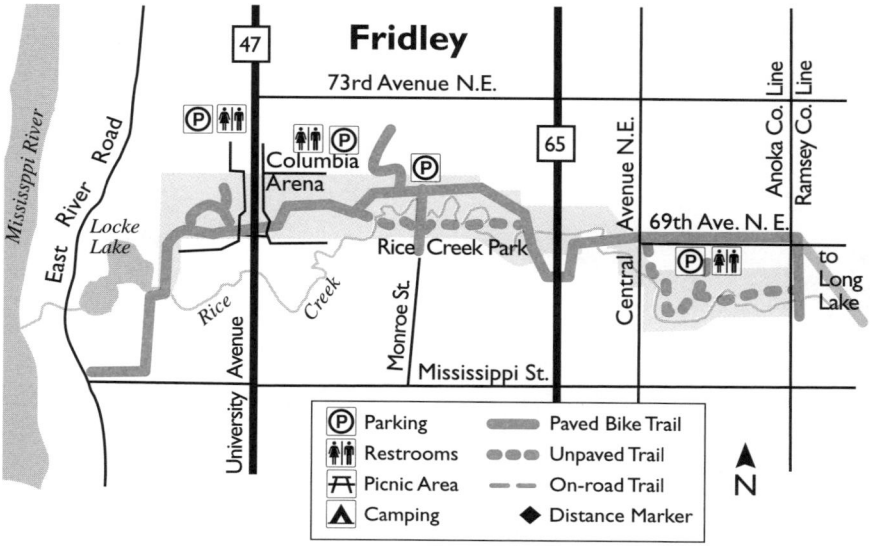

FOR MORE INFORMATION:

Anoka County Parks
550 N.W. Bunker Lake Blvd.
Anoka, MN 55304
612-757-3920

SOUTHWEST REGIONAL LRT-NORTH CORRIDOR

WHERE: Hopkins to Victoria
LENGTH: 15.5 miles
SURFACE: Hard packed limestone, 10' wide
TRAIL USE: 

Trailhead East: At the west side of 8th Avenue North, just north of Main Street in downtown Hopkins. There is parking available at 8th & Excelsior Avenue (County Road 3) on the south side.

Note: To connect to the LRT South Corridor, follow 8th Street south 1½ blocks to Excelsior Avenue, and the parking lot on the south side. The trail is adjacent to the parking lot.

Mid Access: Because the trail traverses from Hopkins to Minnetonka, Deephaven, Greenwood, Excelsior and Shorewood and terminates in Victoria, there are numerous access points.

Trailhead West: At Victoria there is a kiosk at Victoria Drive and Steigor Lake Lane, one block north of Highway 5. The trail actually continues west one-quarter mile but there is no parking available.

With the exception of the half mile of its eastern end in Hopkins, it is surprisingly secluded, with infrequent crossings of streets and roads. This rail bed (as well as the South Corridor route) was acquired by the Hennepin County Regional Railroad Authority and is leased to and managed by the Hennepin County Parks. As is the case with the South Corridor, it may someday become a light rail transportation route instead of a bike trail.

Just west of Hopkins, the trail parallels Minnetonka Boulevard for a time but, as we headed west from the Minnetonka Civic Center, we traveled wooded and remote wetlands most of the way to Excelsior. In Deephaven the trail crosses Carsons Bay with a great view of Lake Minnetonka and the marina. Further west, the trail again affords views of the lake and also crosses St. Albans Bay. At that point, it is necessary to leave the trail and follow well-marked streets through Excelsior to a resumption of the rail bed where you will again ride through secluded and interesting country into Victoria.

FOR MORE INFORMATION:

Hennepin County Parks
French Regional Park
12615 County Road
Plymouth, MN 55441
612-559-9000

Trail Hotline 559-6778

Twin West Chamber of Commerce
10550 Wayzata, Blvd.
Minnetonka, MN 55305
612-540-0234

Shakopee Chamber of Commerce
1801 E. Highway 101
Shakopee, MN 55379
612-445-1660

SOUTHWEST REGIONAL LRT-SOUTH CORRIDOR

WHERE: Hopkins to Chaska
LENGTH: 11.5 miles
SURFACE: Hard packed limestone, 10' wide
TRAIL USE: 

Trailhead East: At the south side of Excelsior Avenue at 8th Street in Hopkins, the Park and Ride lot.

Note: If you wish to connect to the North Corridor LRT, cross Excelsior on 8th Street at the west end of the parking lot. Go 1½ blocks north on 8th and you will see the North Corridor access on the west side of 8th Street.

Mid Access: There are numerous streets and roads that intersect the trail, but for parking availability and easy access we recommend: Evandale Park, Miller Park and Reiley Lake Park.

Trailhead West: The kiosk on Bluff Creek Road, which is about one block west of the Highway 169, 101 and 212 intersection north of Shakopee, where Highway 169 crosses the Minnesota River. Here, you will find parking and portable restrooms. The trail actually extends one-half mile west of the kiosk but there is no access.

The trail surface had a few rough spots, due to recent heavy rains, but was generally excellent. Street crossings are relatively few. Some of the crossings, however, we found less than obvious and/or not well-marked. While riding from the south into Hopkins we totally missed the following crossings: The crossing at Highway 5: Go east via the sidewalk to first stoplight then back on sidewalk to trail. The crossing at Valley View Road: Cross where tail drops down to road level (no stop light), then left a short distance, you will see sign pointing to regain LRT. The crossing at W. 62nd (Crosstown): The trail goes under the bridge and at the top crosses back over the bridge (signs).

The day we rode, we encountered two Rangers patrolling the trail, one by bicycle, and very few trail users. Wherever high grades occur, 6' steel link fences have been installed. Side trips to the swimming beach at Lake Reilly and Shady Oak are easy and we predict you will find this a most enjoyable outing.

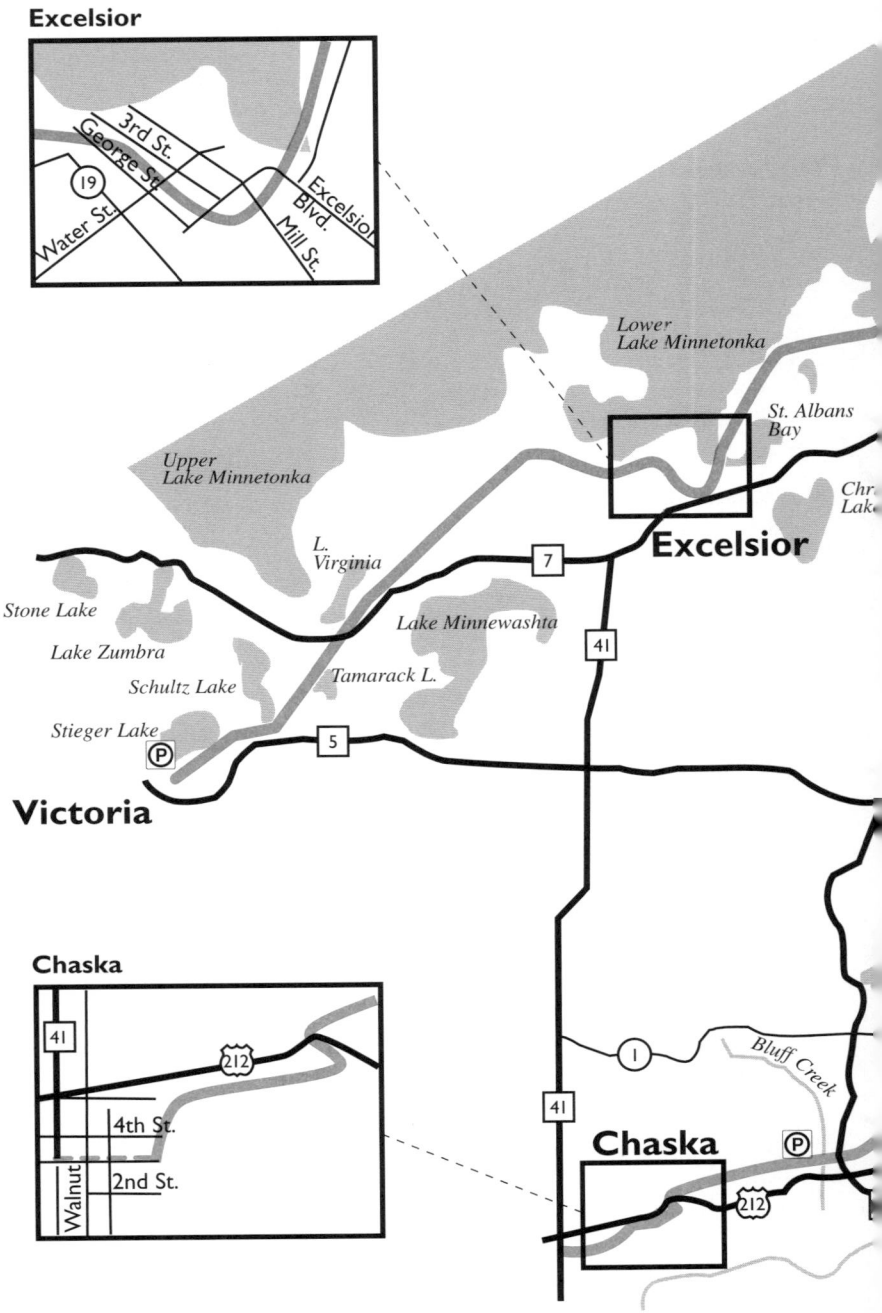
Excelsior
3rd St.
George St.
19
Water St.
Excelsior Blvd.
Mill St.
Lower Lake Minnetonka
St. Albans Bay
Upper Lake Minnetonka
Excelsior
L. Virginia
7
Stone Lake
Lake Minnewashta
41
Lake Zumbra
Tamarack L.
Schultz Lake
Stieger Lake
5
Victoria
Chaska
41
212
4th St.
2nd St.
Walnut
1
Bluff Creek
41
Chaska
212

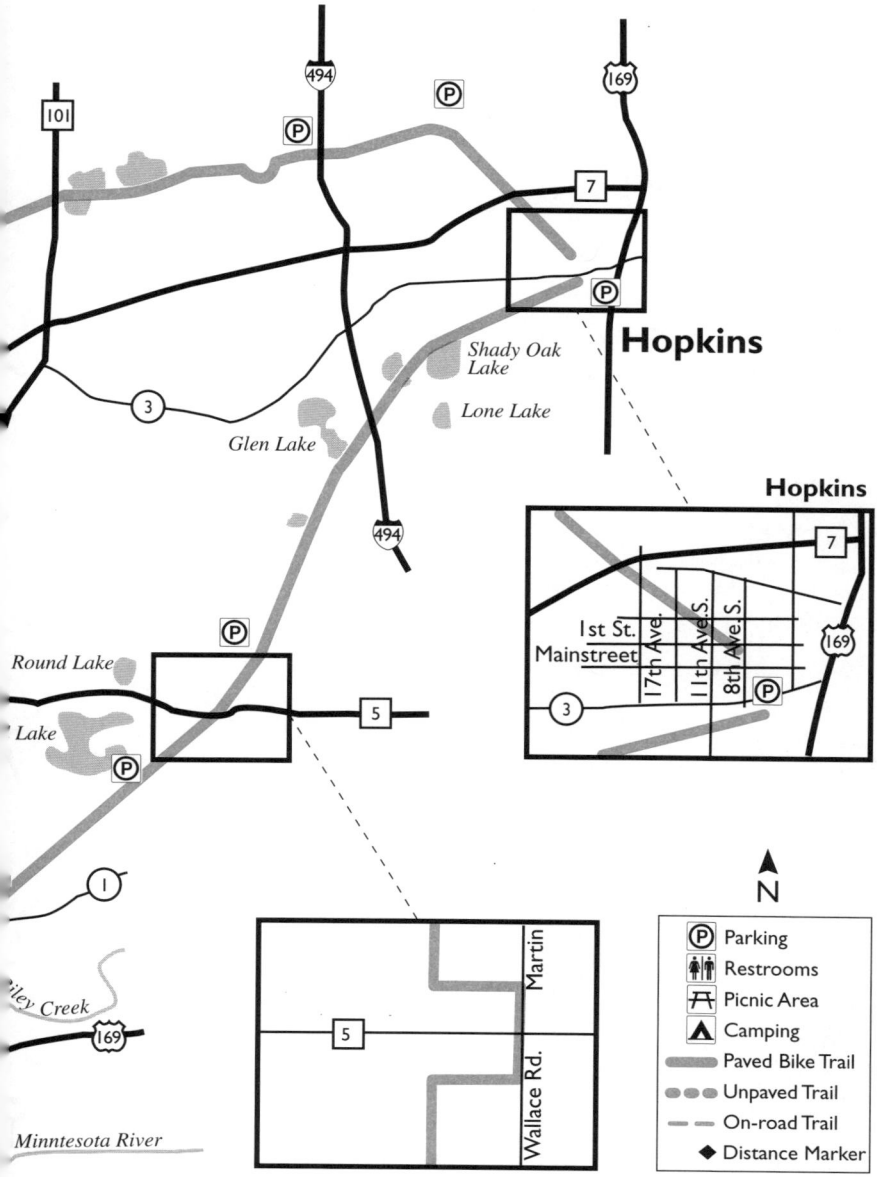

Administered by Minnesota Department of Natural Resources

ST. PAUL GRAND ROUNDS

WHERE: St. Paul
LENGTH: 28 miles
SURFACE: Paved off-road and some paved road shoulder
TRAIL USE: 

Access: At any location throughout the circle route around the city.

For points of interest, convenience, parking and facilities, we especially recommend the following:

Hidden Falls Park
Grand Rounds North
Como Park
(pool, zoo, snacks)
Crosby Farm Park
Phalen Park, beach and restaurants
Indian Mounds Park
(best view in town)
Lower Landing Park at the foot of Jackson Street

Although not entirely off-road, the St. Paul Grand Rounds provides an excellent tour of urban St. Paul and the Mississippi River valley. The Grand Round Loop connects almost all of St. Paul's major parks and parkways (e.g. Mounds Park, Johnson Parkway, Phalen Park, Wheelock Parkway, Como Park, Midway Parkway, Pelham Boulevard and Mississippi River Boulevard, Hidden Falls Park, Crosby Farm Park) and bikeways along the Mississippi. It was first envisioned over a century ago by park system planners and nationally prominent landscape architect Horace W.S. Cleveland.

It will also provide connections to the Munger-Gateway State Trail, the Minneapolis Grand Rounds bikeways, the Stone Arch Bridge and downtown Minneapolis, in addition to the Minneapolis trails bordering the banks of the Mississippi. Other connections will further extend the potential ride to Ft. Snelling and perhaps all the way to Le Sueur.

West Section
The Mississippi River East Bank Trail extends from Emerald Ave. and Mississippi River Boulevard on the north (where it connects to the East River Road segment of the Grand Rounds Parkway System in Mpls.) to south of the Ford Plant and then splits at Hidden Falls Park.

South Section
A branch goes through Hidden Falls and Crosby Farm Park (see page 145). Another branch follows Mississippi River Boulevard past Fort Snelling and the Mendota Bridge to become a separate paved trail paralleling Shepherd Road from I-35E to Randolph Avenue. It also has a paved walking trail, except on bridges, but the trail evaporates at Chestnut Street near downtown St. Paul, necessitating about one mile of on-street riding until a new and wider segment can be picked up going east from Jackson Street, in Lower Landing Park. This new sec-

tion of the Mississippi River Trail is 10' wide paved with a separate walking trail. It extends east nearly 2 miles before ending at the bridge over Childs Road. There is excellent parking at Lower Landing Park. East of Childs and Fish Hatchery Roads the trail bridges over Warner Road to connect to Indian Mounds Park and Johnson Parkway. Another branch goes south to connect with Battle Creek Trail (see page 142) and a route on and along Point Douglas Road.

East Section

The eastern loop of the Grand Rounds follows Johnson Parkway as a marked, on-street route 2½ miles north from Burns Avenue at the north edge of Indian Mounds Park to Wheelock Parkway and the Lake Phalen Park Trail system (see page 156).

North Section

The north loop of the Grand Rounds follows Wheelock Parkway as a well-marked, on-street route west 4 miles to Lake Como and the Como Park System. (See page 143) From Lake Como, the Grand Rounds continues west as an on-street lane on Como Avenue to the intersection with Raymond Street. An alternative route follows Midway Parkway and Commonwealth Avenue through the State Fair Grounds (closed during the State Fair) and the St. Paul campus of the U of M.

Dropping south on Raymond to Myrtle, the on-street trail jogs two blocks over to Pelham where it again heads south to connect with the Mississippi River Trail and the west section.

Now included in the St. Paul trail system is a paved route south of the river from Warner Road and past the Yacht Club on Harriet Island. From the Yacht Club a paved road shoulder follows Water Street all the way to Lilydale Park where it connects to the Big River Trail (see page 135). A word of caution: the road shoulder is 3' wide or less in spots, but road traffic is usually light. Via the Mendota Bridge, this will also provide another link with the Minneapolis Trails. Also new and connecting to the Grand Rounds is an off-road paved trail following the transit way from the St. Paul campus of the University of Minnesota and ending at Energy Park near the Minneapolis campus. This trail will eventually connect to the Minneapolis trail system via the Stone Arch Bridge. There is now a downhill, signed, on street trail from there to Stone Arch Bridge.

FOR MORE INFORMATION:

St. Paul Parks & Recreation
300 City Hall Annex
St. Paul, MN 55102
651-266-6400

University of Minnesota
Como Lake
State Fair Grounds
280
Raymond Ave.
Lexington Ave.
94
Summit Ave.
West 7th
Mississippi River Blvd.
Mississippi River
Shepard Road
35E
Ford Plant
West 7th
Crosby Farm Park
(to Fort Snelling)

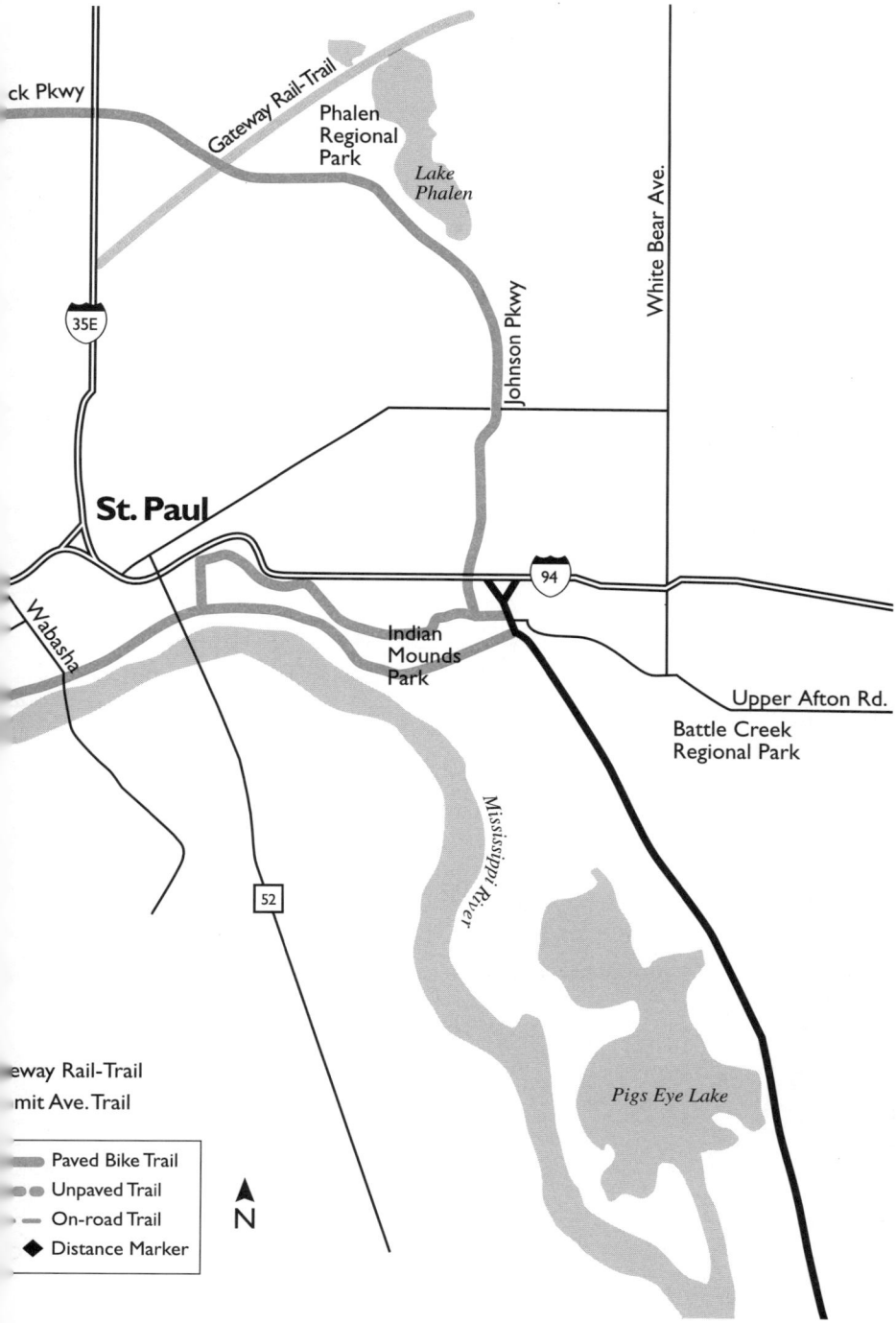
ck Pkwy
Gateway Rail-Trail
Phalen
Regional
Park
Lake
Phalen
White Bear Ave.
Johnson Pkwy
35E
St. Paul
94
Wabasha
Indian
Mounds
Park
Upper Afton Rd.
Battle Creek
Regional Park
Mississippi River
52
Pigs Eye Lake
eway Rail-Trail
mit Ave. Trail
Paved Bike Trail
Unpaved Trail
On-road Trail
Distance Marker
N

SUMMIT AVENUE TRAIL

WHERE: St. Paul
LENGTH: 5 miles
SURFACE: Signed and striped on-street bike lanes
TRAIL USE:

Trailhead West: Connects to the Mississippi River Trail at Mississippi River Road.

Trailhead East: At John Ireland Boulevard and I-94, near the State Capitol and the St. Paul Cathedral. The planned extension of the Munger Gateway State Trail and further extension of this one will eventually connect the two.

This is a well-marked bicycle lane along and through a scenic and historic section of central St. Paul. Summit Avenue is on the longest and best preserved grand Victorian Boulevard in the United States; the entire length of Summit is on the National Register of Historic

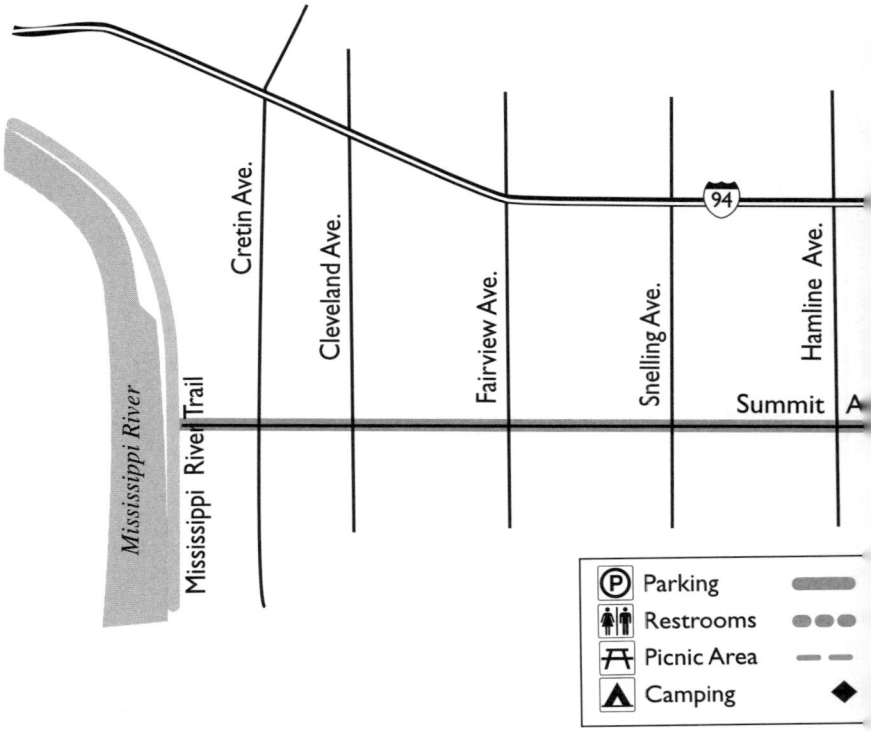

Places. There are numerous good restaurants along Grand Avenue, one block south of Summit, especially near Victoria Street and Macalester College.

For a shorter version (14 miles) of the Grand Rounds, take this, Mississippi River Boulevard, and Shepherd Road past the high bridge to Chestnut, then Chestnut Street north to Summit Avenue.

FOR MORE INFORMATION:

St. Paul Parks & Recreation
300 City Hall Annex
St. Paul, MN 55102
651-266-6400

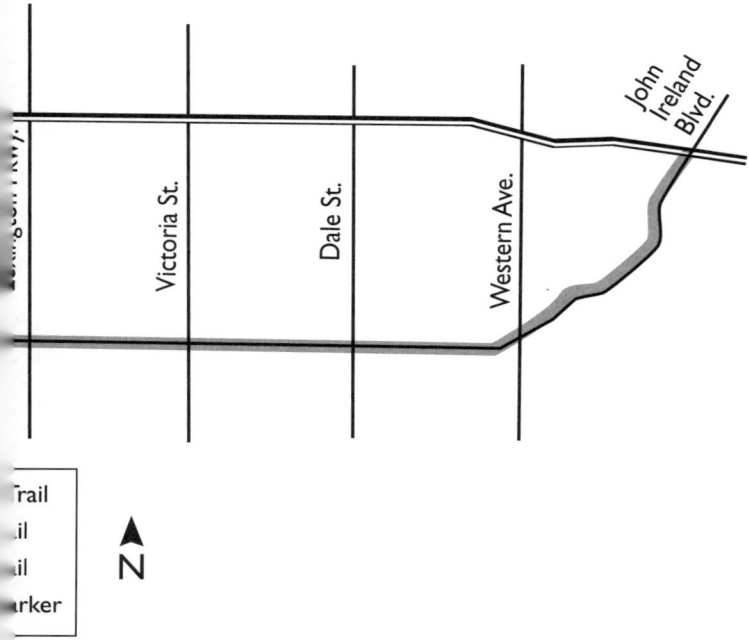

WILLIAM O'BRIEN STATE PARK TRAIL

WHERE: Marine on St. Croix
LENGTH: 2 miles
SURFACE: Paved
TRAIL USE:

Access: State Highway 95 two miles north of Marine-on-St. Croix.

This park was named after William O'Brien, a logger who bought surrounding river front land after it was logged. Now a haven for wildlife and variety of vegetation, this park also offers fine swimming on Lake Alice, canoe and boat rental (for both lake and river). The Interpretive Center and trail center is open year round, offering lots of programs and activities. Bulletin boards post those schedules.

Bike Shorts

Minnesota has more miles of paved rail to trail bikeways than any other state.

The Willard Munger Trail from Hinckley, MN to Duluth, MN is currently the longest paved rail-trail in the nation.

The Heartland Trail in Minnesota, dating to 1975, is the oldest paved rail-trail in the nation.

FOR MORE INFORMATION:

William O'Brien State Park
16821 O'Brien Trail North
Marine on St. Croix, MN 55042
651-433-0500

WILLIAM O'BRIEN STATE PARK TRAIL

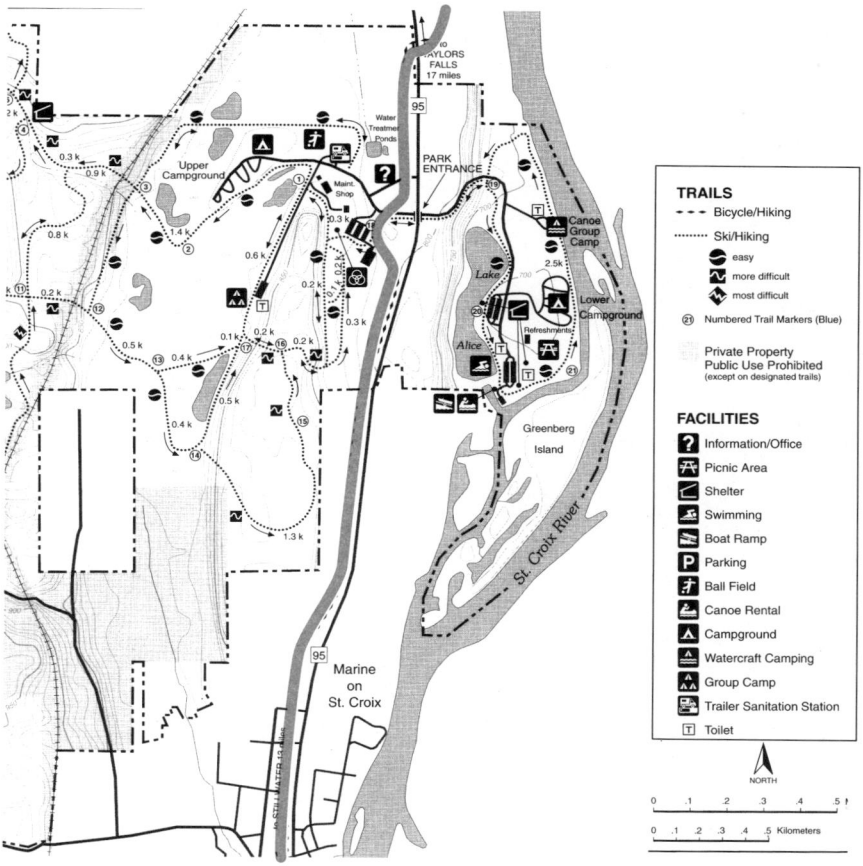

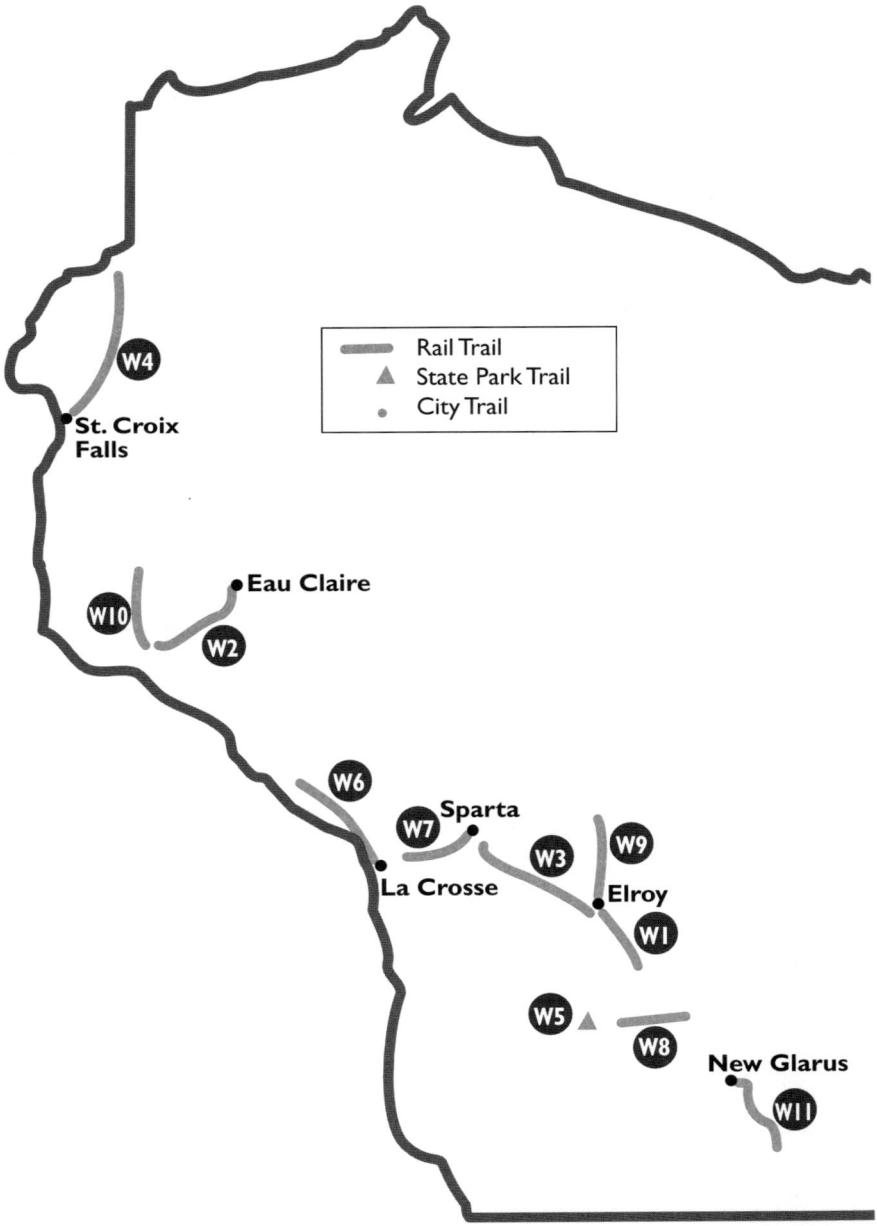
Rail Trail
State Park Trail
City Trail
W4
St. Croix Falls
Eau Claire
W10
W2
W6
W7
Sparta
W3
W9
La Crosse
Elroy
W1
W5
W8
New Glarus
W11

Western Wisconsin

Wisconsin Information. . . . . page 194

Trail

W1. 400 State Trail . . . . . .page 196
W2. Chippewa River State Park Trail . . . . . .page 200
W3. Elroy-Sparta State Park Trail . . . . . .page 204
W4. Gandy Dancer . . . . . .page 208
W5. Governor Dodge State Park . . . . . .page 219
W6. Great River State Park Trail . . . . . .page 212
W7. LaCrosse River State Park Trail . . . . . .page 216
W8. Military Ridge State Trail . . . . . .page 218
W9. Omaha Trail . . . . . .page 222
W10. Red Cedar State Park Trail . . . . . .page 201
W11. Sugar River State Trail . . . . . .page 224

*** Numbers refer to large map on page 11 and opposite page**

WISCONSIN INFORMATION

Although paved trails in Wisconsin are relatively few, the increasing popularity of in-line skating, as well as hiking, is bringing more demand for asphalt. More paving such as was done on the Chippewa River and Omaha Trails can be expected in the future.

The Wisconsin DNR Bureau of Parks and Recreation has a continuing program of expansion and improvement of its off-road biking systems. Wisconsin currently maintains over 470 miles of improved rail bed trails.

Most of the rail bed trails are surfaced with crushed limestone and intersect with numerous small communities providing frequent access, rest and refreshment stops. Quite recently, individual counties have constructed trails with the assistance of and under a memorandum of agreement with the Wisconsin State DNR. In those cases, the county supervises and maintains the trail and may or may not charge the same fee as the state. Current user fees for county trails are indicated with each county trail in this book as is the county headquarters phone number should you desire additional information.

Wisconsin trail hours are 6:00 AM to 11:00 PM. Although most remain surfaced with screened, crushed limestone, there is expanded use of hard surfacing on some of the newest trails.

Wisconsin State Trails require trail user fees. Daily passes are $3.00 per day or a season pass is available for $10.00. Passes are available at all trail headquarters, from rangers you may encounter along the trail, from businesses near the trail in non-headquarter communities (inquire locally), or from DNR at the following address:

Wisconsin Department of Natural Resources
Park Division, P.O. Box 7921
Madison, WI 53707
608-266-2181

The Wisconsin Department of Tourism has available a comprehensive publication, "Wisconsin Biking Guide" which is free. It includes 15 off-road trails, 14 on-road bike tours and 14 mountain bike trails with maps of most of them. Write or call:

The Department of Tourism
201 W. Washington, P.O. Box 7976
Madison, WI 53707-7976
608-266-2161, 800-372-2737.

Individual trail maps are now available from the Bicycle Federation of Wisconsin at the following address. Maps are grouped by each quarter of the state and you will receive all maps within a specified area for $3.95 plus $2.00 handling, or all four maps for $12.95 plus $5.00 handling. Write or call:

Bicycle Federation of Wisconsin
104 King Street, Madison, WI 53707
608-251-4456, 800-362-4537.

Bike Shorts

Biking is second only to walking as the most popular outdoor sport activity in Minnesota. Bikeways have been the most requested recreational facility since 1983.

The most certain way to ride regularly is to develop a group of interested friends.

400 STATE TRAIL

WHERE: Elroy to Reedsburg
LENGTH: 22 miles
SURFACE: Crushed limestone
TRAIL USE:

Trailhead North: At the Commons in Elroy.

Mid Access: At Union Center, Wonewoc and LaValle.

Trailhead South: At Reedsburg.

A scenic ride paralleling the Baraboo River, this trail includes ten river crossings as well as a number of feeder streams. The Baraboo is popular with canoeists and you may also encounter horseback riders because a horse trail runs alongside the 400 between Wonewoc and LaValle.

This trail gets its name from a very well-known passenger train of its day, the old Chicago Northwestern "400" from Chicago to the Twin Cities.

Three Wisconsin bike trails merge in Elroy where the city has recently developed a downtown park with connections to each trail. The Commons provide parking, restrooms, pay showers, lockers, picnic facilities and even a "tot lot." Restaurants, stores and the Elroy Area Historical Society are all nearby.

Note: There is a new country trail connecting Hillsboro and Highway 80 to the 400 Trail at Union Center. It is paved and 3½ miles long. (Wildcat State Park is near Hillsboro)

FOR MORE INFORMATION:

The Depot
240 Railroad Street, P.O. Box 142
Reedsburg, WI 53959-0142
608-524-2850
800-844-3507

Elroy Commons
303 Railroad Street
Elroy WI 53959-0142
608-462-2453
888-606-2453

Bike Shorts

Padded cycling gloves reduce tiring and numbness of hands and wrists.

If it clicks, scrapes, squeaks or rattles, your bike needs fixing.

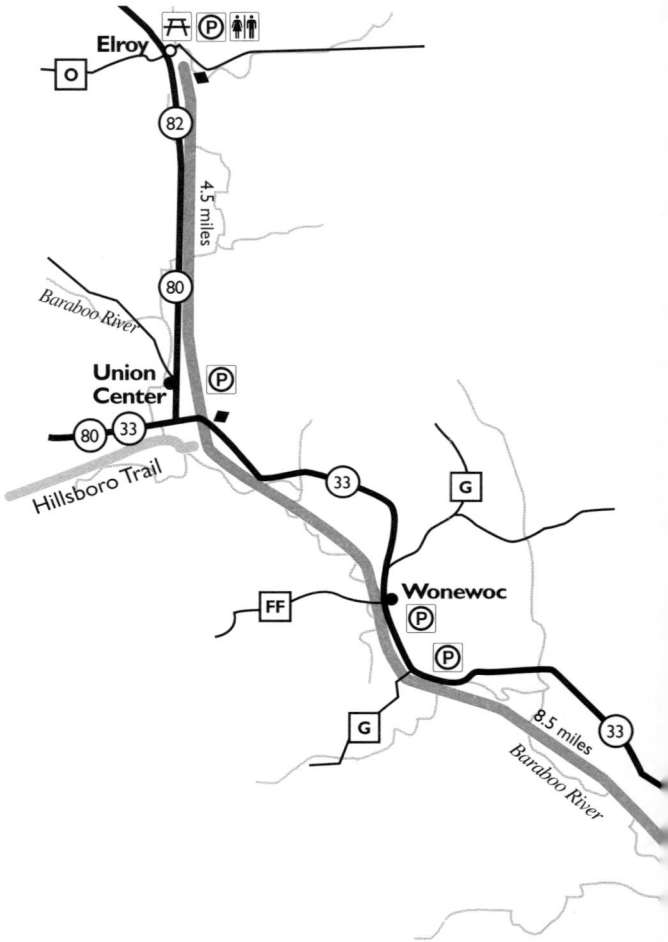
Elroy
O
82
4.5 miles
80
Baraboo River
Union Center
80
33
Hillsboro Trail
33
G
Wonewoc
FF
G
8.5 miles
33
Baraboo River

N
Parking
Restrooms
Picnic Area
Camping
Paved Bike Trail
Unpaved Trail
On-road Trail
Distance Marker

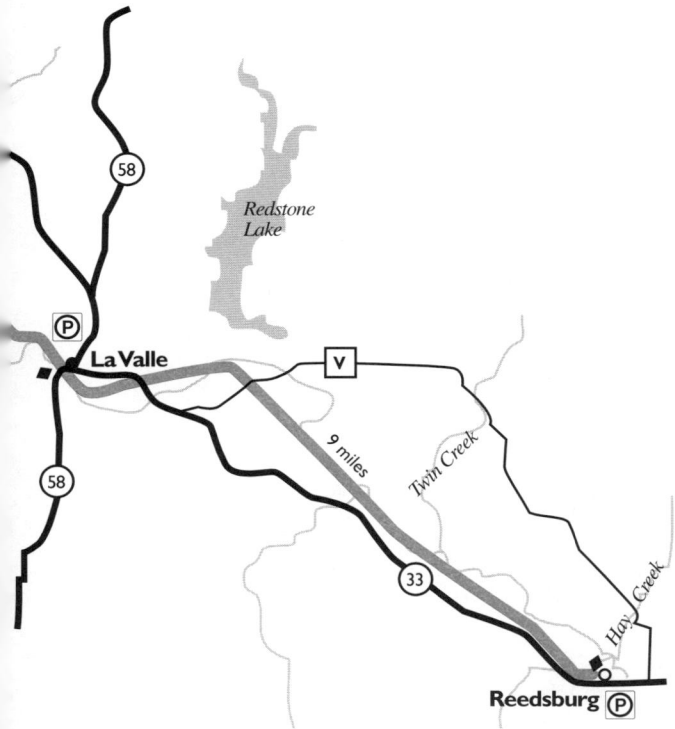
58
Redstone
Lake
P
La Valle
V
9 miles
Twin Creek
58
33
Hay Creek
Reedsburg
P

CHIPPEWA RIVER STATE PARK

WHERE: Eau Claire to Red Cedar State Park Trail
LENGTH: 20 miles
SURFACE: Asphalt from Eau Claire to Caryville. Asphalt emulsion Caryville to the west trailhead.
TRAIL USE:

Trailhead East: The trail begins in downtown Eau Claire, at First Avenue along the Chippewa River. Parking and trail access are also available at the University campus, located at 1st and Water Street.

Mid Access: At Meridean and Caryville. Also at the Highway 85 wayside park, located 8 miles from Eau Claire. The wayside park offers parking, restrooms and water.

Trailhead West: As yet, the Wisconsin DNR has not been successful in obtaining public access to the point where the Chippewa Trail connects with the Red Cedar State Park Trail. The best bet for now is to take County Road Y east at Dunnville, and ride the Red Cedar State Park Trail for the short distance south across the bridge.

This is one of the few Wisconsin State Trails with a surface other than crushed limestone. It is an easy trail, though somewhat open, so wind may be a factor.

See map pages 202.

FOR MORE INFORMATION:

Western Division DNR
1300 W. Clairmont Avenue,
P.O. Box 4001
Eau Claire, Wi 54701-6127
715-839-1607

Eau Claire Area Convention
and Visitors Bureau
800-344-3866

WHERE: Menomonie to Chippewa River State Trail
LENGTH: 14.5 miles
SURFACE: Crushed limestone
TRAIL USE:

Trailhead North: On Highway 29 in west Menomonie at Riverside Park. Take the second exit west of the Highway 29 bridge to the renovated depot.

Mid Access: At Irvington on Highway D (mile 2.7), Downsville on Highway 25 (mile 7.5), and Dunnville on Highway Y (mile 12.5).

Trailhead South: The trail ends after crossing the Chippewa River on an 800-foot trestle at the junction with the Chippewa River State Trail, off of County Road M.

As with most Wisconsin trails, the Red Cedar is surfaced with well-maintained crushed limestone. On this trail, you will pass through woodlands, prairies and unique rock formations. For most of its distance, the trail overlooks the Red Cedar River, which is also popular with canoeists. Several picnic tables have been provided in scenic spots where you can rest and relax.

Just after crossing the Chippewa River, you connect with the western end of the new Chippewa River Trail. We found the wide and sandy shores of the Chippewa to be an excellent picnic spot. This trail also offers riders the opportunity to ride an 800-foot trestle, perhaps the longest of any bike trail, and enjoy a spectacular view in the process.

Since its total length is only 14½ miles, this is a very manageable two-way ride, no matter where you start. Give yourself some extra time for this ride since there are so many interesting things to see and do along the way. In the area you will find the Downsville Cooperative Creamery, which was founded in 1904 and currently houses a restaurant, lounge and four room inn, in addition to the showroom and shop where Dunn County Pottery is designed and created.

See map pages 202.

FOR MORE INFORMATION:

Red Cedar State Park Trail
921 Brickyard Road
Menomonie, WI 54751-9100
715-232-1242

Greater Menomonie Area
Chamber of Commerce
700 Wolske Bay Road, Suite 200
Menomonie, WI 54751
715-235-9087, 800-283-1862

CHIPPEWA RIVER & RED CEDAR STATE PARK

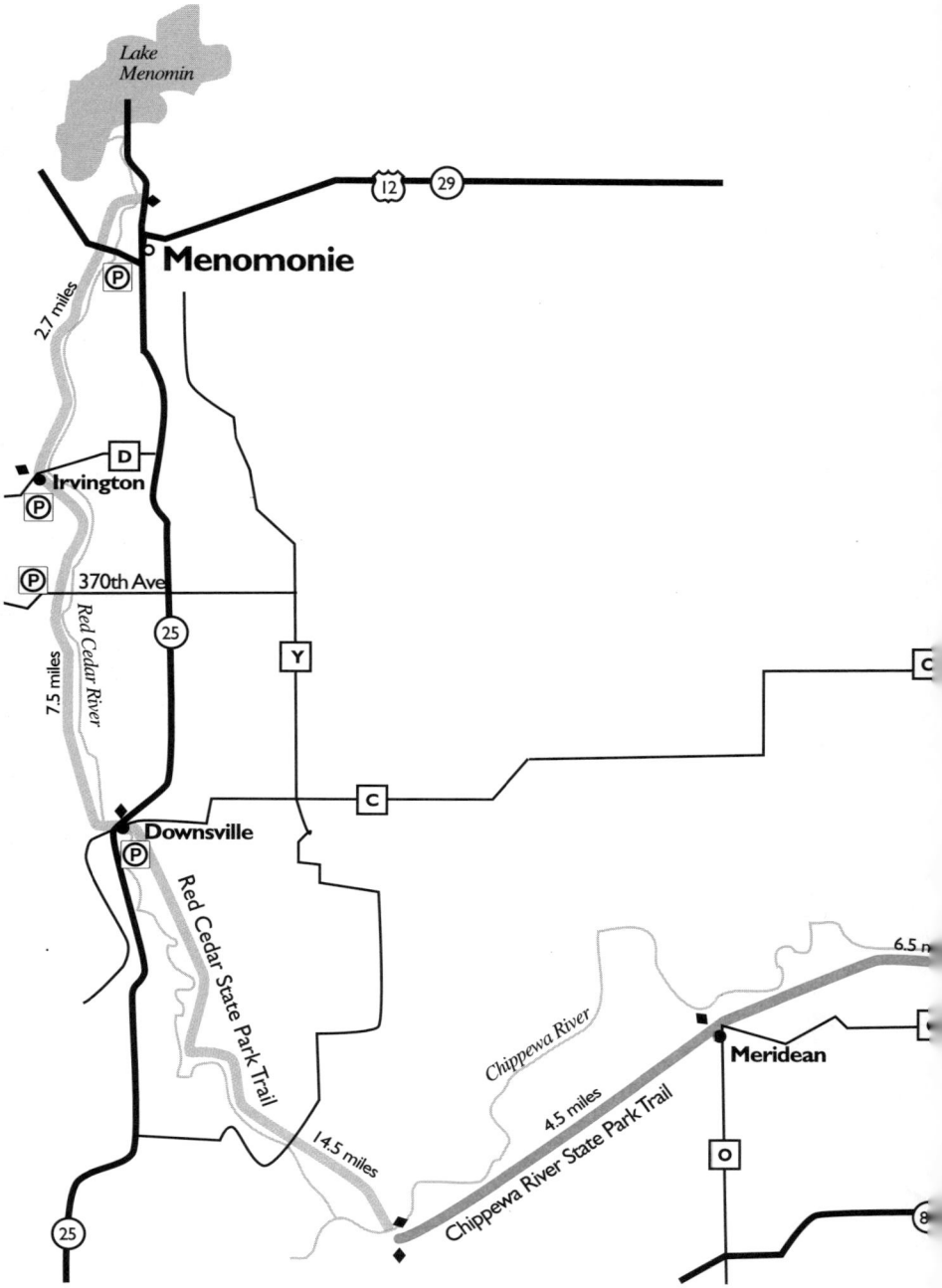

CHIPPEWA RIVER & RED CEDAR STATE PARK

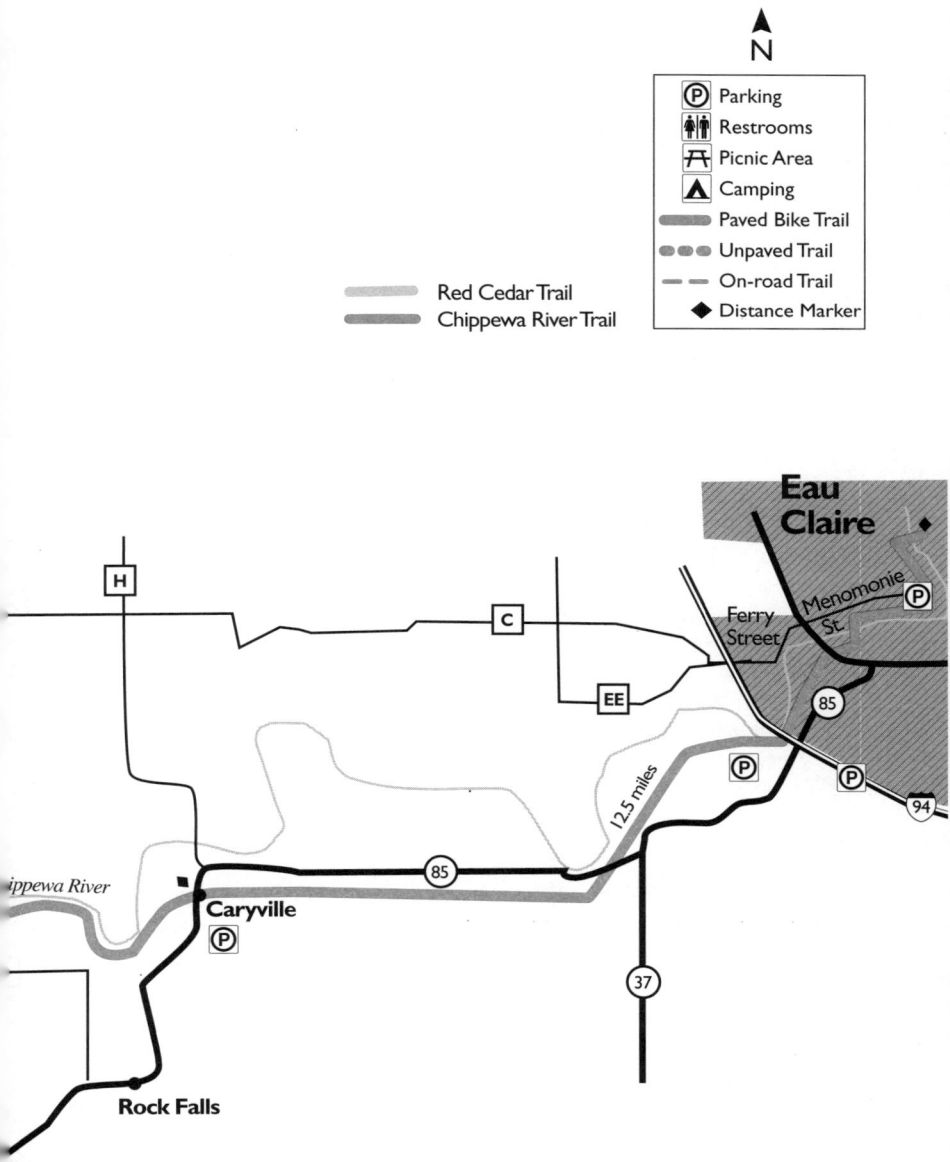

ELROY SPARTA STATE PARK

WHERE: Sparta to Elroy
LENGTH: 32 miles
SURFACE: Crushed limestone
TRAIL USE: 

Trailhead West: At exit I-90 at Highway 27, Sparta. Start at the newly renovated depot at South Water and Milwaukee (also the east terminus of the LaCrosse State Trail, page 216). Follow the well-marked city streets south out of town to the actual trailhead on the left of the road. There is also parking here.

Mid Access: At Norwalk on Highway 71 and County Road T (trail mile 11.9), at Wilton on Highway 71 and County Road M (trail mile 17.3), and at Kendall on Highway 71 and County Road W (trail mile 26.4). The trail headquarters is located at Kendall, 5.7 miles from the east trail access.

Trailhead East: At the west edge of Elroy, just north of Highway 71. Three Wisconsin bike trails merge in Elroy, where the city has recently developed a downtown park with connections to each trail. The Commons provide parking, restrooms, pay showers, lockers, picnic facilities and even a "tot lot." Restaurants, stores and the Elroy Area Historical Society are nearby.

The Elroy-Sparta Trail traverses the Hidden Valley country of Wisconsin providing spectacular scenery as well as great bird watching and possible wildlife sightings. (The entire trail is a wildlife refuge.) The area is heavily-wooded, providing shelter from sun and wind. The woods also make this an extremely popular ride during the fall color season.

The rugged and scenic attraction of the area probably tells you this trail is not the level or gradually-inclined roadbed of the prairie or river bottom. In fact, there are few level stretches, with long, rather steep (for a rail bed) inclines. The long upgrades are matched by equally long downgrades that give you the chance to rest up. This trail does, however, require more physical conditioning and stamina than most 32 mile rides.

There are three upgrades, each leading to tunnel cuts through solid rock. Those tunnels make the trail unique. Tunnel 3, at mile 12.4 from the west end, is seven-tenths of a mile long. Tunnel 2, at mile19.5, is three-tenths of a mile long and tunnel 1, at mile 25.3, is one-quarter of a mile long. For tunnel 3, special equipment not taken along on most bike trips is highly recommended. A three-quarter mile tunnel is long and dark and you will need a flashlight. You may need an extra wrap as tunnels can be both cold and damp. You will need to walk your bike at least through tunnel 3, so it will take awhile. The spirit of adventure provided by the tunnels really adds something special to this trip.

In the valleys between each tunnel (as well as at each end) are interesting small towns that truly welcome bikers and provide food, refreshments and restrooms. Of special interest is the refurbished depot at Kendall which has been designated a national historic landmark. It also serves as the trail headquarters and a railroad museum.

For the casual or weekend biker, a one-way trip is a full day ride. This necessitates staying overnight or dropping a car at one end. Should your party want to drop a car, Highway 71 parallels the trail all the way. If you have only one vehicle, this is one of the few trails that provides a driver service. Take two sets of keys with you and pick up a driver at the Kendall headquarters. The driver will drop you at your starting point and return your car to Kendall. There is a nominal fee and reservations are recommended.

The foresight of responsible individuals and the State of Wisconsin has provided us with a truly exceptional bike trail in an unusually scenic area. It has been maintained and in use since 1965 and has become well known nationally among biking enthusiasts.

While you're in the area, you might want to check out Kendall's annual Labor Day weekend celebration which features a parade, dance and plenty of barbecued chicken and sweet corn. In Wilton, the Lions Club serves pancake breakfasts in the municipal park Sunday mornings from June to September. Finally, you'll find that Sparta has a 34-acre lake.

FOR MORE INFORMATION:

Bike Trail Headquarters
Kendall Depot
P.O. Box 297
Kendall WI 54638-0297
608-463-7109

Elroy Commons
303 Railroad Street
Elroy, WI 53929
608-462-2453,888-606-2453

Sparta Chamber of Commerce
111 Milwaukee Street
Sparta, WI 54656
608-269-4123, 800-354-2453

ELROY SPARTA STATE PARK

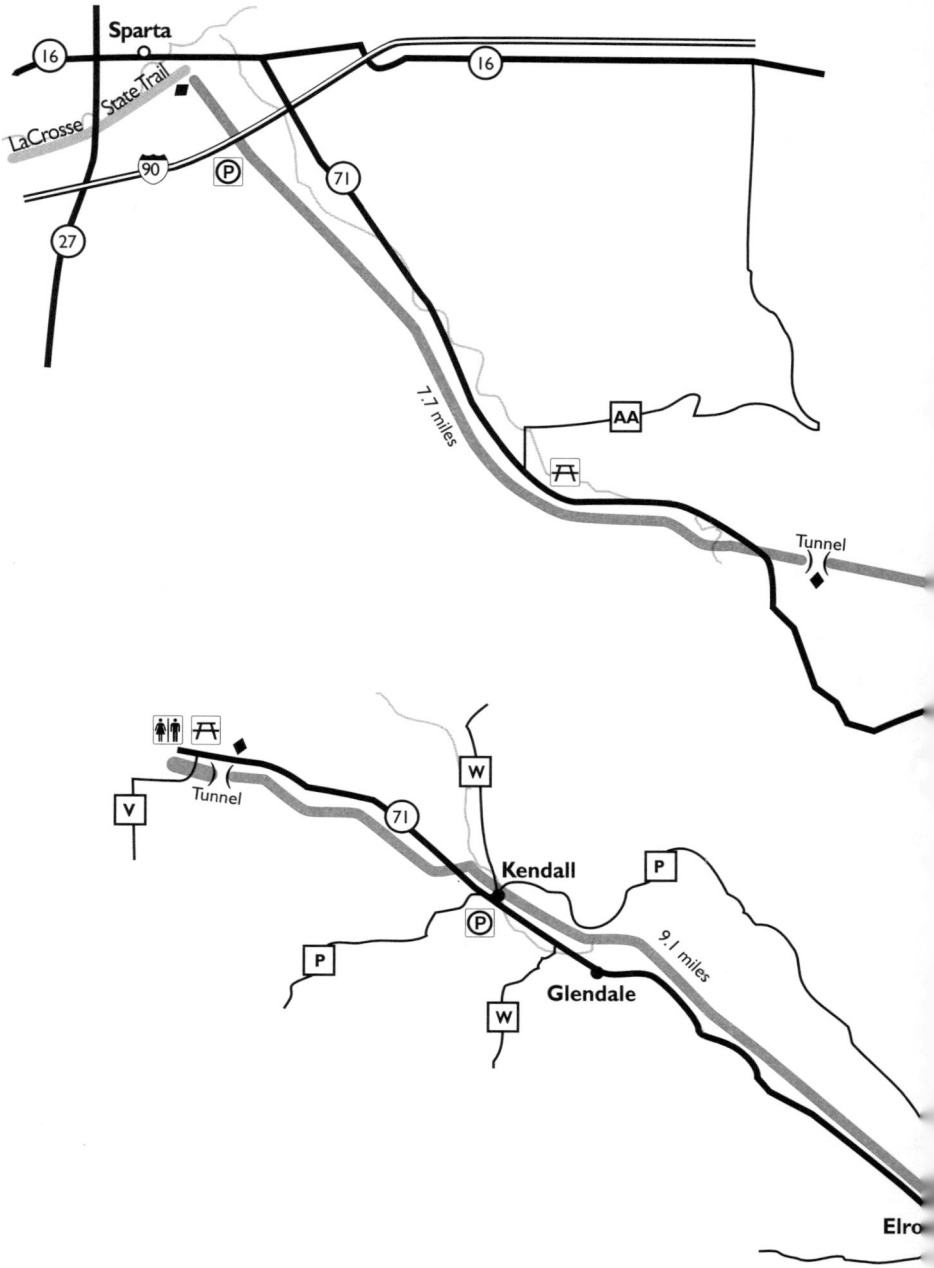

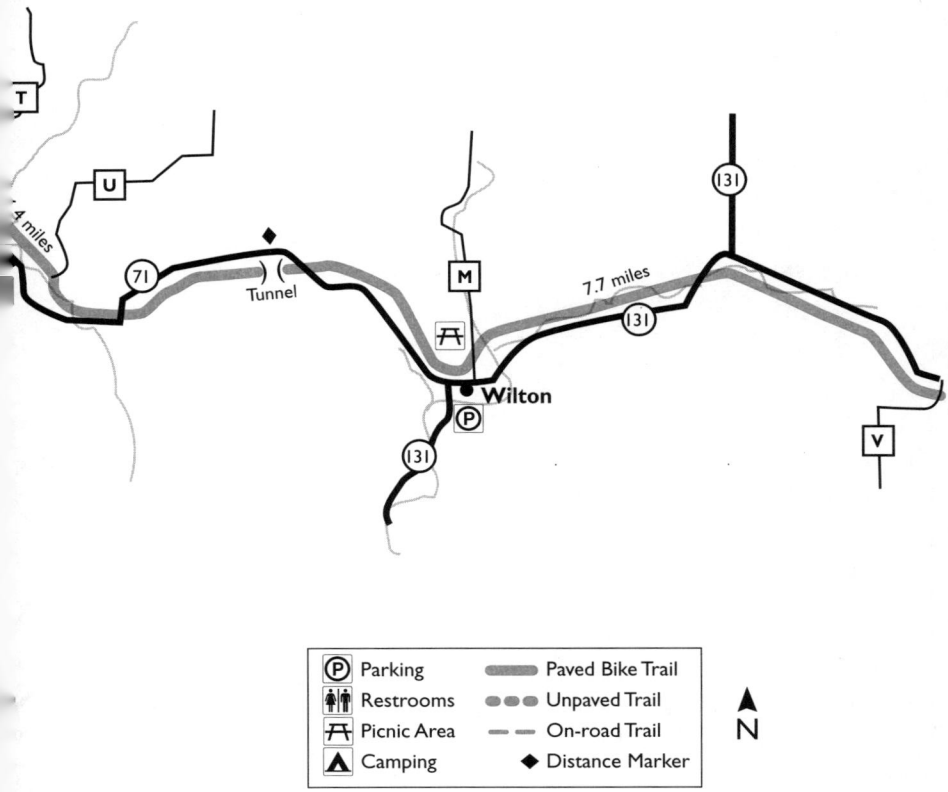
T
U
4 miles
71
Tunnel
M
7.7 miles
131
131
Wilton
P
131
V
Parking
Restrooms
Picnic Area
Camping
Paved Bike Trail
Unpaved Trail
On-road Trail
Distance Marker
N

GANDY DANCER

WHERE: Danbury to St. Croix Falls
LENGTH: 47 miles
SURFACE: 10' wide crushed limestone
TRAIL USE:

Trailhead South: The Polk County Information Center at the Junction of Highways 8 and Highway 35. You will find parking and restrooms there.

Mid Access: The trail passes through Centura, Milltown, Luck, Frederic, Lewis, Siren and Webster. In our opinion, Frederic, Siren and Webster offer the best parking near the trail.

Trailhead North: At Danbury. The trail terminates at Highway 77, on the west edge of town. There is parking here. The ATV, snowmobile and horse trail continues north from Highway 77. The St. Croix State Park, on the Minnesota side of the river, is just a short ride west on Highway 77 from the trail access.

The existence of this trail is the result of unique cooperation between Burnett and Polk Counties, and the Wisconsin Department of Natural Resources. The DNR secured the railroad right-of-way and the counties undertook the construction, maintenance and administration. This trail is jointly administered by Polk and Burnett Counties Park & Forestry Department.

The old rail bed and right-of-way crosses into Minnesota a short distance north of Danbury via a high trestle over the scenic St. Croix River. This unimproved 51-mile segment extends all the way from Danbury to Superior with Minnesota responsible for completing about two-thirds of that and Douglas County, Wisconsin responsible for one-third. Although improvement of this segment is not planned for the near future, the Gandy Dancer will eventually extend a wonderful 98 miles. (Note: A "Gandy Dancer" is the historical nickname for railtrack-laying workmen.)

In Polk County the trail crosses three bridges and utilizes two tunnels under highways. It also features scenic cuts through rock outcroppings, woods and open farmlands that border the trail. In Frederic, the Depot is being refurbished as a museum.

In Burnett County the trail passes through woods, wetlands and farmlands. En route you will cross five bridges and have a good chance of spotting wildlife.

Bike Shorts

A large plastic bag takes little space and makes good emergency rain cover.

Always carry your own water bottle. For a cool drink, fill your water bottle the night before and freeze overnight.

FOR MORE INFORMATION:

Burnett County Forest and Parks Department
7410 County Highway K
Box 106
Siren, WI 54872
715-349-2157

Burnett County Web Site
www.mwd.com/burnett/

Burnett Department of Tourism
7410 County Road K, Box 112
Siren, WI 54872
800-788-3164

Polk County Information Center
710 Highway 35 South
St. Croix Falls, WI 54024
800-222-7655, 715-483-1410

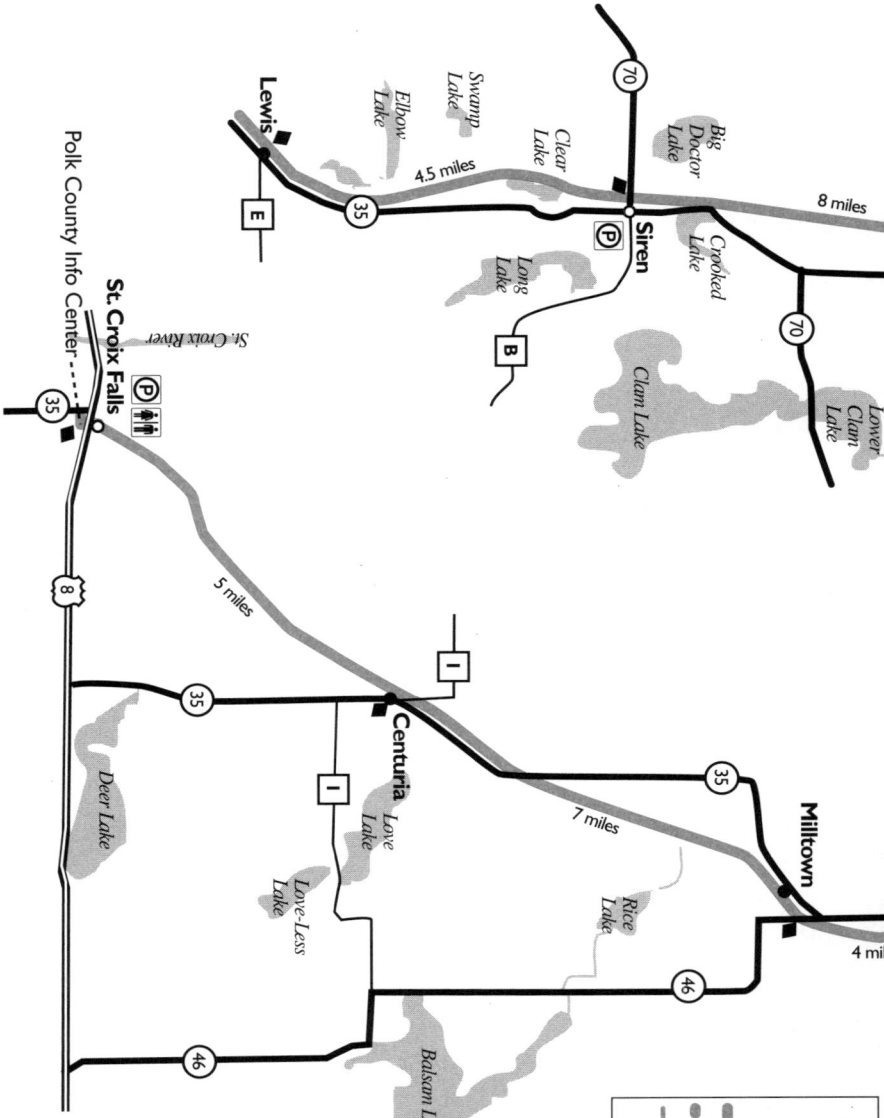
Parking
Restrooms
Picnic Area
Camping
Paved Bike Trail
Unpaved Trail
On-road Trail
Distance Marker
Milltown
4 miles
Lower Clam Lake
Clam Lake
Big Doctor Lake
Crooked Lake
8 miles
Rice Lake
Balsam Lake
Siren
Long Lake
Clear Lake
Swamp Lake
Elbow Lake
Lewis
4.5 miles
Centuria
Love Lake
Love-Less Lake
7 miles
St. Croix Falls
St. Croix River
Deer Lake
5 miles
Polk County Info Center
35
70
46
8
B
E
I

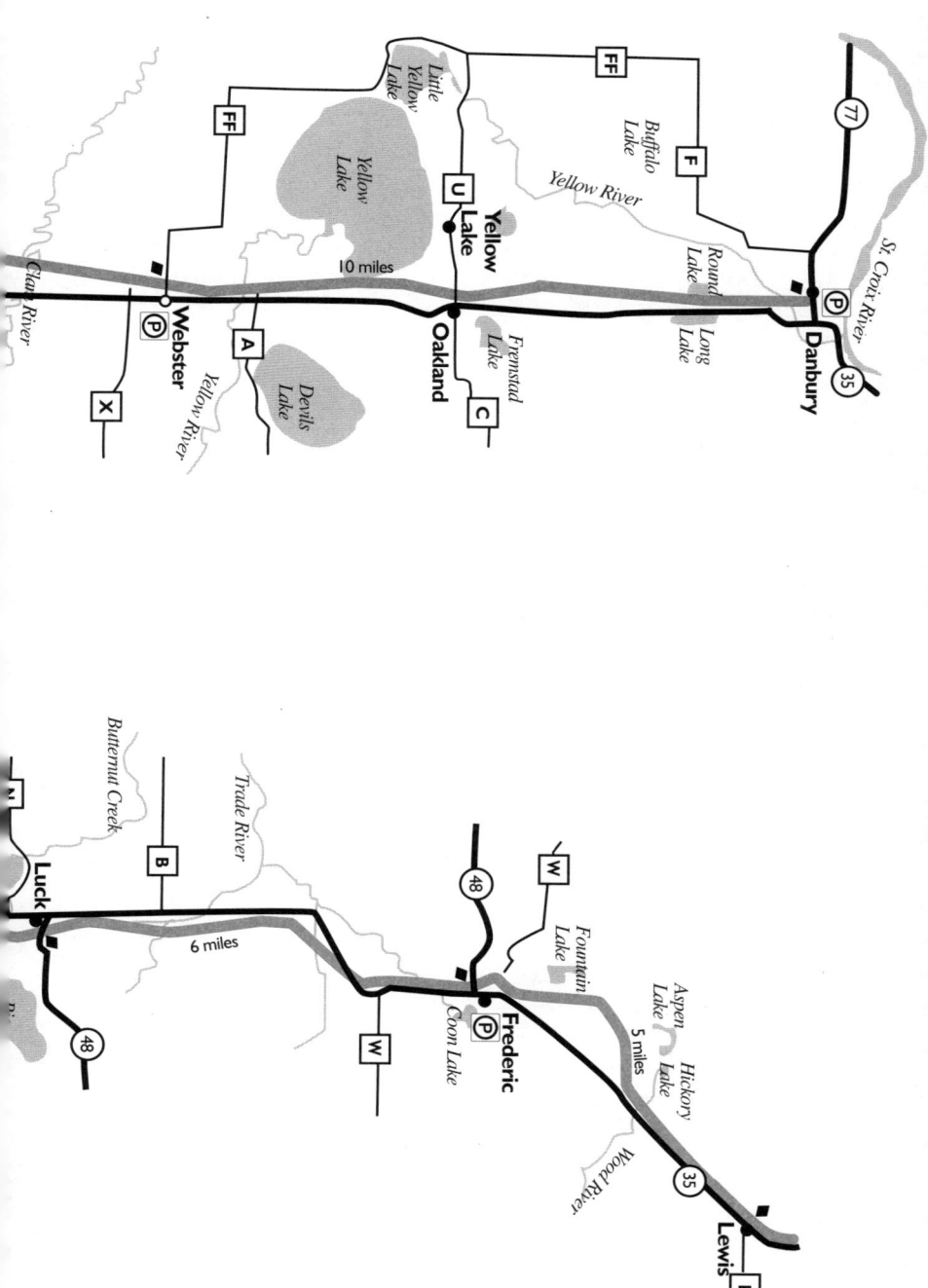
77
St. Croix River
P
35
Danbury
Round Lake
Long Lake
F
Buffalo Lake
FF
Yellow River
Yellow Lake
U
Little Yellow Lake
10 miles
Fremstad Lake
C
Oakland
Clam River
FF
A
Devils Lake
Webster
P
Yellow River
X
W
Fountain Lake
48
Frederic
P
Coon Lake
Aspen Lake
Hickory Lake
5 miles
Wood River
35
Lewis
E
Trade River
Butternut Creek
B
6 miles
W
48
Luck
N

GREAT RIVER STATE PARK

WHERE: South of Marshland to Onalaska
LENGTH: 24 miles
SURFACE: Crushed limestone
TRAIL USE:

Trailhead North: South of Marshland, Wisconsin, on Highway 35, there is a parking lot that serves as the trailhead. There are no restrooms here. The trail does not follow the rail bed until you leave the wildlife refuge. About one mile down the trail you have the option of taking the loop through the refuge. There is no fee to use the trail through the refuge.

Mid Access: There are parking lots at Perrot State Park, Lytles and Midway. Near the city of Trempealeau, on Highway 35, there is a large parking lot with portable restrooms.

Trailhead South: The separate rail bed trail ends near downtown Onalaska where it continues about four blocks on city streets. The streets are well-marked and bring you to the actual trailhead at the Center for Commerce and Tourism, a four-year-old brick building with restrooms and ample paved parking at 800 Oak Forest Road. From the same building, there is a paved connection to the parking lot and west trailhead of the LaCrosse River State Trail (see page 216) just south of Highway 16. At substantial expense, the state recently built a bridge over some active railroad tracks to permit a safe, off-road connection between these two trails.

For a close-up look at waterfowl, wildlife, river bottoms and bluffs, this Wisconsin trail is an excellent choice. Generally sheltered and shaded, it crosses two national refuges and 18 bridges, including one that is 1226 feet long.

Because of the scenery, a side trip through Perrot State Park, and watching a tow lock through Lock & Dam #6, we found this trail took a bit more time than its 24 miles would indicate. Although riding both ways in one day is not unreasonable, you may prefer a more leisurely trip for these same reasons. We found overnighting in Trempealeau suited our schedule, riding south 14 miles and then back one afternoon, and then north the 10 miles and back the next morning.

Bike Shorts

Rail beds provide opportunity for bike trails that require little surface preparation and little tree removal. They also often provide access to scenic vistas not otherwise available.

Footwear is important in biking. Choose shoes with a fairly rigid sole.

FOR MORE INFORMATION:

Perrot State Park
P.O. Box 407
Trempealeau, WI 54661
608-534-6409

Trempealeau Chamber of Commerce
P.O. Box 212
Trempealeau, WI 54661-0212
608-534-6780

Onalaska Tourism
800 Oak Forest Drive
Onalaska, WI 54650
800-873-1901

GREAT RIVER STATE PARK

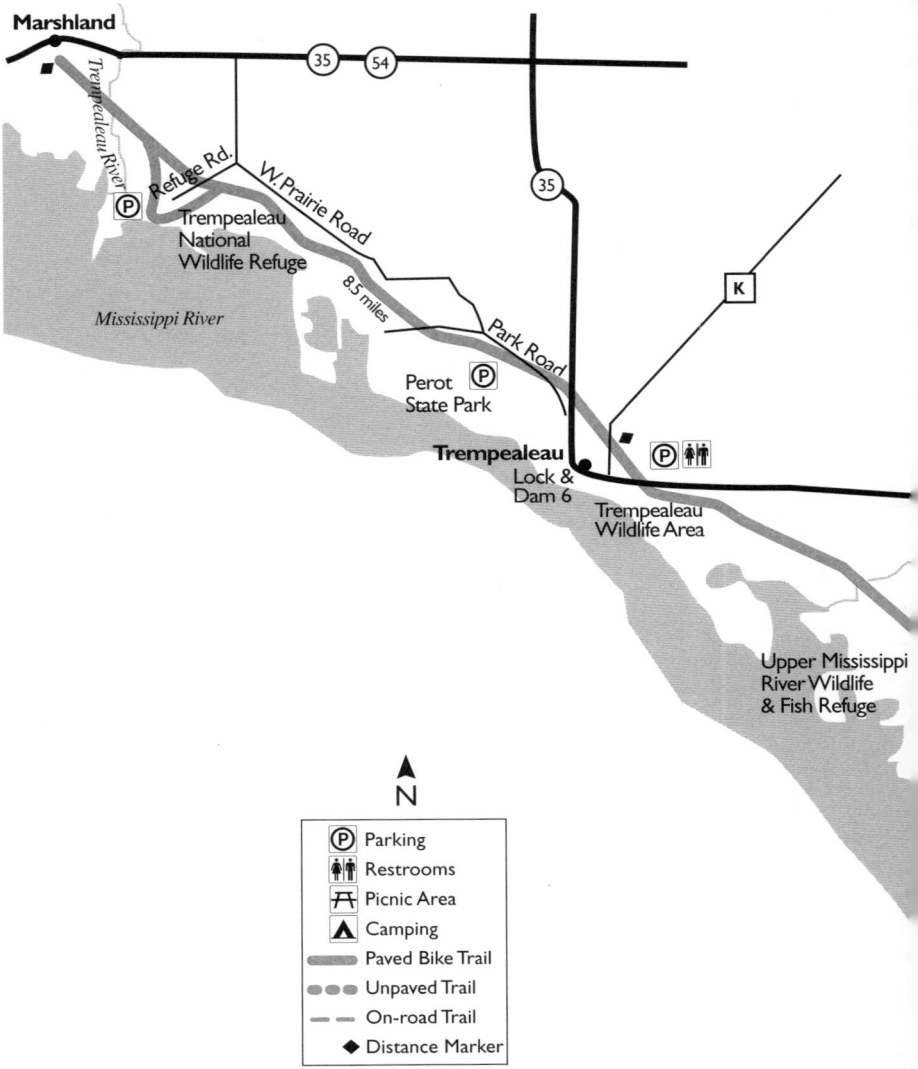

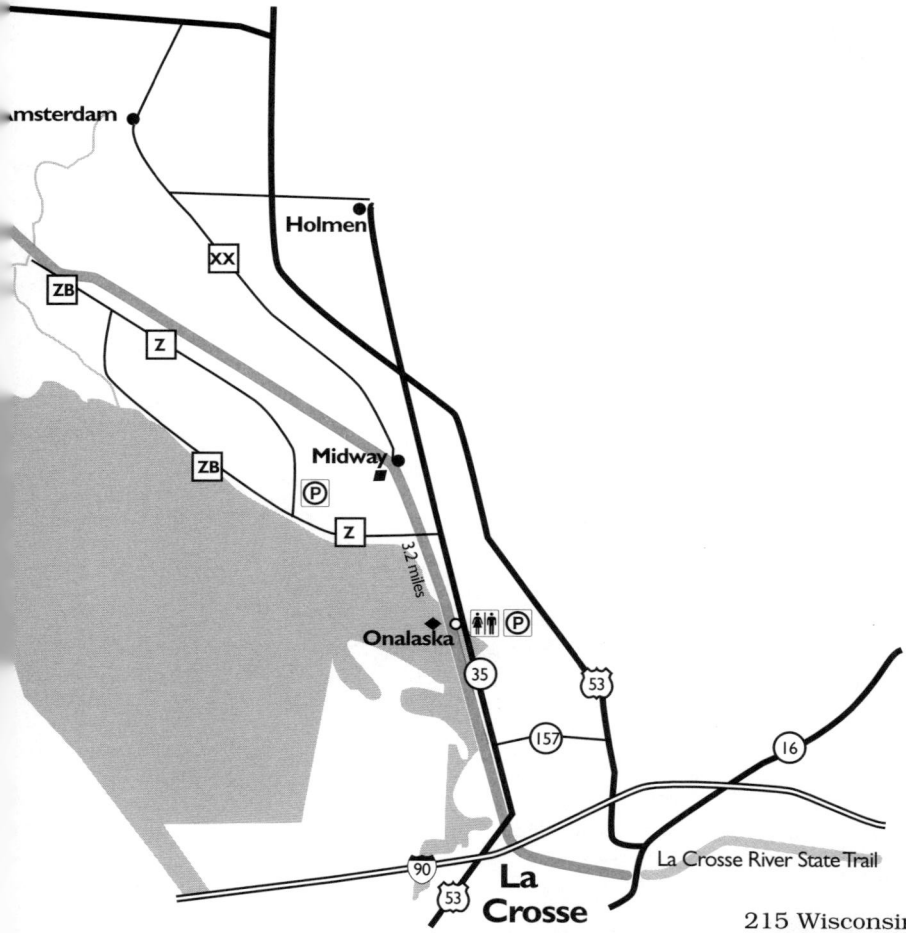
msterdam
Holmen
XX
ZB
Z
ZB
Midway
Z
3.2 miles
Onalaska
35
53
157
16
90
53
La Crosse
La Crosse River State Trail

LACROSSE RIVER STATE PARK

WHERE: LaCrosse to Sparta
LENGTH: 21.5 miles
SURFACE: Crushed limestone
TRAIL USE:

Trailhead West: Exit Highway 16 East at the stop lights at the Highway B intersection in north LaCrosse. Go approximately one-quarter mile on Highway B to the Medary parking lot, on the left.

Mid Access: Highway 108 south of West Salem. Bangor and at intersecting county roads.

Trailhead East: On the south edge of Sparta. Follow the street signs to the renovated depot at the intersection of South Water and Milwaukee in Sparta. You will find ample parking and facilities in Sparta.

This is one of the newer rail-trails in western Wisconsin and connects the Great River and Elroy-Sparta trails. Its roadbed and bridges are in excellent condition and the length provides a challenging two-way ride or an easy one-way day trip.

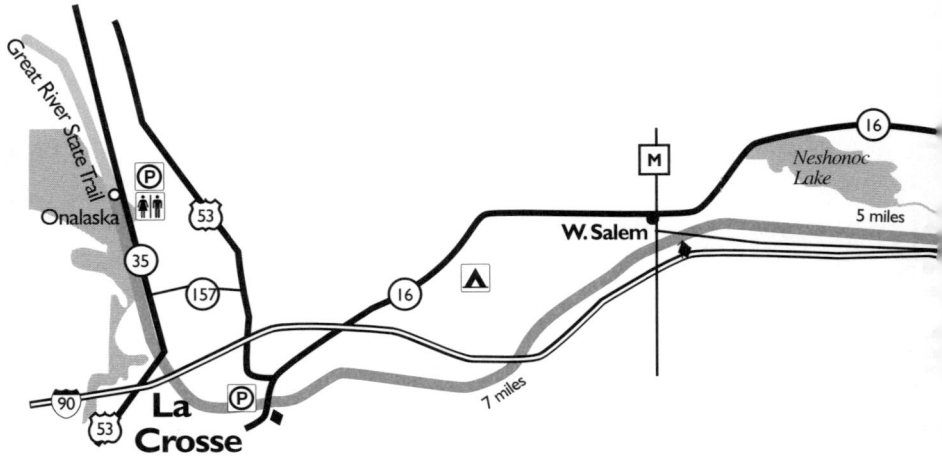

Much of its 21½ miles parallels the LaCrosse River and provides a variety of scenery including farmlands, hardwood forests and wetlands. It also parallels I-90 for much of the distance between north LaCrosse and Sparta. Unfortunately, there are some points where this detracts somewhat from the serenity of the ride. The connection to the Great River State Trail takes you north on County Road B, under Highway 16 and over a recently completed bridge spanning active rail tracks. From the bridge, the paved connection continues to the Onalaska Center for Commerce and Tourism at 800 Oak Forest Road. The latter is the southern trailhead of the Great River State Trail (see page 212).

FOR MORE INFORMATION:

LaCrosse River State Trail
P.O. Box 99
Ontario, WI 54651
608-337-4775

Onalaska Tourism
800 Oak Forest Drive
Onalaska, WI 54650
800-873-1901
Open weekends May-October

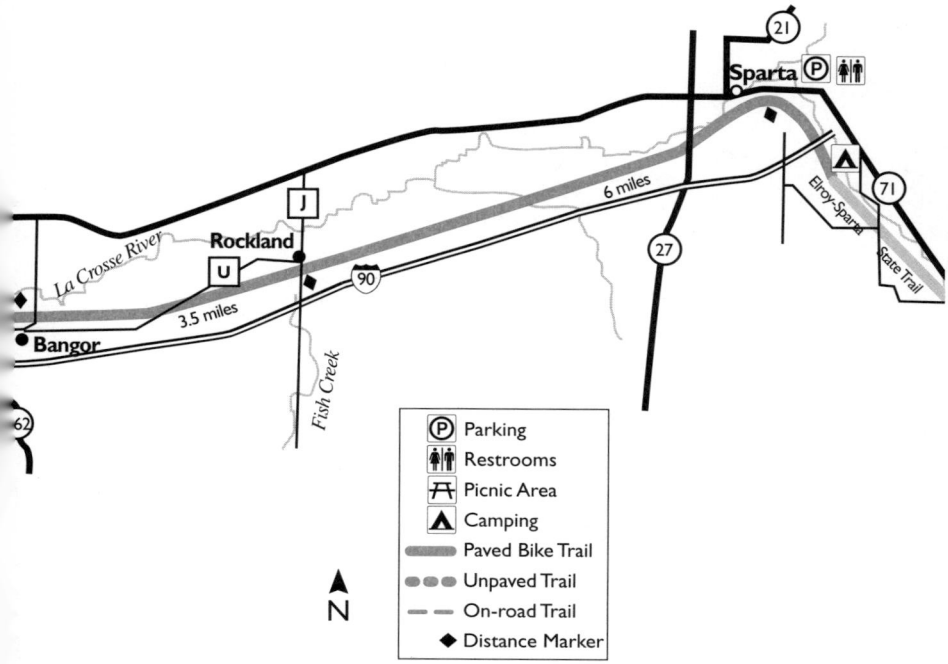

MILITARY RIDGE

WHERE: Verona to Dodgeville
LENGTH: 39.6 miles
SURFACE: Crushed limestone
TRAIL USE:

Trailhead East: The trail actually begins one mile east of Verona but this location offers no facilities. The trail runs through Verona where you will find everything you need including parking, restrooms, bike repair and trail passes.

Mid Access: At Riley at County Road J, Klevenville on County Road P, Barneveld at County Road T, Ridgeway at County Road H, and Mt. Horeb, the trail's midpoint, which has a trailside parking lot, but no restrooms, located 1½ blocks south of County Road PD on either 1st or 2nd Street. Also, the Blue Mounds State Park has parking and restrooms.

Trailhead West: At Dodgeville, just east of Highway 23 and County Road YZ. At the 2½ mile connection to Governor Dodge State Park you will find parking but no restrooms. Parking and facilities are available in other sections of the park (see page 219 for park trails)

Military Ridge Trail follows a route originally traveled by buffalo and Indians. Part of this route was converted to a Highway by General Zachary Taylor and subsequently the path became a rail bed.

This is an historic and scenic ride with a maximum grade of one-half percent. Along the route you will encounter 48 planked bridges. We found the Mt. Horeb to Verona portion to be the most scenic although it is also the more difficult of the two halves. The grade rises almost all the way west from Verona back to Mt. Horeb.

This is one of the oldest trails in Wisconsin and has shelters and picnic tables at scattered locations, but most facilities are provided by the communities and businesses along the trail.

In the area you will find the Blue Mounds, Governor Dodge State Parks, Little Norway and the trolls of Mt. Horeb. Finally, Madison is only a short distance from Verona.

FOR MORE INFORMATION:

Military Ridge State Park Trail
P.O. Box 98
Blue Mounds, WI 53517
608-935-5119

Dodgeville Chamber of Commerce
Dodgeville, WI 53533
608-935-5993

GOLD MINE TRAIL: 2.5 miles
MEADOW VALLEY: 6.8 miles
MILL CREEK: 3.3 miles
USER FEES: The park honors State Trail passes
TRAIL USE:

Located just north of Dodgeville, this park is one of the largest in Wisconsin. With over 12 miles of paved trail and a paved connection to the well-known Military Ridge State Park Trail, this park should be considered as a scenic addition to any Military Ridge trip. These are not rail-trails so expect some hills. The park trails connect with Military Ridge Trail just east of County Road Z in north Dodgeville (see page 218).

The Gold Mine loop is a short meandering trail through scenic woods and meadows, with a minimum of hills. The Meadow Valley loop begins at the Cox Hollow Lake beach. It has some steep hills, but is very scenic. Also beginning at the Cox Hollow Lake beach, the Mill Creek trail connects with the Military Ridge Trail to the south.

On any of the park trails you will encounter hikers, and some portions also allow horse riders. As a result, caution is advised.

FOR MORE INFORMATION:

Governor Dodge State Park
4175 State Highway 23 North
Dodgeville, WI 53533
608-935-2315

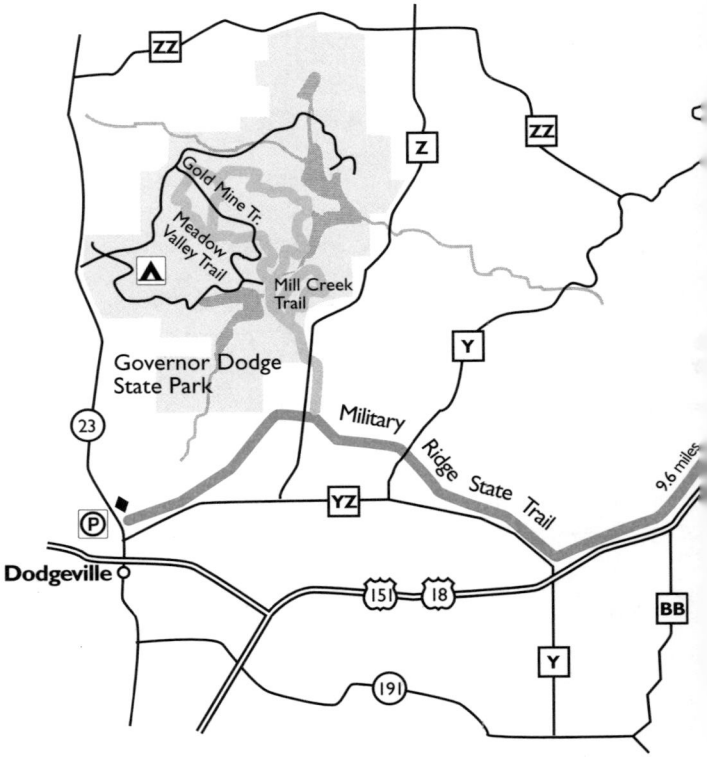
ZZ
Z
ZZ
Gold Mine Tr.
Meadow Valley Trail
Mill Creek Trail
Y
Governor Dodge State Park
23
Military Ridge State Trail
9.6 miles
YZ
Dodgeville
151
18
BB
Y
191

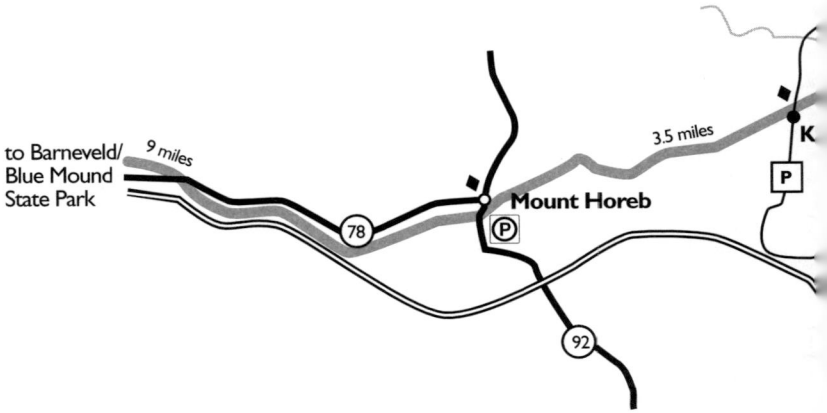
to Barneveld/ Blue Mound State Park
9 miles
78
Mount Horeb
3.5 miles
K
P
92

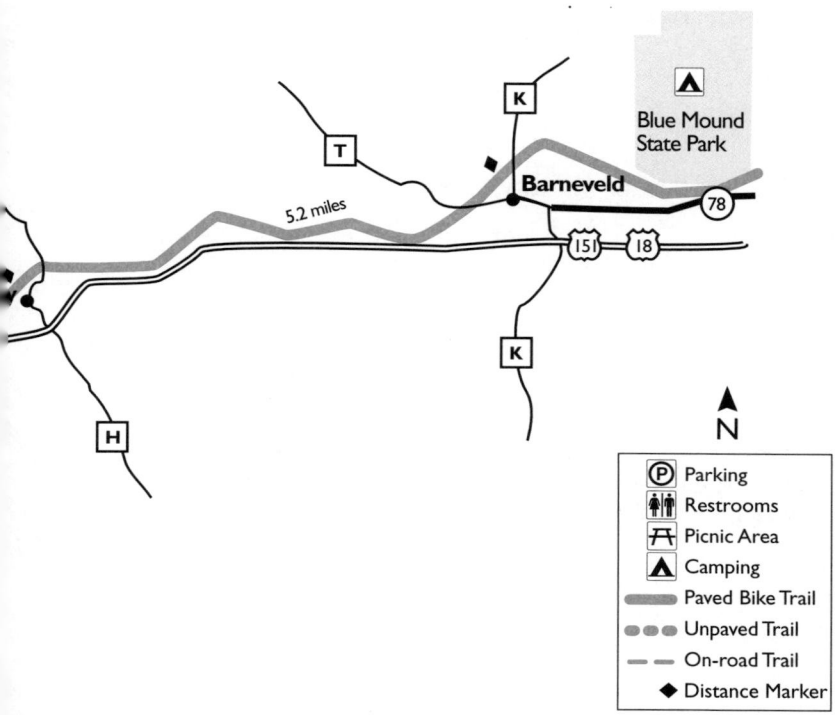
Blue Mound State Park
K
T
Barneveld
78
5.2 miles
151
18
K
H
N
Parking
Restrooms
Picnic Area
Camping
Paved Bike Trail
Unpaved Trail
On-road Trail
Distance Marker

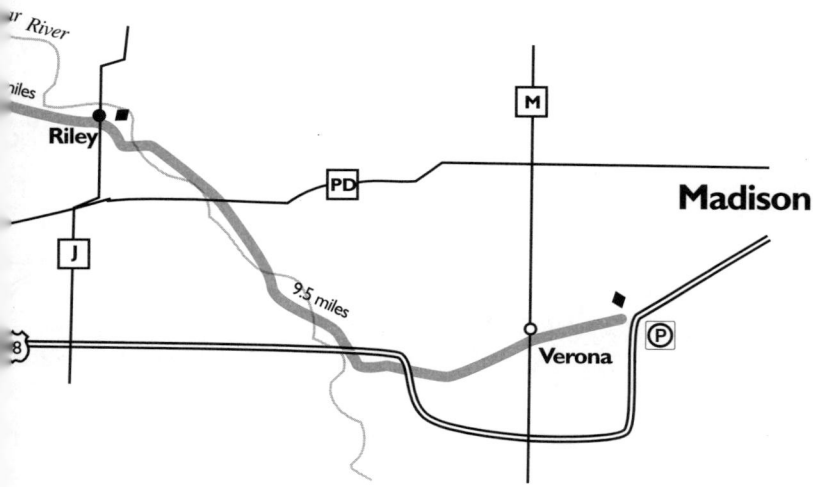
River
Riley
M
PD
Madison
J
9.5 miles
Verona

OMAHA

LENGTH: 12.5 miles
SURFACE: Paved
TRAIL FEE: $1.00 per day or $5.00 for the season.
TRAIL USE:

Trailhead South: At the Commons in downtown Elroy. You will find full facilities here including pay showers, lockers, restrooms and a picnic area.

Mid Access: At Hustler, on County Road A. The city park has parking and restrooms.

Trailhead North: At Camp Douglas, one-half mile south of I-94 at exit 55.

This trail is county owned and constructed. It is one of the newer trails in the state. Connecting to the Sparta-Elroy and the 400 Trail at Elroy, it is a beautiful ride by itself, or as an addition to either of the DNR Trails out of Elroy.

This trail traverses wooded, rolling and open vistas. It also includes 12 bridges, an overpass over Highway 80, and a tunnel over 600 feet long. At the tunnel, you will find a small park and picnic area with restrooms.

FOR MORE INFORMATION:

Juneau County Forestry and Parks
250 Oak Street
Mauston, WI 53948
608-847-9389

Elroy Commons
303 Railroad Street
Elroy, WI 53929
888-606-2453
608-462-2453

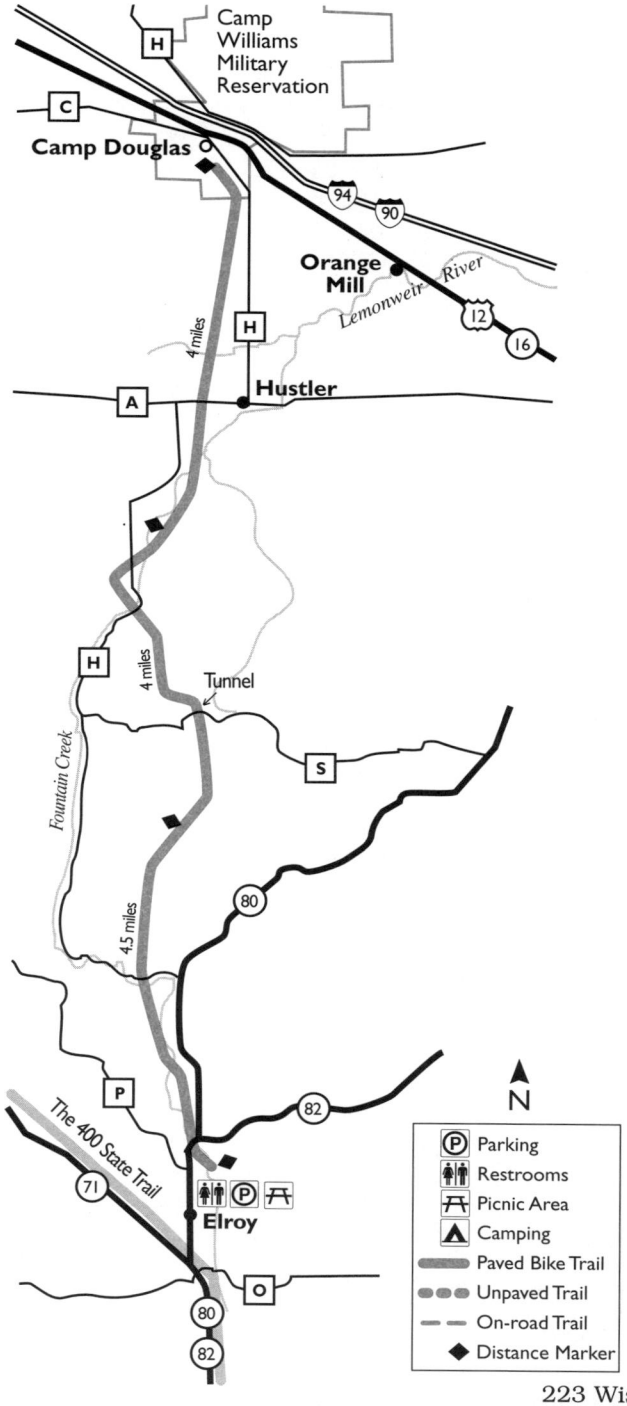
Camp Williams Military Reservation
H
C
Camp Douglas
94
90
Orange Mill
Lemonweir River
12
16
H
4 miles
A
Hustler
H
4 miles
Tunnel
S
Fountain Creek
80
4.5 miles
P
82
The 400 State Trail
71
Elroy
O
80
82
N
Parking
Restrooms
Picnic Area
Camping
Paved Bike Trail
Unpaved Trail
On-road Trail
Distance Marker

SUGAR RIVER STATE PARK

WHERE: New Glarus to Brodhead
LENGTH: 22.6 miles
SURFACE: Crushed limestone
TRAIL USE:

Trailhead North: The trail headquarters is located in the old depot at Highway 69 and 39 in New Glarus. You will find parking and restrooms there. You may get your permit here, rent a bike and inquire about shuttle service.

Mid Access: At Monticello on Highway 69 you will find trailside restrooms, water and parking.

Trailhead South: At Brodhead on Highway 11. There are trailside restrooms, water and parking located at west 3rd Avenue and Exchange Street.

An interesting and scenic ride through the heart of the Swiss Community of southwest Wisconsin, referred to as the Uplands, this trail runs through beautiful countryside from New Glarus to Brodhead, Wisconsin. The trail is flat and smooth and offers appropriate biking for the entire family.

The trail is packed with limestone screening for comfortable travel through picturesque rolling hills, verdant meadows and state wildlife refuges. The trestle bridges over rushing streams have planked floors and safety railings.

New Glarus is home to some of the Midwest's finest specialty foods. The butcher shops feature kalberwurst, landjaeger and homemade bratwurst. The baker makes Swiss bratzeli cookies, fastnacht juechli and a holiday stollen that is shipped all over the nation during the holidays. The trail's surrounding countryside is where some of the finest cheeses in the United States are made. There are many great restaurants here, too. Wisconsin's #1 tourist attraction, Frank Lloyd Wright's House on the Rock at Spring Green, is nearby as well as historical Mineral Point.

FOR MORE INFORMATION:

Sugar River State Trail
PO Box 781
New Glarus, WI 53574
608-527-2334

Bike Shorts

Allow for less efficient braking in wet weather or after riding through a puddle. Water on your rims and brakes can double required stopping distance.

Time your ride to avoid rush hour traffic. Midday on weekdays and weekends are the safest times to ride.

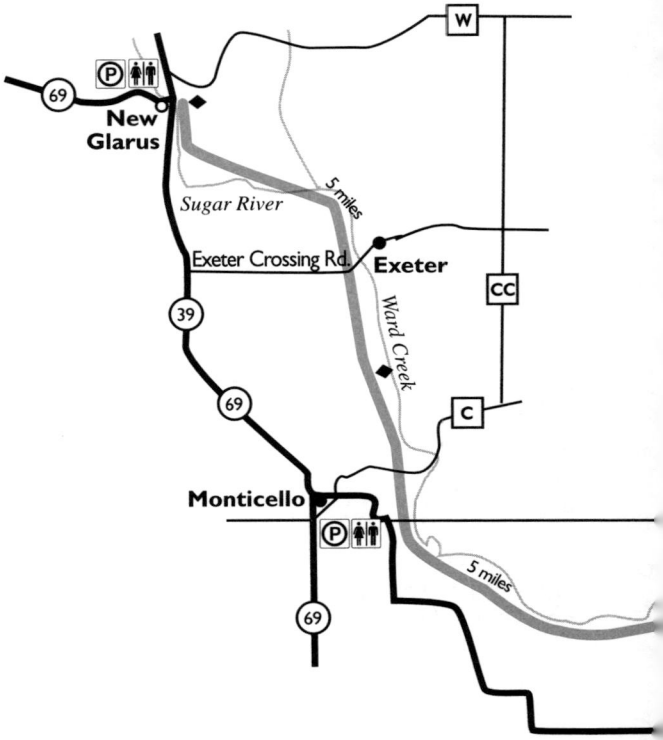

Parking	Paved Bike Trail	N
Restrooms	Unpaved Trail	
Picnic Area	On-road Trail	
Camping	Distance Marker	

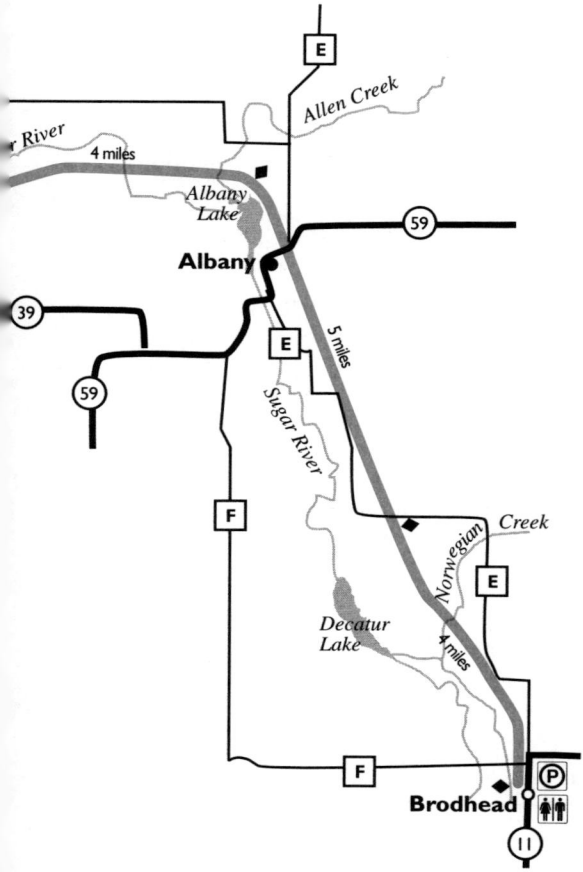
E
Allen Creek
r River
4 miles
Albany Lake
59
Albany
39
E
5 miles
59
Sugar River
F
Creek
Norwegian
E
Decatur Lake
4 miles
F
P
Brodhead
11

Minnesota has a continuing rail-to-trail acquisition and development program which will improve existing trail systems and take advantage of some of the hundreds of miles of abandoned rail bed remaining in the state. Present plans include the following, which will be incorporated in future editions of this book as they are added to the trail system.

Paul Bunyan
The continuation from Hackensack to connect to the Heartland Trail just south of Walker. 218-828-2693

Glacial Lakes
Extending the trail from New London to Richmond — 25 miles. Presently crushed rock from New London to Hawick, undeveloped to Richmond. 320-354-4940

Taconite Trail
The challenge to completing the trail north and east out of Grand Rapids is terrain, not right-of-way. 218-327-4408

Gateway Trail
The 1998 Legislature appropriated funds, planning to extend the Gateway from Pine Point Park to O'Brien State Park on the St. Croix River. 651-772-7935

Mill Towns Trail
A paved recreational trail in the works that would link the Cannon Valley Trail (Cannon Falls to Red Wing) and the Sakatah Singing Hills Trail (Faribault to Mankato). Call Northfield Chamber of Commerce for updated information. 507-645-5604

Harmony–Preston Valley
A six mile paved spur from Preston trail headquarters west to Forestville State Park is planned to be added as soon as funds become available. 507-467-2552

Blufflands Trail System
An extensive trail system is in the planning stages for Fillmore and Houston counties. Already named are the Blazing Star, Prairie Wildflower and Shooting Star. 507-467-2552, 800-428-2030

Agassiz Trail
A Joint Powers Board is developing an old rail bed through Polk, Clay and Norman Counties running from Ulen north. Thirty-five miles are now open to mountain biking. Eventually this will be a 72-mile trail. 218-584-5169

Soo Line Trail
Extensions 20 miles west from Onamia to Genola and east from Isle to Munger and Duluth is in this trail's future. 320-983-2561

Willard Munger
Much remains to be done to span the gap between the north end of the Gateway Segment and the Hinckley-to-Duluth segments. 218-485-5410

Gandy Dancer
A 90-mile trail originating and ending in Wisconsin, the Minnesota segment enters at Danbury and parallels the state line to exit just south of Superior. See Wisconsin Rail-Trail section page 192. 715-349-2157

Minnesota Valley National Wildlife Refuge and Recreation Trail
Most of the right-of-way has been secured to permit an 86-mile multi-use trail from Fort Snelling State Park to Le Sueur. 612-492-6400

BICYCLE HEADGEAR

Reprinted from July 1989 "Mayo Clinic Health Letter" with permission of Mayo Foundation, for Medical Education and Research, Rochester, Minnesota.

Bicycle Helmets

Protective headgear can be a lifesaver.

It's as easy as falling off a bicycle.

The adage has been around for decades. Unfortunately, it makes light of the potential for tragedy if you should take a serious fall while riding a bicycle.

With an increasing number of people riding bicycles on our streets and highways, the risk of injury, in particular head injury, continues to rise. Each year, nearly 50,000 bicyclists suffer serious head injuries. According to the most recent statistics, head injuries are the leading cause of death in the approximately 1-300 bicycle-related fatalities that occur annually. To a large extent, these head injuries are preventable.

Wearing a helmet can make a difference. Until recently, advocates of the use of protective headgear for cyclists found their stance lacked scientific support. But wearing protective headgear clearly makes a difference. Recent evidence confirms that a helmet can reduce your risk of serious head and brain injury by almost 90 percent should you be involved in a bicycle accident.

What to look for in a bicycle helmet
We endorse these guidelines for bicycle helmets recommended by the American Academy of Pediatrics:

The helmet should meet the voluntary testing standards of one of these two groups: American National Standards Institute (ANSI) OR Snell Memorial Foundation. Look for a sticker on the inside of the helmet.

1) Select the right size. Find one that fits comfortably and doesn't pinch.

2) Buy a helmet with a durable outer shell and a polystyrene liner. Be sure it allows adequate ventilation.

3) Use the adjustable foam pads to ensure a proper fit at the front, back and sides.

4) Adjust the strap for a snug fit. The helmet should cover the top of your forehead and not rock side to side or back and forth with the chain strap in place.

5) Replace your helmet if it is involved in an accident.

EQUIPMENT

The proper equipment for your intended level of biking is an important factor in your safety and enjoyment. All bike shops offer a wide selection of equipment, accessories and clothing and can best advise you on your specific needs.

Basic Equipment

1) Most bicycle shops have "fit kits" to precisely advise on proper fit for your body. A rule of thumb is to straddle the bike with feet flat on the floor and close together. There should be 2 to 3 inches clearance. Your bike shop professional will help you with this.

2) Touring seats and handlebars are more comfortable for casual biking. Racing handlebars put considerable pressure on wrists and hands in addition to the strain on your neck from riding with your hands so low. Touring seats are wider and generally carry more padding–something most people appreciate. You can buy seat pads filled with gel or made of soft and comfortable sheepskin.

3) The angle of the seat is critical. It should be level and the height set so the leg is nearly fully extended when the pedal is in the full down position.

Accessories

Realizing there are a multitude of accessories available, we will confine our comments to a very few which we have found to be most beneficial to our biking safety and pleasure. Of course, the most important is a good helmet but we also suggest the following to increase your comfort and enjoyment.

1) Seat pads filled with gel provide multiple return on the investment in the form of added comfort.

2) Padded bike shorts reduce chafing, absorb moisture and provide additional padding.

3) A rear view mirror (either helmet or handle bar mounted) is primarily a safety accessory but it also saves neck strain.

4) Padded gloves help reduce discomfort of weight and tension on the hands when subject to long periods in the same position.

5) Frame-mounted water bottle should be translucent to keep track of supply.

Special Equipment:
It is not necessary for certain equipment to be carried by everyone, but it is desirable that someone in the group carry a tire pump, patching material and some basic tools.

For example:
Screwdriver
6" or 8" adjustable wrench
Pair of small pliers
Accurate tire pressure gauge

Everyone should carry at least one bike bag. How many, size and style depend on the type of ride and length of trip you intend to make.

We recommend a handle bar bag for clothing and personal items on every bike. One insulated rear wheel bag is adequate for every two people. This may require a rear carrier bracket. Use one or two reusable containers of frozen liquid to ensure cold drinks and preserve food.

If your bike trip is an overnight, you will require larger saddle bag storage for extra clothing. Panniers are available for either front or back wheels.

Minnesota Bikeways Maps

We recommend the Explore Minnesota Bikeways maps published by the Minnesota Department of Transportation and the Wisconsin Division of Tourism (see Wisconsin information, page 194). The Minnesota Bikeways maps include DNR and county-maintained rail-trails and maps of trails and bike paths in towns and along highways suitable for extended biking and of particular interest to long distance runners. Roads are color coded for biking suitability and contain information regarding road analysis for bicycle usage, paved road shoulders, off-road bikeways, bike-pedestrian bridges, controlled access roads (bicycles prohibited), historical and cultural attractions, public parklands and facilities. Maps are not current.

Map	Includes inset of cities with trails:
Northeast	Duluth, Cloquet, Virginia, Hibbing, International Falls, Brainerd, Grand Rapids
Northwest	Detroit Lakes, Fargo/Moorhead, Little Falls, Grand Forks/E. Grand Forks, Bemidji, Thief River Falls, Fergus Falls, Crookston
Southeast	Owatonna, Mankato/N. Mankato, Albert Lea, Faribault, Austin, Rochester, Northfield, St. Cloud/Sauk Rapids, Red Wing, Winona, Stillwater, Hastings
Southwest	Marshall, New Ulm, Hutchinson, Worthington, Fairmont, Alexandria, Willmar
Metro East	
Metro West	

Each map is $3.00 except the metro maps which are $2.00. There is a $2.00 mailing charge per order and a 6.5% sales tax (for MN residents only). Prices are subject to change without notice. Mail map orders to:

Minnesota Department of Transportation
John Ireland Boulevard, Room B-20
St. Paul, MN 55155
(no phone orders accepted)

or

Minnesota Bookstore
117 University Avenue (Ford Building)
St. Paul, MN 55155
612-297-3000 or 1-800-657-3757
Phone orders accepted
Mastercard, Visa, Discover, American Express

State Bicycle Advisory Board

Minnesota has a full-time bicycle coordinator and State Bicycle Advisory Board. For additional information, safety brochures, etc. Contact:

State Bicycle Coordinator
State Bicycle Advisory Board
440 Transportation Building
395 John Ireland Boulevard
St. Paul, MN 55155

Minnesota DNR

Individual maps of the 18 bicycle trails, state parks with bicycle paths and mountain bike opportunities are available at no charge.

Contact:

Minnesota Department of Natural Resources
Outdoor Information Center
Box 40, 500 Lafayette Road
St. Paul, MN 55155
612-296- 6157
Within Minnesota, toll free 888-646-6367

Minnesota Office of Tourism

The Minnesota Office of Tourism has developed free directories for accommodations that you may order by phone or mail. *Explore Minnesota Hotels, Explore Minnesota Motels, Explore Minnesota Resorts, Explore Minnesota Campgrounds, Explore Minnesota Bed and Breakfast and Historic Inns*, all available from:

Minnesota Office of Tourism
100 Metro Square
121 Seventh Place East
St. Paul, MN 55101
800-657-3700 Metro Area: 296-5029